IFIP Advances in Information and Communication Technology 762

IFIP Advances in Information and Communication Technology

The IFIP AICT series publishes state-of-the-art results in the sciences and technologies of information and communication. The scope of the series includes: foundations of computer science; software theory and practice; education; computer applications in technology; communication systems; systems modeling and optimization; information systems; ICT and society; computer systems technology; security and protection in information processing systems; artificial intelligence; and human-computer interaction.

Edited volumes and proceedings of refereed international conferences in computer science and interdisciplinary fields are featured. These results often precede journal publication and represent the most current research.

The principal aim of the IFIP AICT series is to encourage education and the dissemination and exchange of information about all aspects of computing.

More information about this series at https://link.springer.com/bookseries/6102

Elizabeth Kurkowski · Sujeet Shenoi
Editors

Advances in Digital Forensics XXI

21st IFIP WG 11.9 International Conference New Delhi, India, January 6–7, 2025 Revised Selected Papers

Springer

Editors
Elizabeth Kurkowski
Johns Hopkins University Applied Physics Laboratory
Laurel, MD, USA

Sujeet Shenoi
University of Tulsa
Tulsa, OK, USA

ISSN 1868-4238 ISSN 1868-422X (electronic)
IFIP Advances in Information and Communication Technology
ISBN 978-3-032-09801-6 ISBN 978-3-032-09802-3 (eBook)
https://doi.org/10.1007/978-3-032-09802-3

This Springer imprint is published by the registered company Springer Nature Switzerland AG
The registered company address is: Gewerbestrasse 11, 6330 Cham, Switzerland

Preface

Digital forensics deals with the acquisition, preservation, examination, analysis and presentation of electronic evidence. Computer networks, cloud computing, smartphones, embedded devices, automobiles and the Internet of Things have expanded the role of digital forensics beyond traditional computer crime investigations. Practically every crime now involves some aspect of digital evidence; digital forensics provides the techniques and tools to articulate this evidence in legal proceedings. Digital forensics also has myriad intelligence applications; furthermore, it has a vital role in cyber security – investigations of security breaches yield valuable information that can be used to design more secure and resilient systems.

This book, *Advances in Digital Forensics XXI*, is the twenty-first volume in the annual series produced by the IFIP Working Group 11.9 on Digital Forensics, an international community of scientists, engineers and practitioners dedicated to advancing the state of the art of research and practice in digital forensics. The book presents original research results and innovative applications in digital forensics. Also, it highlights some of the major technical and legal issues related to digital evidence and electronic crime investigations.

This volume contains ten revised and edited chapters based on papers presented at the Twentieth IFIP WG 11.9 International Conference on Digital Forensics held in New Delhi, India on January 6–7, 2025. A total of 25 full-length papers were submitted for presentation at the conference. Each paper was refereed in a single-blind manner by three members of the conference program committee, all of them internationally recognized experts in digital forensics. The ten post-conference manuscripts submitted by the authors were required to be rewritten to accommodate the suggestions provided by the referees and by the conference attendees. The manuscripts were subsequently revised by the editors to produce the final chapters published in this volume.

The chapters in this volume are organized into four thematic sections: Image and Video Forensics, Large Language Model Applications, Forensic Investigations and Digital Forensics Frameworks. The coverage of topics highlights the richness and vitality of the digital forensics discipline and offers promising avenues for future research.

This book is the result of the combined efforts of several individuals. In particular, we thank Kam-Pui Chow and Gaurav Gupta for their tireless work on behalf of IFIP Working Group 11.9 on Digital Forensics. We also acknowledge the support provided by the U.S. National Science Foundation, U.S. National Security Agency and U.S. Secret Service.

June 2025

Elizabeth Kurkowski
Sujeet Shenoi

Organization

General Chair

Gaurav Gupta	Ministry of Electronics and Information Technology, India

Organizing Chair

Somitra Sanadhya	Indian Institute of Technology Jodhpur, India

Program Chairs

Elizabeth Kurkowski	Johns Hopkins University Applied Physics Laboratory, USA
Sujeet Shenoi	University of Tulsa, USA

Program Committee

Stefan Axelsson	Stockholm University, Sweden
Harald Baier	University of the Bundeswehr Munich, Germany
Raymond Chan	Singapore Institute of Technology, Singapore
Kam-Pui Chow	University of Hong Kong, China
Yong Guan	Iowa State University, USA
Gaurav Gupta	Ministry of Electronics and Information Technology, India
Al Holt	U.S. Department of Defense, USA
Umit Karabiyik	Purdue University, USA
Alan Lin	Air Force Office of Scientific Research, USA
Jigang Liu	Metropolitan State University, USA
Michael Losavio	University of Louisville, USA
Duohe Ma	Chinese Academy of Sciences, China
James Okolica	Air Force Institute of Technology, USA
Martin Olivier	University of Pretoria, South Africa
Gilbert Peterson	Air Force Institute of Technology, USA
Emmanuel Pilli	Malaviya National Institute of Technology, India

Huw Read	Norwich University, USA
Jason Staggs	University of Tulsa, USA
Iain Sutherland	Noroff University College, Norway
Robin Verma	Marshall University, USA
Konstantinos Xynos	Mycenx Consultancy, Germany

Contents

Digital Forensics Frameworks

Contributors

Sheeba Armoogum University of Mauritius, Reduit, Mauritius

Anurag Chandra Defence and Aviation, New Delhi, India

Kam-Pui Chow University of Hong Kong, Hong Kong, China

Fuqiang Du Chinese Academy of Sciences, Beijing, China; University of Chinese Academy of Sciences, Beijing, China

Pulkit Garg Indian Institute of Technology Jodhpur, Karwar, India

Krishnendu Ghosh College of Charleston, Charleston, SC, USA

Gaurav Gupta Ministry of Electronics and Information Technology, New Delhi, India

Catherine Hoffmann College of Charleston, Charleston, SC, USA

Weiqing Huang Chinese Academy of Sciences, Beijing, China

Cheuk-Yu Ip University of Hong Kong, Hong Kong, China

Jianguo Jiang Chinese Academy of Sciences, Beijing, China; University of Chinese Academy of Sciences, Beijing, China

Yi-Anson Lam University of Hong Kong, Hong Kong, China

Boquan Li Harbin Engineering University, Harbin, China

Gang Li Deakin University, Burwood, Australia

Zhihao Li Institute of Forensic Science, Beijing, China

Yachao Liang Chinese Academy of Sciences, Beijing, China; University of Chinese Academy of Sciences, Beijing, China

Yueheng Mao Chinese Academy of Sciences, Beijing, China; University of Chinese Academy of Sciences, Beijing, China

Xiang Meng Chinese Academy of Sciences, Beijing, China

Digambar Pawar University of Hyderabad, Hyderabad, India

Pranitha Sanda C.R. Rao Advanced Institute of Mathematics, Statistics and Computer Science, Hyderabad, India

Keshav Shrivas C.R. Rao Advanced Institute of Mathematics, Statistics and Computer Science, Hyderabad, India

Vishal Srivastava Indian Institute of Technology Jodhpur, Karwar, India

Radha Vedala Institute for Development and Research in Banking Technology, Hyderabad, India

Huan Wang Chinese Academy of Sciences, Beijing, China;
University of Chinese Academy of Sciences, Beijing, China

Jiawen Wang Illinois Institute of Technology, Chicago, IL, USA

Lanchi Xie Institute of Forensic Science, Beijing, China

Ruiyao Yang Beijing University of Posts and Telecommunications, Beijing, China

Yaotian Yang Beijing University of Posts and Telecommunications, Beijing, China

Yu Yang Beijing University of Posts and Telecommunications, Beijing, China

Siu-Ming Yiu University of Hong Kong, Hong Kong, China

Min Yu Chinese Academy of Sciences, Beijing, China;
University of Chinese Academy of Sciences, Beijing, China

Pengbo Zhang Chinese Academy of Sciences, Beijing, China;
University of Chinese Academy of Sciences, Beijing, China

Linna Zhou Beijing University of Posts and Telecommunications, Beijing, China

Jixin Zou Institute of Forensic Science, Beijing, China

Image and Video Forensics

Self-Supervised Steganalysis Targeting Generative-Adversarial-Network-Based Steganographic Image Variants by Maximizing Commonality Features

Ruiyao Yang, Yu Yang, and Linna Zhou

Beijing University of Posts and Telecommunications, Beijing, China
yangyu@bupt.edu.cn

Abstract. Generative-adversarial-network-based steganographic methods typically create images through adversarial confrontations between a generator and discriminator. However, these steganographic methods are characterized by the specificity of their structures, which makes them prone to generating large numbers of variants that are not easy to detect. Unfortunately, limited research has focused on detecting variants of generative-adversarial-network-based steganographic images.
This chapter describes a framework for detecting generative-adversarial-network-based steganographic image variants. The framework is developed by controlling and guiding the features of images in the middle layer of a neural network and by constructing image samples that capture the common characteristics of generative-adversarial-network-based steganographic images. A detector trained on these images has improved generalization ability when faced with generative-adversarial-network-based steganographic image variants. Experimental results demonstrate the effectiveness of the approach compared with other generative-adversarial-network-based models.

Keywords: Generative Adversarial Network · Image Steganography · Image Analysis · Image Detection

1 Introduction

Criminal entities often use image steganography to hide secret information for nefarious purposes [1, 17]. As a result, researchers have been working on steganalysis techniques to detect steganography and deter its misuse.

Traditional steganographic algorithms are designed to minimize distortion [5]. Steganography algorithms such as HUGO [23], WOW [8], S-UNIWARD [9], HILL [16] and MiPOD [25] securely embed steganographic information by minimizing embedding distortion.

Traditional steganalysis algorithms such as SPAM [22] and SRM [6] detect steganography by extracting the statistical features of images and engaging integrated classifiers [13]. In recent years, steganalysis techniques leveraging convolutional neural networks (CNNs) [15] have demonstrated significant

Published by Springer Nature Switzerland AG 2026
E. Kurkowski and S. Shenoi (Eds.): DigitalForensics 2025, IFIP AICT 762, pp. 3–26, 2026.
https://doi.org/10.1007/978-3-032-09802-3_1

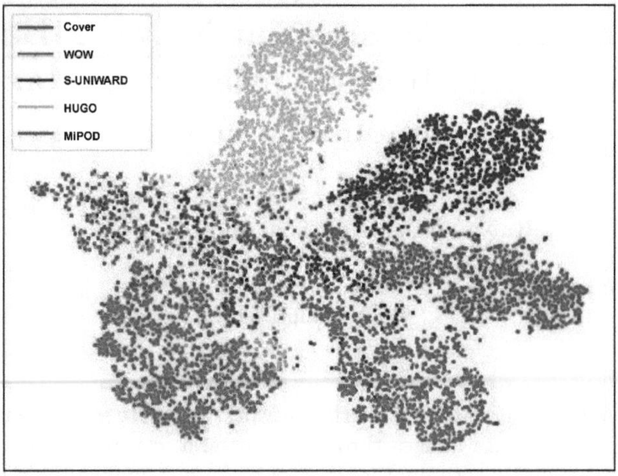

Fig. 1. t-SNE distributions of images produced by steganographic algorithms.

performance improvements over traditional methods. Representative techniques include XuNet [31], YeNet [33], Yedroudj-Net [34], SRNet [3], Zhu-Net [37], SiaStegNet [35] and LWENet [29].

Since the development of generative adversarial networks (GANs) [7], various GAN-based steganographic algorithms such as ASDL-GAN [28], UT-GAN [32], SPAR-RL [27] and Steg-GMAN [10] have been proposed. These algorithms typically leverage a generator and discriminator. The generator incorporates a feature extraction network to create probability maps whereas the discriminator incorporates a steganalyzer to distinguish steganographic images. Secret information is securely embedded in steganographic images via adversarial training between the generator and discriminator.

Detecting GAN-based steganographic images is more important than traditional steganographic images because GAN-based steganographic images have high security and their structure makes it very easy to generate variants. Indeed, GAN-based steganographic methods can generate variants simply by modifying their generators or discriminators. In contrast, generating variants using traditional steganographic methods requires modifications to their embedding distortion functions that are time-consuming and have long cycle times. Additionally, traditional one-on-one trained steganalyzers exhibit reduced detection accuracy when faced with GAN-based steganographic image variants and struggle to respond effectively. This significantly impacts the effectiveness of traditional steganalysis on GAN-based steganographic images.

Naseer et al. [21] have shown that feature distortion affects the transferability of attack methods. Maximizing deep feature distortions generates generic attack methods and improves the abilities of defensive models. To perform steganalysis, steganographic images should have multiple classes of steganographic features if model transferability is the optimization goal. Figure 1 shows the t-distributed

Table 1. Detection accuracy of steganalyzers in the face of algorithmic mismatch.

Dataset	Steganography Algorithms Used for Training			
	WOW	**S-UNIWARD**	**HUGO**	**MiPOD**
WOW (0.4bpp)	**93.70%**	91.48%	78.20%	90.38%
S-UNIWARD (0.4bpp)	89.80%	**93.00%**	76.90%	89.33%
HUGO (0.4bpp)	73.38%	81.28%	**91.10%**	82.15%
MiPOD (0.4bpp)	82.38%	85.15%	74.65%	**89.60%**

stochastic neighbor embedding (t-SNE) distributions of images produced by various steganographic algorithms. Clearly, the steganographic images generated by the MiPOD algorithm are more distributed in the intersection region of the WOW, S-UNIWARD and HUGO algorithms, which have common features.

Table 1 shows the detection accuracy of steganalyzers trained by four mainstream steganographic algorithms in the face of algorithmic mismatch. The best accuracy obtained for a dataset is indicated in bold font and the second-best accuracy is underlined. The results indicate that the generalization ability of MiPOD-trained models is better than that of the models trained by WOW and S-UNIWARD. This is consistent with the t-SNE results in Figure 1.

To address this phenomenon, a self-supervised steganalysis framework – MLC-GAN – is proposed to detect GAN-based steganographic image variants. A dataset that captures the common features of multiple GAN-based steganographic image variants is constructed for model training. The core idea is to generate samples that share common steganalysis features by reducing the Euclidean distance between middle layer features. As shown in Figure 2, a middle layer controller (MLC) controls the cover image features (Feat-C) and steganographic image features (Feat-S). A steganalyzer trained using these samples can effectively detect GAN-based steganographic image variants despite algorithmic and steganographic payload mismatches.

2 Related Work

This section discusses GAN-based steganographic frameworks and methods for enhancing their generalization ability.

2.1 GAN-Based Steganographic Frameworks

GAN-based steganographic frameworks seek to produce artificial samples that are almost indistinguishable from real samples through adversarial interactions between a generator and discriminator. The following are four typical GAN-based steganographic frameworks:

- **ASDL-GAN:** ASDL-GAN [28] was the first automatic steganographic distortion learning framework based on GANs. It is able to learn the pixel embedding change probability and transform it to embedding distortion. The

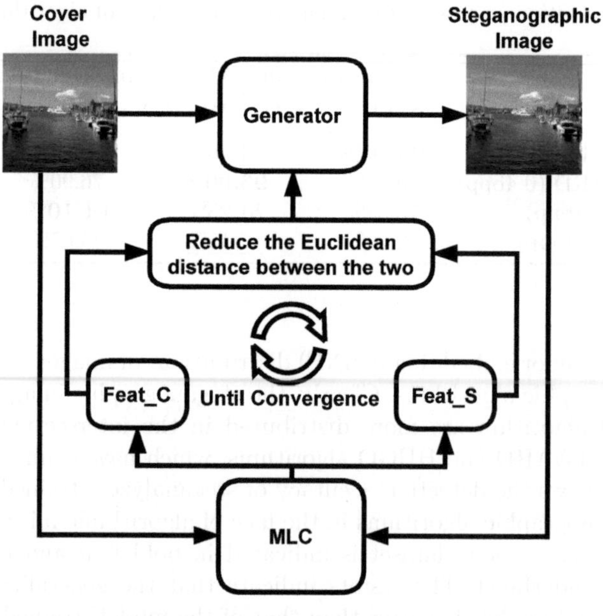

Fig. 2. Controlling cover and steganographic features.

framework incorporates a generator that uses a KV high-pass filter [12] and has 25 convolutional layers. The discriminator is XuNet [31].

- **UT-GAN:** UT-GAN [32] uses U-Net [24] as the generator and XuNet as the discriminator. It employs the double-tanh function instead of a ternary embedding simulator (TES), which eliminates the need for pre-training, reduces computation time and maintains minimizability. The discriminator incorporates multiple high-pass filters for preprocessing to enhance the adversarial effect.
- **SPAR-RL:** SPAR-RL [27] is a deep-reinforcement-learning-based embedding cost learning framework that learns embedding strategies for steganographic images on a pixel-by-pixel basis with the goal of maximizing the overall reward of steganalysis and generating content-adaptive embedding costs. A policy network acts as the generator and the environment network acts as the discriminator.
- **Steg-GMAN:** Steg-GMAN [10] was the first framework to incorporate multiple steganalyzers in a discriminator. It employs a new adaptive parameter update strategy to enhance discriminator performance and balances the capabilities of the generator and discriminator to improve overall performance.

The core structure in all of the above GAN-based steganographic frameworks is the generator-discriminator combination. The GAN-based framework employing a multilayer controller (MLC-GAN) described in this chapter enables steganographic image variants to be generated by simply changing the generator, discriminator or embedding strategy.

2.2 Improving Generalization Performance

The relationship between steganography and steganalysis is similar to that of attack and defense. The common goal is to enhance model generalization to address steganographic samples or unknown attacks. The following are relevant methods in the two domains.

- **Neural Representation Purifier:** Traditional adversarial training relies on task-specific objectives or label spaces. Neural Representation Purifier [21] employs a task-independent approach to adversarial training. It acts as a purified model to recover images from adversarial perturbations without relying on task-specific goals and serves as a generalized defense mechanism for multiple tasks. A self-supervised adversarial training mechanism is employed to generate perturbations in feature space, avoiding the label leakage problem [14] and providing the model with a stronger generalized defense against a range of unseen attacks.
- **J-Net:** J-Net [38] employs a new deep adaptive network architecture. It is optimized based on the joint maximum mean difference (JMMD) [20] that reduces the difference in the feature distribution between the training and testing sets, improving the generalization ability on different distributed datasets.
- **FME-Net:** FME-Net [36] is a deep steganalysis network that fuses supervised information in the source domain with unsupervised information in the target domain to enhance the performance of the classifier in cases involving coverage source mismatch (CSM). Target features are modeled using a multivariate Laplace distribution (MLD) and source features are enhanced along the transformed direction of the MLD samples to make them closer to the target features, thereby improving the generalization ability.

The methods described above exhibit improved generalization performance on traditional datasets. However, no method currently exists that effectively detects GAN-based steganographic image variants.

3 MLC-GAN Framework

Figure 3 shows the MLC-GAN process for generating commonality samples. The common steganographic image generation module contains the conditional constraint module. Samples that meet the three constraints of the conditional constraint module are commonality steganographic images.

Common steganographic images can be generated using the fast gradient descent (FGD) algorithm [26] for embedding steganographic information or a GAN-based framework for generating steganographic image samples. Figure 4

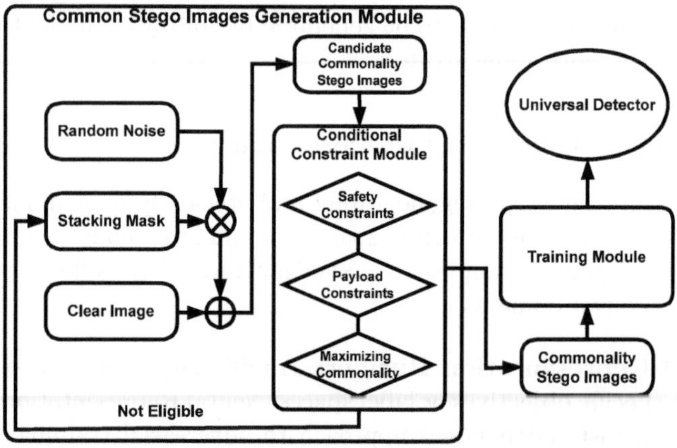

Fig. 3. MLC-GAN process for generating commonality samples.

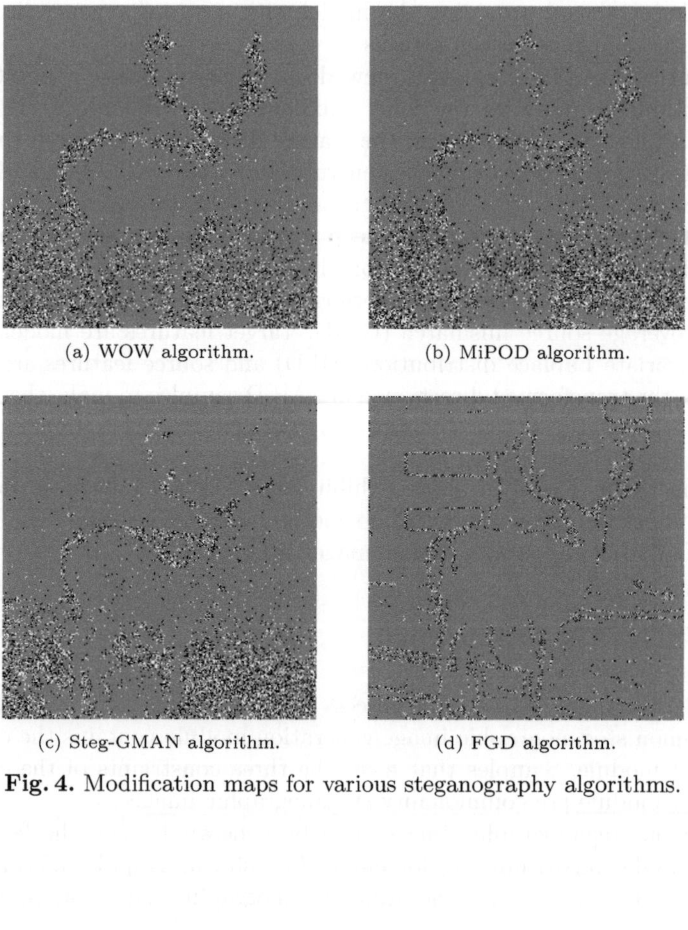

(a) WOW algorithm. (b) MiPOD algorithm.

(c) Steg-GMAN algorithm. (d) FGD algorithm.

Fig. 4. Modification maps for various steganography algorithms.

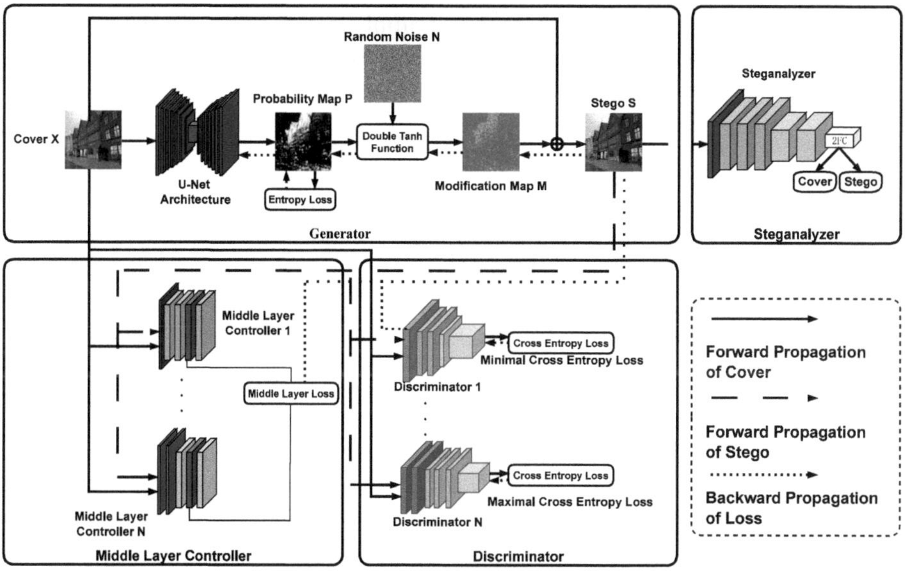

Fig. 5. MLC-GAN framework architecture.

shows the embedding locations generated by the WOW, MiPOD, Steg-GMAN and FGD-based algorithms on 8.pgm from the BOSSbase 1.01 dataset [2]. Although the FGD algorithm generates steganographic images quickly, its main problem is that the security of the embedding positions in the images is not high, which makes it difficult for a steganalyzer to learn the relevant features.

The MLC-GAN steganographic framework described in this chapter is designed to generate more secure steganographic image samples with common features and to decouple them from specific generation methods. Figure 5 shows the entire framework architecture. It incorporates four modules – generator, discriminator, middle layer controller and steganalysis detector.

3.1 Generator Design

The role of the generator is to turn a cover image into an embedding probability map and combine the map with steganographic information to produce the final steganographic image. The generator has two stages – embedding probability map creation and steganographic information embedding.

Embedding Probability Map Creation. In the self-supervised steganographic image generation task, the generator with the U-Net architecture converts a cover image to an embedding probability map. The size of the embedding probability map is kept consistent with the cover image and the value of each pixel is distributed in the range $[0, 0.5]$, which represents the probability that the pixel can be embedded with steganographic information and the probability that the pixel value is augmented by one and the pixel value is decremented by one are equal to ensure embedding rationality:

$$p_{i,j}^{+1} = p_{i,j}^{-1} = p_{i,j}/2$$

where $p_{i,j}$ is the probability that pixel (i, j) is modified.

The generator creates a probability map through a combination of downsampling and upsampling. The resulting feature values are processed by a feature mapping module, which uses the sigmoid and ReLU functions to map the embedded probabilities to the range $[0, 0.5]$.

Steganographic Information Embedding. In the simulated information embedding part, a differentiable simulation is performed through the double-tanh function. A random noise matrix $\mathrm{R} = (r_{i,j})^{H,W}$ is generated, where each element $r_{i,j}$ is an independent and uniformly distributed random number on the interval $[0, 1]$. Subsequently, the modification mapping $\mathrm{M} = (m_{i,j})^{H,W}$ is determined based on the embedding probability $p_{i,j}$ and random noise $r_{i,j}$. The steganographic images are then obtained by overlaying the modification mapping with the cover images.

The double-tanh function [32] is used as an embedding simulator because it is microscopic, enabling the generator parameters to be optimized by backpropagation. The double-tanh function is defined as follows:

$$m_{i,j} = -0.5 \times \tanh(\lambda(p_{i,j} - 2 \times r_{i,j})) + 0.5 \times \tanh(\lambda(p_{i,j} - 2 \times (1 - r_{i,j})))$$

$$tanh = \frac{e^x - e^{-x}}{e^x + e^{-x}}$$

where the parameter λ is set to 60 as in [32].

After the training is completed, the embedding of steganographic information is accomplished using syndrome-trellis coding. The embedding cost ρ is computed as:

$$\rho = \begin{cases} \rho_{i,j}^{+1} = \ln(\frac{1}{p_{i,j}^{+1}} - 2) \\ \rho_{i,j}^{-1} = \ln(\frac{1}{p_{i,j}^{-1}} - 2) \\ \rho_{i,j}^{0} = 0 \end{cases}$$

where $p_{i,j}$ is the embedding probability obtained from model training and $\rho_{i,j}$ is the embedding cost.

3.2 Discriminator Design

The discriminator plays a key role in a GAN-based steganographic method. Its principal function is to render the steganographic images produced by the generator more resistant to detection. Discriminator performance affects the generator

– inaccurate decision boundaries produced by a weak discriminator provides limited feedback to the generator [11, 30]. Additionally, stronger steganalyzers are able to make steganographic images samples more secure when acting as target steganalyzers [18, 19].

Research has shown that using modern steganalyzers can enhance discriminator performance, but selecting only stronger steganalyzers without other interventions can lead to the rapid convergence of discriminator loss to zero. This leads to the disappearance of the gradient and, consequently, valid information cannot be provided to the discriminator. Therefore, a new training strategy is incorporated to maintain the dynamic balance between the discriminator and generator. The discriminator still adopts the basic Steg-GMAN strategy [10].

3.3 Middle Layer Controller Design

The middle layer controller makes the feature values of the cover image X and steganographic image Y created by the generator as close as possible to each other in one of the controller layers that is referred to as M. The feature distortion $\Delta(X, Y$ is computed as:

$$\Delta(X, Y) = \|(M(X;\theta)|_n, M(Y;\theta)|_n)\|_2$$

where $M(x;\theta)|_n$ is the feature representation of images x in the n-th layer of the middle layer controller and $\| - \|_2$ is a distance metric based on the Euclidean distance with mean square error (L2 norm).

The middle layer controller narrows the Euclidean distance between the cover image X and steganographic image Y. It can make the generated steganographic images have the commonality of multiple GAN-based steganographic image variants, enhancing the generalization ability of the steganalyzer. Additionally, experiments have shown that the middle layer controller does not rely on a specific network, but can choose the appropriate network based on different GAN-based frameworks. The optimization strategy is:

$$\underset{Y}{\text{Min}}\ \Delta(X, Y) \rightarrow 0$$

so that the distance between X and Y converges to zero for the L2 norm.

3.4 Loss Function Design

The framework employs three loss functions – feature discrepancy loss, discriminator loss and generator loss. The three loss functions work together to guide the process of generating the final steganographic images.

Feature Discrepancy Loss. The middle layer controller reduces the feature distance between cover images and steganographic images. The feature discrepancy loss L_f, a variant of the L2 loss, is computed as:

$$L_f = \sum_{i=1}^{n}(M(X) - M(Y))^2/n$$

where M is the middle layer controller, X is the cover image, Y is the steganographic image and n is the batch size. The parameters of the middle layer controller are not involved in the update, but only guide the parameter update process of the generator.

Discriminator Loss. The purpose of the discriminator is to determine whether images are cover images or steganographic images. An adversarial relationship exists between the discriminator and generator throughout the framework. As pointed out by Huang et al. [10], the use of a single or weak steganalyzer in a GAN-based steganography method can limit the security performance. Therefore, in the proposed framework, the discriminator employs multiple steganalyzers and updates the weakest steganalyzer in each iteration.

The discriminator loss l_D is computed as:

$$l_D = \underset{i \in \{1,2,...N\}}{\text{Max}} \{-z_0 log(D_i(X)) - z_1 log(D_i(Y))\}$$

where $D_i(X)$ and $D_i(Y)$ are the discrimination results of the discriminator for cover image X and steganographic image Y in the softmax layer denoted as a 2-D normalized vector with value unity and $z_0 = (1 \quad 0)^T$ and $z_1 = (0 \quad 1)^T$ are the true labels of the cover image X and steganographic image Y, respectively.

The performance of the steganalyzer is determined by the binary cross entropy E_i computed as:

$$E_i = -z_0 log(D_i(X)) - z_1 log(D_i(Y))$$

where a larger value of E_i denotes worse steganalyzer performance. The loss l_D then selects the steganalyzer with the largest E_i value for update.

Generator Loss. The generator embeds steganographic information in images in a secure manner to produce steganographic images that evade detection by the discriminator. The generator has three main objectives, fraud discrimination, image generation corresponding to a payload and steganographic image generation.

The fraud discriminator loss l_G^1 is computed as:

$$l_G^1 = \underset{i \in \{1,2,...N\}}{\text{Min}} \{-z_0 log(D_i(X)) - z_1 log(D_i(Y))\}$$

Unlike the discriminator loss l_D, the fraud discriminator loss l_G^1 chooses the best discriminator to compute the opponent loss.

The loss of an image corresponding to a payload l_G^2 is computed as:

$$l_G^2 = (-(\sum_{\forall(i,j)} \sum_{\forall m} p_{i,j}^{(m)} \cdot \log_2(p_{i,j}^{(m)})) - (\mathrm{H} \times \mathrm{W} \times q))^2$$

where H and W are the height and width of the input image, respectively ($1 \leq i \leq H, 1 \leq j \leq W$), m is the number of embedding modifications ($m \in \{-1, 0, +1\}$) and q is the payload.

The loss in generating a steganographic image with smaller distances from the features of a cover image is computed as:

$$l_G^3 = \sum_{i=1}^{n}(M(X) - M(Y))^2/n$$

The overall generator loss l_G is computed as:

$$l_G = -\alpha_1 \cdot l_G^1 - \alpha_2 \cdot l_G^2 + \alpha_3 \cdot l_G^3$$

where α_1,α_2 and α_3 are the weights of the three loss values, respectively.

As a result of the positive and negative relationships of the three weights, steganographic images with stronger deception ability, more accurate payloads and smaller distances from the features of cover images can be obtained.

4 Experiments and Results

This section describes the experimental setup, dataset and results.

4.1 Experimental Setup

The experiments used the BOSSbase 1.01 dataset comprising 10,000 512 × 512 images resized to 256 × 256 images via Matlab's bilinear interpolation and split into training, validation and testing sets in a 6:2:2 ratio.

For the middle layer controller GAN (MLC-GAN) training phase, the Adam optimizer learning rate was set to 0.0001, the batch size was 24 and 52 rounds of training were performed. The training set was 1-6000.pgm, validation set was 6001-8000.pgm and testing set was 8001-10000.pgm.

The generator employed the U-Net architecture and the discriminators included various combinations of XuNet, Yedroudj-Net, SRNet and LWENet. If the number of discriminators was greater than one, the generator with the weakest capability was selected as the steganalyzer to be updated and the generator with strongest capability was selected as the generator to be updated.

During the training phase of the steganalysis model, 200 rounds of training were performed using the Adamax optimizer with a learning rate of 0.0001, $\beta_1 = 0.9$, $\beta_2 = 0.999$, $\epsilon = 1e - 8$, L2 regularization coefficient of 0.0001 and batch size of 32. The experiments were conducted using an NVIDIA GeForce RTX 3090 CPU with Python 3.8 and PyTorch 2.0.1.

Special model notation is employed to simplify the discussion. The detector trained by the MLC-GAN framework without the middle layer controller is abbreviated as SG. The detector trained by the MLC-GAN framework with the middle layer controller is abbreviated as SD.

Table 2 shows the discriminator abbreviations. For example, SG(Xu+Yed+LWE) is the combination of discriminators XuNet, Yedroudj-Net and LWENet without a middle layer controller. SD(Xu+Yed+LWE, Xu) indicates that XuNet is used as the middle layer controller while keeping the original discriminators, XuNet, Yedroudj-Net and LWENet, intact.

Table 2. Discriminator abbreviations.

Discriminator	Abbreviation
XuNet	Xu
Yedroudj-Net	Yed
SRNet	SR
LWENet	LWE

Table 3. Dataset generator models.

Dataset	Generator Model
D1	SG(Xu)
D2	SG(LWE)
D3	SG(Xu+Yed)
D4	SG(Yed+SR)
D5	SG(Xu+Yed+SR)
D6	SG(Xu+Yed+LWE)

4.2 Datasets

Six datasets were generated via traditional GAN-based steganography. Each dataset had two versions with steganographic rates of 0.4bpp and 0.2bpp. Table 3 lists the datasets and their generator models.

4.3 Model Performance

The first set of experiments evaluated the performance of the models trained using the GAN-based steganographic method under steganographic payload mismatch and algorithmic mismatch. Scenario 1 corresponds to the case where a model encounters an unknown algorithm for the dataset to be tested. Scenario 2 corresponds to the case where the algorithm is known (algorithmic mismatch).

The performance of the MLC-GAN models was evaluated by comparing the GAN-based steganographic algorithms and traditional steganographic algorithms using the dataset. The 14 models are designated as: I: WOW, II: S-UNIWARD, III: HUGO, IV: MiPOD, V: HILL, VI: SG(Xu), VII: SG(SR), VIII: SG(LWENet), IX: SG(Xu+Yed), X: SG(Xu+SR), XI: SG(Yed+SR), XII: SG(Xu+Yed+SR), XIII: SG(Xu+Yed+LWE) and XIV: SD(Xu+Yed+SR, Xu).

Table 4 shows the detection accuracy (%) results of the 14 models trained using the GAN-based steganographic method under steganographic payload mismatch and algorithmic mismatch. The 14 models were used to first generate steganographic images and then train the steganalyzer. The Scenario 1 models are labeled I to V (unboxed data items) and the Scenario 2 models are labeled VI to XIV (boxed data items). The best accuracy obtained for a dataset is indicated in bold font and the second-best accuracy is underlined.

Table 4. Performance comparison.

Dataset	Payload	Model Numbers													
		I	II	III	IV	V	VI	VII	VIII	IX	X	XI	XII	XIII	XIV
D1	0.4bpp	74.28	79.33	59.45	78.35	77.33	87.58	82.73	<u>85.62</u>	84.75	83.03	82.67	84.28	84.57	**86.30**
	0.2bpp	57.25	62.60	50.82	58.43	60.90	70.35	64.98	66.92	67.30	66.15	65.50	66.92	<u>67.62</u>	**69.97**
D2	0.4bpp	78.08	80.17	70.97	81.62	79.67	<u>84.95</u>	78.45	86.98	80.15	83.85	80.85	80.58	84.60	**85.80**
	0.2bpp	60.85	64.12	54.93	62.80	63.25	66.95	63.20	71.38	64.70	67.00	65.10	65.10	<u>67.50</u>	**69.60**
D3	0.4bpp	71.85	78.97	58.20	77.72	76.95	**87.17**	84.52	85.40	87.02	83.08	84.03	85.55	85.25	<u>86.83</u>
	0.2bpp	55.30	60.95	50.85	56.57	58.58	<u>69.55</u>	66.47	65.58	69.75	65.15	65.28	68.60	66.67	**70.08**
D4	0.4bpp	74.58	81.85	62.10	78.67	78.70	<u>85.95</u>	82.73	85.47	83.95	85.78	85.32	84.42	85.80	**87.05**
	0.2bpp	55.80	63.52	51.75	57.67	60.75	68.27	65.97	66.62	67.95	<u>69.27</u>	69.23	68.60	68.95	**71.92**
D5	0.4bpp	72.32	79.55	60.30	76.53	77.22	<u>86.08</u>	83.38	85.35	85.42	83.85	83.85	84.67	84.60	**86.78**
	0.2bpp	55.77	59.15	51.12	58.98	60.52	<u>66.25</u>	63.75	65.25	65.03	65.18	63.92	68.00	63.50	**69.23**
D6	0.4bpp	78.05	82.55	61.22	83.10	82.23	<u>86.05</u>	80.33	85.87	82.97	84.05	84.47	83.83	88.30	**86.55**
	0.2bpp	59.33	61.70	51.25	63.50	64.90	64.42	57.50	63.83	62.12	<u>65.60</u>	63.80	64.83	68.42	**68.00**

The detection accuracies of the proposed Model XIV SD(Xu+Yed+SR, Xu) on datasets D1 to D6 are all better than those of the other 13 models. For traditional steganography algorithms, Model I to Model V, the detection accuracies are improved by 16.12%, 10.08%, 28.63%, 14.25% and 11.5%, respectively. For the GAN-based steganography algorithms, Model VI to Model XIII, the highest detection accuracy improvement is 5.22%, which is 2.98% ahead of the second-best accuracy, Even without prior knowledge of LWENet, the proposed Model XIV SD(Xu+Yed+SR, Xu) has higher detection accuracy than SG(Xu+Yed+LWE) on dataset D2.

The results in Table 4 show that the number and combination of discriminators impact model detection performance. Increasing the number of discriminators does not necessarily improve the generalization performance. For example, consider Model VI versus Model IX. Although Model IX has a larger number of discriminators, the detection accuracy of Model IX is not as good as that of Model VI that only uses XuNet. However, Model VII shows a significant improvement in generalization ability with the addition of XuNet compared with Model X. Similarly, the generalization ability is improved by adding XuNet and Yedroudj-Net in Model VIII versus Model XIII. According to the literature [3, 4, 29, 34], the steganalysis ability of XuNet is not as good as that of Yedroudj-Net, SRNet and LWENet. However, as shown by Huang et al. [10], the use of an overly strong discriminator leads to a rapid convergence of the discriminator loss, which fails to provide the generator with an effective gradient. This reduces the security of steganographic images and negatively impacts the generalization performance of the steganalyzer.

4.4 Training Process with Middle Layer Controller

The second set of experiments evaluated the training process with the middle layer controller. Figure 6 shows that the MLC-GAN model gradually concentrates the regions with high embedding probability in the texture and edge regions of the images as the epochs increase. This indicates that the middle layer controller does not reduce the security of the steganographic images when expressing the commonality.

Figure 7 shows the difference between the steganographic locations of the MLC-GAN model and the traditional GAN-based steganographic model. The embedding locations of the different steganographic image variants are different, but all of them are concentrated in the texture and edge regions. The steganographic information of the MLC-GAN model is more concentrated in the texture region, which is in line with the high-density region feature of the steganographic algorithm and improves the generalization performance of the detector.

Figure 8 shows the variation of loss value with epochs when combining XuNet, Yedroudj and SRNet in the discriminator. The middle layer feature loss of the MLC-GAN model is overall lower than that of the traditional GAN-based steganographic model. This is consistent with the fact that the middle layer controller reduces the distances between cover images and steganographic images.

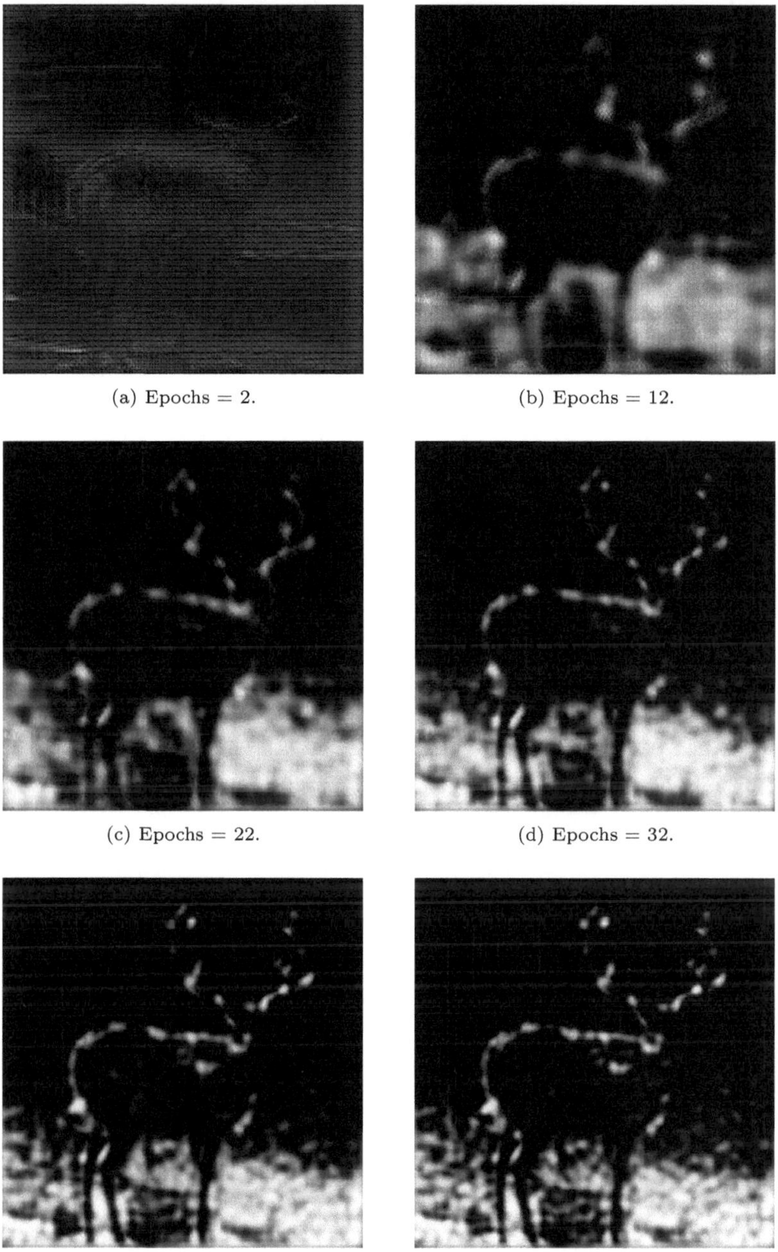

(a) Epochs = 2. (b) Epochs = 12.

(c) Epochs = 22. (d) Epochs = 32.

(e) Epochs = 42. (d) Epochs = 52.

Fig. 6. Embedded probability maps with varying epochs.

(a) Original image 8.pgm.

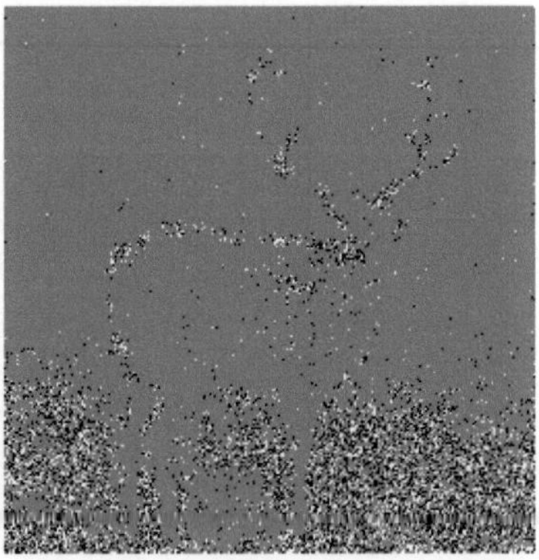

(b) SG(Xu).

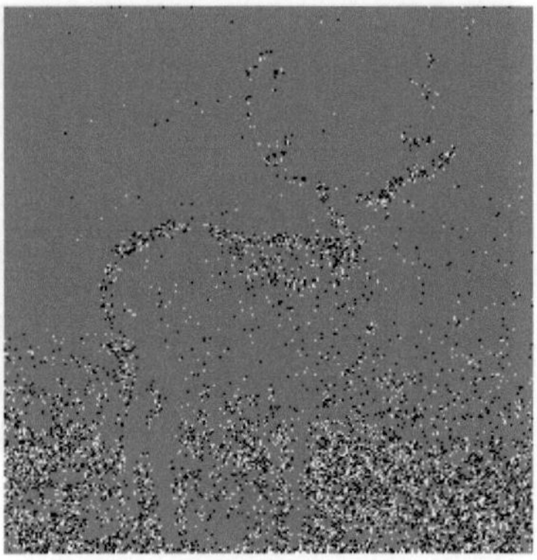

(c) SG(LWE).

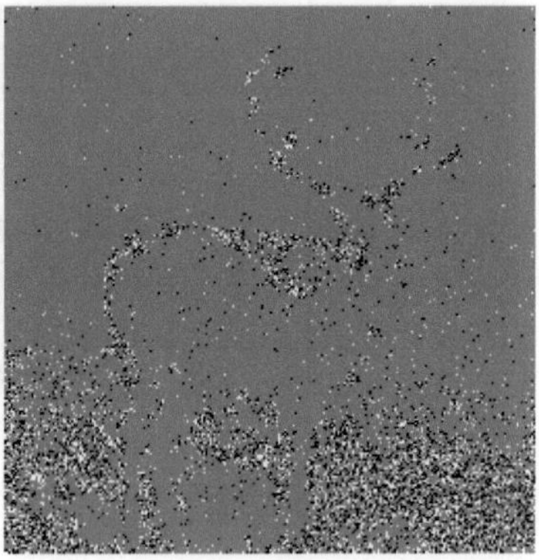

(d) SG(Xu+Yed).

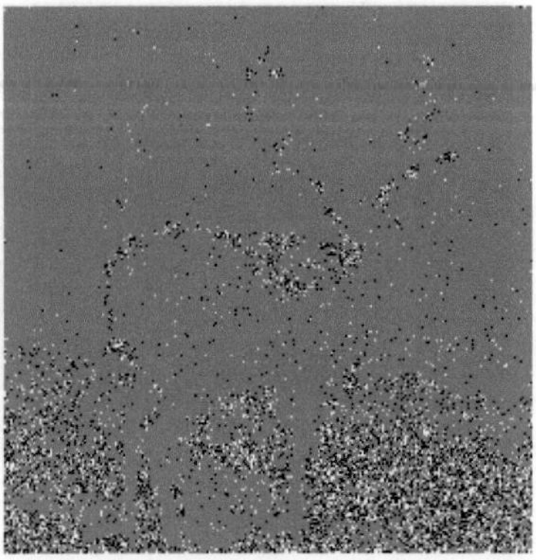

(e) SG(Xu+Yed+SR).

(d) SD(Xu+Yed+SR, Xu).

Fig. 7. Embedding locations in GAN-based steganographic image variants.

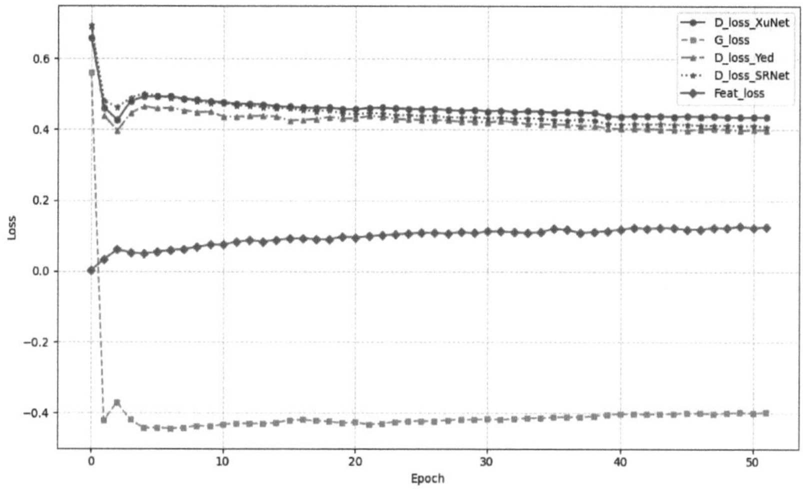

(a) SG(Xu+Yed+SR).

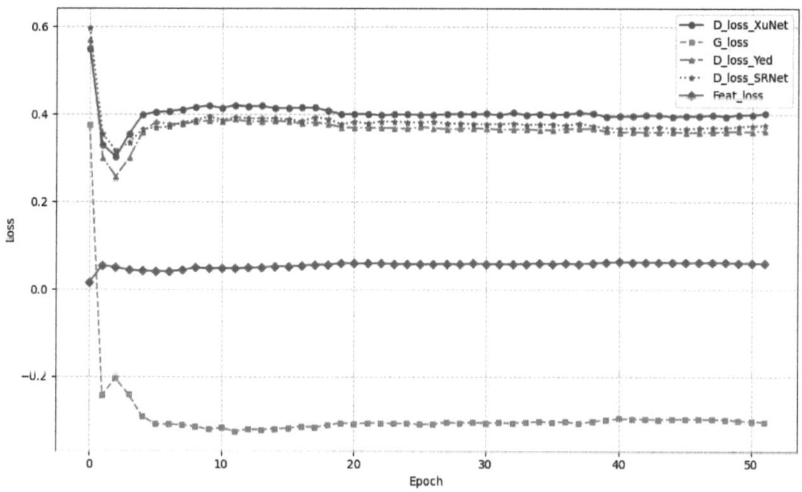

(b) SD(Xu+Yed+SR, Xu).

Fig. 8. Variations of loss values over epochs with and without the MLC.

4.5 Optimal Combination of Middle Layer Controller Models

The third set of experiments evaluated the optimal combination of middle layer controller models. Table 5 shows the detection accuracies of different model combinations introduced into the middle layer controller in the generative dataset in the face of algorithmic and steganographic payload mismatches. The best accuracy obtained for a dataset is indicated in bold font. The results indicate that the combination of middle layer controller and discriminator significantly affects model performance. Model VII achieved the highest detection rates in eight out of the 12 datasets. Model I with a single discriminator (XuNet) outperformed Model II (SRNet) and Model III (LWENet), indicating that XuNet has an advantage when serving as a discriminator or a middle layer controller.

Comparison of Models I, IV and VII reveals that increasing the number of discriminators improves detection performance. Different combinations using XuNet and SRNet as middle layer controllers were tested for the models with three discriminators – Models VII, VIII and IX. The experimental results show that the combination in Model VII achieved the best detection performance. Therefore, the three-discriminator configuration with XuNet as the middle layer controller was selected for subsequent ablation studies.

4.6 Middle Layer Controller Loss Weights

The fourth set of experiments evaluated the impacts of middle layer controller loss weights ranging from 0.1 to 100 on detection performance. Table 6 shows that the middle layer controller had minimal influence when the loss weight was 0.1 and the detection accuracy was close to that of models without a middle layer controller. The detection accuracy gradually improved as the loss weight increased with Model VI (weight = 100) achieving a 4.7% higher detection accuracy than Model I (weight = 0.1). The increase in model weight signifies a greater influence of the middle layer controller in the framework. Combined with the improvement in accuracy, this confirms the effectiveness of the middle layer controller in enhancing the generalization ability of detectors for GAN-based steganographic image samples.

4.7 Optimal Location of Model Middle Layer

The location of the model middle layer has a large impact on the steganographic images and the fifth set of experiments evaluated the optimal location of the middle layer. Table 7 shows the detection accuracies with the best accuracy obtained for a dataset indicated in bold font. In the case of XuNet, there are five possible groups, the shallower groups extracting shallow features and the deeper groups extracting deep abstract features. Comparison of Model I and Model IV shows that the generalization performance improvement brought by pulling the shallow layer features closer was not as effective as pulling the middle layer features closer. The shallow layer mainly extracts texture features and steganographic information is difficult to distinguish as a weak signal whereas the middle layer captures more abstract features and is suitable for feature control of cover images and steganographic images. Comparison of Model IV and Model V reveals that, as the network level deepens, the feature independence increases, the deep layer control becomes less effective and the commonality region decreases. Therefore, the layer selected for the middle layer controller should not be too deep.

Table 5. Performance comparison for combinations of middle layer controller models.

Dataset	Payload	I-SD (Xu,Xu)	II-SD (SR,SR)	III-SD (LWE Net, LWE ENet)	IV-SD (Xu+Yed, Xu)	V-SD (Yed+SR, Yed)	VI-SD (Yed+SR, SR)	VII-SD (Xu+Yed+ SR,Xu)	VIII-SD (Xu+Yed+ SR,SR)	IX-SD (Xu+Yed+ +LWE,Xu)
D1	0.4bpp	**86.75%**	84.25%	85.10%	85.65%	80.45%	84.72%	86.30%	82.93%	84.75%
	0.2bpp	69.73%	67.22%	67.92%	69.83%	60.22%	69.35%	**69.97%**	65.70%	66.88%
D2	0.4bpp	84.88%	82.80%	**86.42%**	84.05%	83.53%	85.42%	85.80%	78.67%	81.90%
	0.2bpp	67.95%	66.50%	**70.53%**	68.12%	65.00%	69.53%	69.60%	63.78%	65.28%
D3	0.4bpp	86.55%	85.32%	85.62%	86.78%	79.15%	85.80%	**86.83%**	85.52%	86.05%
	0.2bpp	69.08%	67.30%	66.22%	**70.10%**	58.70%	69.23%	70.08%	67.60%	67.90%
D4	0.4bpp	85.70%	84.80%	85.12%	85.05%	82.33%	84.40%	**87.05%**	82.55%	84.72%
	0.2bpp	68.85%	67.85%	66.75%	69.97%	61.52%	66.97%	**71.92%**	66.77%	68.70%
D5	0.4bpp	86.42%	84.72%	85.15%	85.45%	81.23%	84.88%	**86.78%**	83.73%	85.28%
	0.2bpp	65.58%	66.57%	65.30%	67.90%	59.80%	67.97%	**69.23%**	63.08%	66.35%
D6	0.4bpp	86.48%	83.40%	85.90%	84.97%	85.05%	85.50%	**86.55%**	81.53%	84.38%
	0.2bpp	65.72%	62.10%	63.90%	66.60%	63.60%	67.77%	**68.00%**	59.40%	63.65%

Table 6. Performance comparison for various middle layer controller loss weights.

Dataset	Payload	I-Loss=0.1	II-Loss=1	III-Loss=3	IV-Loss=10	V-Loss=20	VI-Loss=50	VII-Loss=100
D1	0.4bpp	84.95%	82.88%	**86.70%**	86.45%	84.85%	86.17%	86.30%
	0.2bpp	67.40%	66.42%	69.90%	69.27%	67.70%	69.55%	**69.97%**
D2	0.4bpp	82.03%	83.05%	**86.05%**	85.12%	81.30%	85.22%	85.80%
	0.2bpp	65.42%	67.10%	69.53%	68.17%	65.28%	69.83%	**69.60%**
D3	0.4bpp	86.95%	83.58%	87.17%	**87.80%**	86.12%	86.95%	86.83%
	0.2bpp	69.12%	65.55%	69.45%	**70.50%**	68.67%	**70.50%**	70.08%
D4	0.4bpp	84.25%	86.72%	86.35%	86.67%	83.97%	86.35%	**87.05%**
	0.2bpp	68.23%	70.97%	70.75%	70.93%	68.23%	70.58%	**71.92%**
D5	0.4bpp	85.45%	84.28%	86.42%	86.60%	84.88%	86.22%	**86.78%**
	0.2bpp	66.53%	65.88%	68.62%	68.10%	65.67%	67.67%	**69.23%**
D6	0.4bpp	83.58%	**86.65%**	86.15%	85.65%	83.35%	85.80%	86.55%
	0.2bpp	63.30%	**68.17%**	67.22%	66.50%	62.48%	65.72%	68.00%

Table 7. Performance comparison for various model middle layer locations.

Dataset	Payload	I-Group1	II-Group2	III-Group3	IV-Group4	V-Group5
D1	0.4bpp	85.08%	85.75%	85.25%	**86.30%**	86.02%
	0.2bpp	67.35%	69.70%	69.12%	**69.97%**	**69.97%**
D2	0.4bpp	82.17%	84.55%	**85.88%**	85.80%	84.72%
	0.2bpp	65.38%	69.23%	**70.05%**	69.60%	68.10%
D3	0.4bpp	85.80%	86.90%	85.30%	86.83%	**87.12%**
	0.2bpp	67.92%	69.25%	68.77%	**70.08%**	70.00%
D4	0.4bpp	85.30%	86.62%	86.45%	**87.05%**	86.17%
	0.2bpp	69.33%	71.70%	71.03%	**71.92%**	70.38%
D5	0.4bpp	85.22%	86.10%	85.75%	**86.78%**	86.28%
	0.2bpp	67.40%	67.27%	69.45%	69.23%	**69.55%**
D6	0.4bpp	83.43%	85.88%	**87.62%**	86.55%	85.78%
	0.2bpp	64.12%	66.50%	**70.58%**	68.00%	68.17%

Table 8. Performance comparison for varying numbers of middle layer controllers.

Dataset	Payload	I-SD (Xu+Yed+SR, Xu)	II-SD (Xu+Yed+SR, Xu+SR)	III-SD (Xu+Yed+SR, Xu+Yed+SR)
D1	0.4bpp	**86.30%**	85.10%	86.28%
	0.2bpp	**69.97%**	67.67%	68.65%
D2	0.4bpp	**85.80%**	84.42%	84.30%
	0.2bpp	**69.60%**	67.55%	68.17%
D3	0.4bpp	86.83%	86.00%	**87.40%**
	0.2bpp	**70.08%**	68.58%	69.73%
D4	0.4bpp	**87.05%**	86.30%	86.65%
	0.2bpp	**71.92%**	70.97%	71.15%
D5	0.4bpp	**86.78%**	85.78%	86.55%
	0.2bpp	**69.23%**	67.27%	68.65%
D6	0.4bpp	**86.55%**	85.60%	85.52%
	0.2bpp	**68.00%**	65.85%	66.00%

4.8 Number of Middle Layer Controllers

The final set of experiments evaluated the impacts of different combinations of middle layer controllers on generalization performance. Table 8 shows the detection accuracies with the best accuracy obtained for a dataset indicated in bold font. The results reveal that the middle layer controller using only XuNet is more effective than the combination of XuNet with Yedroudj-Net and SRNet. In fact, the improvement is up to 2.3%. This provides evidence of the efficacy of using a single steganalysis network as a middle layer controller.

5 Conclusions

The novel self-supervised MLC-GAN framework described in this chapter is designed to detect GAN-based steganalyzer variants. The framework controls and guides the features of images in the middle layer of a neural network by constructing image samples that capture the common characteristics of GAN-based steganographic images. The detector trained using these image samples exhibits superior generalized detection performance.

The experimental results demonstrate the effectiveness of the MLC-GAN framework at detecting GAN-based steganalyzer variants. Additionally, the results of ablation experiments demonstrate the relevance of the various framework modules to improving detection performance and generalizability. Limited research has focused on the detection of GAN-based steganographic images. It is hoped that this work will stimulate new efforts focused on the challenging problem of detecting GAN-based steganalyzer variants.

Acknowledgement

This research was supported by the National Key R&D Program of China under Grant no. 2022YFC3300803, Opening Project of the Intelligent Policing Key Laboratory of Sichuan Province under Grant no. ZNJW2023KFMS008, Natural Science Foundation of China under Grant no. 62172053, 111 Project under Grant no. B21049 and Open Foundation of Guizhou Provincial Key Laboratory of Public Big Data under Grant no. 2018BDKFJJ019.

References

1. A. Ansari, M. Mohammadi and M. Parvez, A comparative study of recent steganography techniques for multiple image formats, *International Journal of Computer Network and Information Security*, vol. 11(1), pp. 11–25, 2019.
2. P. Bas, T. Filler and T. Pevny, "Break our steganographic system" – The ins and outs of organizing BOSS, in *Information Hiding*, T. Filler, T. Pevny, S. Craver and A. Ker (Eds.), Springer, Berlin Heidelberg, Germany, pp. 59–70, 2011.
3. M. Boroumand, M. Chen and J. Fridrich, Deep residual network for steganalysis of digital images, *IEEE Transactions on Information Forensics and Security*, vol. 14(5), pp. 1181–1193, 2019.
4. X. Deng, B. Chen, W. Luo and D. Luo, Fast and effective global covariance pooling network for image steganalysis, *Proceedings of the ACM Workshop on Information Hiding and Multimedia Security*, pp. 230–234, 2019.
5. J. Fridrich and T. Filler, Practical methods for minimizing embedding impact in steganography, *Proceedings of SPIE: Security, Steganography and Watermarking of Multimedia Contents IX*, vol. 6505, pp. 13–27. 2007.
6. J. Fridrich and J. Kodovsky, Rich models for steganalysis of digital images, *IEEE Transactions on Information Forensics and Security*, vol. 7(3), pp. 868–882, 2012.
7. I. Goodfellow, J. Pouget-Abadie, M. Mirza, B. Xu, D. Warde-Farley, S. Ozair, A. Courville and Y. Bengio, Generative adversarial nets, *Communications of the ACM*, vol. 63(11), pp. 139–144, 2020.

8. V. Holub and J. Fridrich, Designing steganographic distortion using directional filters, *Proceedings of the IEEE International Workshop on Information Forensics and Security*, pp. 234–239, 2012.
9. V. Holub, J. Fridrich and T. Denemark, Universal distortion function for steganography in an arbitrary domain, *EURASIP Journal on Information Security*, vol. 2014, article no. 1, 2014.
10. D. Huang, W. Luo, M. Liu, W. Tang and J. Huang, Steganography embedding cost learning with a generative multi-adversarial network, *IEEE Transactions on Information Forensics and Security*, vol. 19, pp. 15–29, 2024.
11. Y. Jin, Y. Wang, M. Long, J. Wang, P. Yu and J. Sun, A multi-player minimax game for generative adversarial networks, *Proceedings of the IEEE International Conference on Multimedia and Expo*, 2020.
12. J. Kodovsky, J. Fridrich and V. Holub, On the dangers of overtraining steganography to incomplete cover models, *Proceedings of the Thirteenth ACM Multimedia Workshop on Multimedia and Security*, pp. 69–76, 2011.
13. J. Kodovsky, J. Fridrich and V. Holub, Ensemble classifiers for steganalysis of digital media, *IEEE Transactions on Information Forensics and Security*, vol. 7(2), pp. 432–444, 2012.
14. A. Kurakin, I. Goodfellow and S. Bengio, Adversarial Machine Learning at Scale, arXiv: 1611.01236v2 (`arxiv.org/abs/1611.01236v2`), 2017.
15. Y. LeCun, L. Bottou, Y. Bengio and P. Haffner, Gradient-based learning applied to document recognition, *Proceedings of the IEEE*, vol. 86(11), pp. 2278–2324, 1998.
16. B. Li, M. Wang, J. Huang and X. Li, A new cost function for spatial image steganography, *Proceedings of the IEEE International Conference on Image Processing*, pp. 4206–4210, 2014.
17. J. Liu, Y. Ke, Z. Zhang, Y. Lei, J. Li and M. Zhang, Recent advances in image steganography with generative adversarial networks, *IEEE Access*, vol. 8, pp. 60575–60597, 2020.
18. M. Liu, W. Luo, P. Zheng and J. Huang, A new adversarial embedding method for enhancing image steganography, *IEEE Transactions on Information Forensics and Security*, vol. 16, pp. 4621–4634, 2021.
19. M. Liu, T. Song, W. Luo, P. Zheng and J. Huang, Adversarial steganography embedding via stego generation and selection, *IEEE Transactions on Dependable and Secure Computing*, vol. 20(3), pp. 2375–2389, 2023.
20. M. Long, H. Zhu, J. Wang and M. Jordan, Deep transfer learning with joint adaptation networks, *Proceedings of the International Conference on Machine Learning*, vol. 70, pp. 2208–2217.
21. M. Naseer, S. Khan, M. Hayat, F. Khan and F. Porikl, A self-supervised approach for adversarial robustness, *Proceedings of the IEEE/CVF Conference on Computer Vision and Pattern Recognition*, pp. 259–268, 2020.
22. T. Pevny, P. Bas and J. Fridrich, Steganalysis by subtractive pixel adjacency matrix, *IEEE Transactions on Information Forensics and Security*, vol. 5(2), pp. 215–224, 2010.
23. T. Pevny, T. Filler and P. Bas, Using high-dimensional image models to perform highly undetectable steganography, in *Information Hiding*, R. Bohme, P. Fong and R. Safavi-Naini (Eds.), Springer, Berlin Heidelberg, Germany, pp. 161–177, 2010.
24. O. Ronneberger, P. Fischer and T. Brox, U-Net: Convolutional networks for biomedical image segmentation, in *Medical Image Computing and Computer-Assisted Intervention – MICCAI 2015*, N. Navab, J., Hornegger, W. Wells and A. Frangi (Eds.), Springer, Cham, Switzerland, pp. 234–241, 2015.

25. V. Sedighi, R. Cogranne and J. Fridrich, Content-adaptive steganography by minimizing statistical detectability, *IEEE Transactions on Information Forensics and Security*, vol. 11(2), pp. 221–234, 2016.
26. R. Sutton, H. Maei, D. Precup, S. Bhatnagar, D. Silver, C. Szepesvari and E. Wiewiora, Fast gradient-descent methods for temporal-difference learning with linear function approximation, *Proceedings of the Twenty-Sixth Annual International Conference on Machine Learning*, pp. 993–1000, 2009.
27. W. Tang, B. Li, M. Barni, J. Li and J. Huang, An automatic cost learning framework for image steganography using deep reinforcement learning, *IEEE Transactions on Information Forensics and Security*, vol. 16, pp. 952–967, 2021.
28. W. Tang, S. Tan, B. Li and J. Huang, Automatic steganographic distortion learning using a generative adversarial network, *IEEE Signal Processing Letters*, vol. 24(10), pp. 1547–1551, 2017.
29. S. Weng, M. Chen, L. Yu and S. Sun, Lightweight and effective deep image steganalysis network, *IEEE Signal Processing Letters*, vol. 29, pp. 1888–1892, 2022.
30. Y. Wu, H. Shuai, Z. Tam and H. Chiu, Gradient normalization for generative adversarial networks, *Proceedings of the IEEE/CVF International Conference on Computer Vision*, pp. 6353–6362, 2021.
31. G. Xu, H. Wu and Y. Shi, Structural design of convolutional neural networks for steganalysis, *IEEE Signal Processing Letters*, vol. 23(5), pp. 708–712, 2016.
32. J. Yang, D. Ruan, J. Huang, X. Kang and Y. Shi, An embedding cost learning framework using GAN, *IEEE Transactions on Information Forensics and Security*, vol. 15, pp. 839–851, 2020.
33. J. Ye, J. Ni and Y. Yi, Deep learning hierarchical representations for image steganalysis, *IEEE Transactions on Information Forensics and Security*, vol. 12(11), pp. 2545–2557, 2017.
34. M. Yedroudj, F. Comby and M. Chaumont, Yedroudj-Net: An efficient CNN for spatial steganalysis, *Proceedings of the International Conference on Acoustics, Speech and Signal Processing*, pp. 2092–2096, 2018.
35. W. You, H. Zhang and X. Zhao, A Siamese CNN for image steganalysis, *IEEE Transactions on Information Forensics and Security*, vol. 16, pp. 291–306, 2021.
36. L. Yu, Z. Zhang, S. Weng, P. Cao and G. Cao, A deep steganalysis network combining source-supervised and target-unsupervised information for cover-source mismatch, *Expert Systems with Applications*, vol. 255(D), article no. 124790, 2024.
37. R. Zhang, F. Zhu, J. Liu and G. Liu, Depthwise separable convolutions and multi-level pooling for efficient spatial CNN-based steganalysis, *IEEE Transactions on Information Forensics and Security*, vol. 15, pp. 1138–1150, 2020.
38. X. Zhang, X. Kong, P. Wang and B. Wang, Cover-source mismatch in deep spatial steganalysis, in *Digital Forensics and Watermarking*, H. Wang, X. Zhao, Y. Shi, H. Kim and A. Piva (Eds.), Springer, Cham, Switzerland, pp. 71–83, 2020.

Practical Benchmarks for Evaluating Deepfake Detectors

Jianguo Jiang[1,2], Huan Wang[1,2], Fuqiang Du[1,2], Kam-Pui Chow[3], Jiawen Wang[4], Yachao Liang[1,2], Boquan Li[5], Lanchi Xie[6], and Min Yu[1,2]

[1] Chinese Academy of Sciences, Beijing, China
[2] University of Chinese Academy of Sciences, Beijing, China
yumin@iie.ac.cn
[3] University of Hong Kong, Hong Kong, China
[4] Illinois Institute of Technology, Chicago, Illinois, USA
[5] Harbin Engineering University, Harbin, China
[6] Institute of Forensic Science, Beijing, China

Abstract. Deepfake images have raised significant security concerns due to their malicious use. Deepfake detection algorithms based on deep learning have achieved promising performance. However, the algorithms face challenges in real-world deployments, especially in digital forensic applications. Therefore, it is essential to develop evaluation methods for deepfake detectors that characterize their reliability, security and efficiency.

This chapter specifies practical benchmarks for evaluating deepfake detectors. An evaluation platform for deepfake image detectors is employed. The platform, comprising a sample generation engine, an interaction engine and a real-time analysis engine, significantly reduces the manual analysis efforts. A comprehensive, multidimensional quantitative evaluation system for deepfake detectors is described. The evaluation system has three primary metrics, ten secondary metrics and 21 tertiary metrics that provide holistic evaluations of detection, security and efficiency. Extensive experiments demonstrate the usability of the platform and the effectiveness of the evaluation system.

Keywords: Image Forensics · Deepfake Images · Deepfake Detector · Evaluation · Detection · Security · Efficiency

1 Introduction

Rapid advancements in generative artificial intelligence technology have contributed to the proliferation of sophisticated deepfake images and videos. Deepfake images and videos are increasingly being misused, raising significant security concerns.

Researchers have developed various detection algorithms to detect deepfake images and videos. Algorithms that leverage deep learning techniques have

Published by Springer Nature Switzerland AG 2026
E. Kurkowski and S. Shenoi (Eds.): DigitalForensics 2025, IFIP AICT 762, pp. 27–42, 2026.
https://doi.org/10.1007/978-3-032-09802-3_2

achieved considerable success [1, 2, 5, 11]. However, while these algorithms perform well under controlled laboratory conditions, they face challenges in real-world deployments, especially in digital forensic applications. The principal reason is that the deepfake detection algorithms exhibit uncertain performance and security in real-world environments.

To address the limitations, attention has focused on evaluating deepfake detection algorithms and implementations, including establishing metrics such as accuracy, robustness and generalization [3, 6, 13, 18, 29]. The research has progressed in two areas, evaluation of deepfake detection models and evaluation of deepfake detection systems.

Efforts related to deepfake detection model evaluation have applied conventional methods to models developed in controlled laboratory settings. For example, Li et al. [18] have introduced a cross-dataset evaluation protocol that assesses the generalization ability of deepfake detection models on previously-unseen data. While these evaluations reflect model performance to some extent, the complexities encountered in real-world scenarios make it difficult to gauge their deployment capabilities.

Efforts related to deepfake detection system evaluation tend to leverage the interfaces of deployed systems to conduct extensive black-box testing using large numbers of samples. For example, Wang et al. [29] have evaluated the accuracy, generalizability and robustness of deepfake detection systems using application programming interfaces from three vendors. However, one limitation is that the test results still require manual analysis. Another limitation is that the evaluation metrics are neither systematic nor comprehensive, which hinders their ability to fully reflect the underlying deepfake model capabilities, especially with regard to security.

This research has attempted to address the limitations by developing an evaluation platform for conducting automated quantitative assessments of deepfake detectors that target real-world application scenarios. The evaluation platform interacts with deepfake detectors via application programming interfaces and supports provides testing, real-time analysis and real-time attack functionality. The platform engages test samples from seven deepfake models as well as adversarial samples generated by seven adversarial attack methods – four common perturbation generation algorithms and three black-box attack algorithms. Additionally, the platform supports a comprehensive, multidimensional quantitative evaluation system for deepfake detectors. The evaluation system incorporates three primary metrics, ten secondary metrics and 21 tertiary metrics that provide holistic evaluations of the detection, security and efficiency characteristics of deepfake detectors.

2 Related Work

This section describes research on deepfake generation and deepfake detection. Also, it discusses efforts related to the evaluation of deepfake detectors.

2.1 Deepfake Generation

Deepfake generation techniques have evolved significantly since their inception. Initial models using variational autoencoders (VAEs) [15] and generative adversarial networks (GANs) [9] enabled the generation of synthetic images with increasing realism. Generative adversarial networks, in particular, revolutionized the field, enabling high-quality image and video synthesis by learning the underlying distributions of real data via generator-discriminator interactions.

Subsequent advancements led to more sophisticated models such as StyleGAN [14] that enables controlled and detailed image synthesis by learning disentangled latent representations. Recent work has seen the integration of attention mechanisms and transformer architectures in generative models, which significantly improves the quality of the generated media.

Diffusion models [12] have gained prominence for generating high-fidelity images by iteratively refining noisy images. Nichol and Dhariwal [24] extended this concept, achieving state-of-the-art results in image synthesis using continuous-time diffusion processes.

Meanwhile, tools such as DeepFaceLab [20] and FaceSwap have made deepfake technology accessible to a wider audience, raising concerns about its misuse. Indeed, the widespread availability of these tools has made it increasingly important to develop detection systems capable of identifying deepfakes created by a broad range of methods [22].

2.2 Deepfake Detection

Several deepfake detection methods have been developed to combat the growing threats posed by deepfake images and videos. Early methods focused on detecting artifacts in deepfake videos by analyzing inconsistencies in facial landmarks [16] and eye-blinking patterns [17]. However, the reliance of these methods on handcrafted features limits their generalizability.

With the advent of deep learning, convolutional neural networks have become the *de facto* basis for detecting deepfakes. A prominent exemplar is MesoNet [1], a convolutional neural network architecture designed specifically for detecting manipulated videos. MesoNet has demonstrated promising results, but struggles with generalization across different types of deepfakes. Building on this work, Nguyen et al. [23] employed capsule networks for deepfake detection. The method provides improved robustness to facial manipulations by capturing spatial hierarchies.

Several large-scale datasets, such as FaceForensics++ [26], DFDC [7] and Celeb-DF [18], have been released to help benchmark deepfake detection models. These datasets play a crucial role in evaluating model generalization ability and continue to facilitate the development of deepfake detection models with improved robustness and scalability.

Beyond individual models, integrated detection systems have been deployed in practical applications. For example, social media platforms such as Facebook and Twitter have implemented real-time deepfake detection systems to identify and remove manipulated content. However, these systems face challenges related to scalability, false positives and detection speed, highlighting the need to develop more efficient deepfake detection frameworks [10].

2.3 Deepfake Detector Evaluation

Deepfake detectors have traditionally been evaluated using standard machine learning metrics such as accuracy, precision, recall and F1-score [8]. While these metrics provide basic performance assessments, they do not adequately capture the complexities of real-world deepfake detection scenarios where adversarial attacks, generalization across different datasets and ethical implications of biased models must be considered.

Recent research has focused on developing more comprehensive deepfake detector evaluation frameworks. For example, Li et al. [18] have introduced a cross-dataset evaluation protocol that assesses the generalization ability of detection models on unseen data. Their work revealed that many state-of-the-art models overfit to specific datasets and fail to generalize to new types of deepfakes, underscoring the need for more robust evaluations of detection models and systems.

Adversarial robustness has become an important factor in evaluating deepfake detection models. Carlini and Wagner [3] demonstrated that deepfake detectors can be vulnerable to adversarial samples, where small, imperceptible perturbations in the input data cause model misclassification. Evaluating models for robustness to such attacks is critical to ensuring their reliability in real-world applications.

Several frameworks have been proposed for holistic evaluations. For example, Hussain et al. [13] developed a multi-faceted evaluation system that includes metrics for accuracy, robustness to adversarial attacks, generalization across datasets and efficiency in large-scale deployments. The work serves as a foundation for developing evaluation protocols that provide more comprehensive assessments of deepfake detection models.

Despite these research efforts, a significant gap exists in evaluating the scalability and efficiency of deepfake detectors in real-world settings. Evaluating detection models and systems for their ability to process large volumes of data in real-time while maintaining high accuracy and robustness is essential to successful practical deployments [28].

3 Evaluation Methodology

This section describes the proposed evaluation methodology for deepfake detectors. It presents the architecture of the automated evaluation platform and provides a detailed description of the evaluation system.

3.1 Evaluation Platform Architecture

The evaluation platform architecture is tailored to assess deepfake detectors in real-world applications. The design principles are simplicity, real-time capabili-

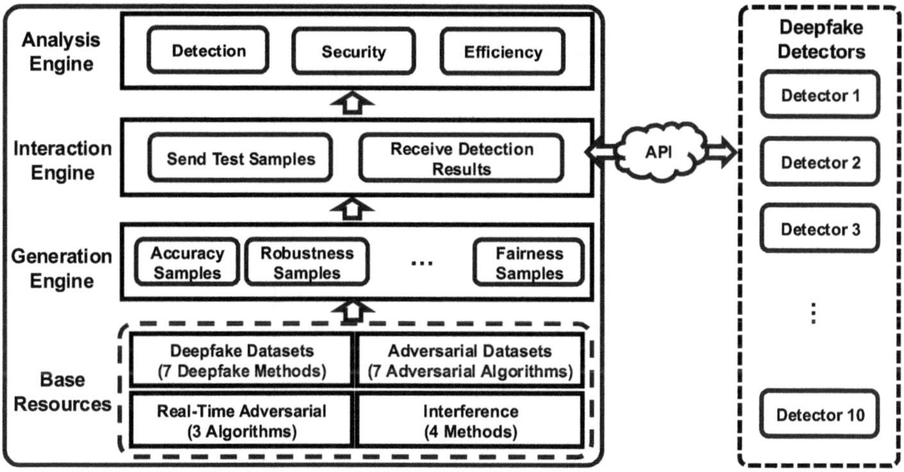

Fig. 1. Evaluation platform architecture.

ties and automation. Simplicity focuses on the ease of interaction between users and the platform. Real-time capability requires the platform to generate samples, perform tests and provide real-time analyses of the desired metrics at any point during testing. Automation ensures that the platform can perform automated testing and analysis throughout the evaluation cycle.

Figure 1 shows the architecture of the evaluation platform that incorporates a generation engine, an interaction engine and an analysis engine.

The generation engine is responsible for constructing diverse test samples. Since sample testing is fundamental to evaluating deepfake detectors, extensive preparatory work was conducted. Seven deepfake generation techniques were employed to generate test samples and seven adversarial sample generation methods were engaged to generate adversarial test samples. Additionally, four perturbation algorithms are implemented for the real-time generation of samples with added noise/interference, and three real-time adversarial attack algorithms are implemented for dynamic adversarial testing. The sample generation engine leverages the samples and algorithms to construct tailored testing datasets specific to the deepfake detector being evaluated.

The interaction engine facilitates communications between the evaluation platform and deepfake detector being evaluated. Since a black-box testing approach is employed, the interaction engine sends test samples to the deepfake detector via its application programming interface and receives the detector's results. The returned detection results include information such as timestamps, probability scores and other relevant data. The interaction engine supports the collection of a large volume of detection results.

The analysis engine implements automated processing and analysis of the results in real time. The metrics and evaluation methods are engaged by the

Table 1. Primary detection metric and its secondary and tertiary metrics.

Primary	Secondary	Tertiary	Description
Detection (11)	Accuracy (6)	acc	Overall accuracy
		auc	Area under the curve
		prec	Precision of predictions
		rec	Ability to retrieve relevant cases
		f1	Harmonic mean of precision and recall
		fpr	False positive rate
	Robustness (4)	$\mathrm{dev_n}$	Deviation under noise
		$\mathrm{dev_b}$	Deviation under blur
		$\mathrm{dev_c}$	Deviation under compression
		$\mathrm{dev_r}$	Deviation under rotation
	Generalization (1)	fdr	Forgery detection rate

analysis engine, which aggregates and analyzes multiple test outcomes. Comprehensive evaluation results covering multiple metric dimensions and levels are presented to users in an intuitively appealing manner.

3.2 Evaluation System

A multidimensional, multilevel evaluation system is proposed to address the limitations of current deepfake evaluation schemes. The evaluation system is designed to facilitate comprehensive assessments of deepfake detectors. Specifically, it offers a holistic characterization of deepfake detectors covering three key dimensions – detection, security and efficiency.

Detection Metric. This primary metric expresses the overall detection performance of a deepfake detector. In real-world scenarios, the images to be detected are often unknown and numerous interference factors may arise during network transmission. Therefore, the detection metric has three secondary metrics – accuracy, robustness and generalization. Accuracy measures how precisely a deepfake detector can identify deepfakes. Robustness measures the ability to detect deepfakes under typical interference conditions. Generalization measures the ability to detect deepfakes created using unknown methods.

Table 1 shows the primary detection metric, its three secondary metrics and eleven tertiary metrics. The secondary accuracy metric has six tertiary metrics (acc, auc, prec, rec, f1 and fpr). The secondary robustness metric has four tertiary metrics ($\mathrm{dev_n}$, $\mathrm{dev_b}$, $\mathrm{dev_c}$ and $\mathrm{dev_r}$). The secondary generalization metric has one tertiary metric (fdr).

Table 2. Primary security metric and its secondary and tertiary metrics.

Primary	Secondary	Tertiary	Description
Security (6)	Anti Deepfake (1)	det_s	Detection success rate
	Anti Adversarial Sample (1)	asr	Attack success rate
	Anti Real-Time Attack(3)	flag	Weathering an attack
		query	Number of queries
		drop	Dropped detection rate
	Fairness (1)	dev_a	Deviation under different age

The secondary accuracy metric score is computed as:

$$\text{Accuracy} = \frac{1}{6}(\text{acc} + \text{auc} + \text{prec} + \text{rec} + \text{f1} + (1 - \text{fpr}))$$

The secondary robustness metric score is computed as:

$$\text{Robustness} = 100 \cdot \left(1 - \frac{1}{4}\sum_{i=1}^{4} \frac{\text{dev}_i}{\text{Accuracy}}\right)$$

where dev_i ($i \in \{1, 2, 3, 4\}$) correspond to dev_n, dev_b, dev_c and dev_r, respectively. Furthermore, each dev_i is computed as:

$$\text{dev}_\text{i} = \text{Accuracy} - \text{Accuracy}_i$$

where Accuracy_i denotes the Accuracy score under perturbation i.

The secondary generalization metric score is computed as:

$$\text{Generalization} = \text{f1}$$

where f1 is the F1-score (harmonic mean of precision and recall) computed using the generalization testing set.

Finally, the primary detection metric score is computed as:

$$\text{Detection} = \lambda_1 \cdot \text{Accuracy} + \lambda_2 \cdot \text{Robustness} + \lambda_3 \cdot \text{Generalization}$$

Security Metric. This primary metric expresses the security risk associated with a deepfake detector. The security risk of a deepfake detector is assessed based on its performance in various attack scenarios, including novel deepfake attacks, adversarial sample attacks and real-time adversarial attacks. Additionally, the fairness of the deepfake detector is considered.

Table 2 shows the primary security metric, its four secondary metrics and six tertiary metrics. The secondary anti deepfake metric has one tertiary metric

(det_s). The secondary anti adversarial sample metric has one tertiary metric (asr). The secondary anti real-time attack metric has three tertiary metrics (flag, query and drop). The secondary fairness metric has one tertiary metric (dev_a).

The secondary anti deepfake metric score is computed as:

$$\text{Anti Deepfake} = 100 \cdot \text{Min}\left(\frac{\text{det}_\text{s}}{\text{f1}}, 1\right)$$

where det_s is the recall on the novel deepfake sample set and f1 is the tertiary metric score corresponding to the primary detection metric (Table 1).

The secondary anti adversarial sample metric score is computed as:

$$\text{Anti Adversarial Sample} = 100 \cdot \text{Min}\left(1 - \frac{\text{asr}}{\text{acc}}, 1\right)$$

where asr is the tertiary metric score corresponding to the primary security metric (Table 2) and acc is the tertiary metric score corresponding to the primary detection metric (Table 1).

The secondary anti real-time attack metric score is computed as:

$$\text{Anti Real-Time Attack} = 100 \cdot \left(1 - (1 - \text{flag}) \cdot \frac{\text{drop}}{\text{prob}_\text{init}}\right)$$

where flag has a value of 0 or 1 (0 corresponds to an unsuccessful attack and 1 corresponds to a successful attack) and prob_init is the initial probability value of a single sample.

Finally, the secondary fairness metric score is computed as:

$$\text{Fairness} = 100 \cdot \left(1 - \frac{\text{dev}_a}{\text{Accuracy}}\right)$$

where

$$\text{dev}_\text{a} = \text{Accuracy}_1 - \text{Accuracy}_2$$

and Accuracy_1 and Accuracy_2 are the acc tertiary metric scores corresponding to the primary detection primary metric (Table 1) for two testing datasets of different ages.

Finally, the primary security metric score is computed as:

$$\begin{aligned}\text{Security} = {} & \lambda_4 \cdot \text{Anti Deepfake} + \lambda_5 \cdot \text{Anti Adversarial Sample} \\ & + \lambda_6 \cdot \text{Anti Real-Time Attack} + \lambda_7 \times \text{Fairness}\end{aligned}$$

Efficiency Metric. This primary metric expresses the responsiveness of a deepfake detector. Providing prompt responses is crucial in real-world scenarios with large data volumes and stringent timeliness requirements. Therefore, time consumption, space consumption and detection speed are selected as secondary metrics for assessing deepfake detector efficiency.

Table 3. Primary efficiency metric and its secondary and tertiary metrics.

Primary	Secondary	Tertiary	Description
Efficiency (4)	Time Consumption (2)	rt	Response time
		ait	Average inference time
	Space Consumption (1)	mu	Memory used
	Detection Speed (1)	thr	Number per unit time

Table 3 shows the primary efficiency metric, its three secondary metrics and four tertiary metrics. The secondary time consumption metric has two tertiary metrics (rt and ait). The secondary space consumption metric has one tertiary metric (mu). The secondary detection speed metric has one tertiary metric (thr).

4 Experiments and Results

This section describes the deepfake detector evaluation experiments and the evaluation results.

4.1 Experiments

This section describes the deepfake detectors evaluated in the experiments, the datasets used in the experiments and the evaluation method used in the experiments.

Table 4. Detectors and training datasets.

Detector (Release Date)	Training Dataset
MesoInception [1] (2018)	FaceForensics++(c23)
Xception [4] (2018)	FaceForensics++(c23)
EfficientB4 [27] (2022)	FaceForensics++(c23)
Capsule [23] (2019)	FaceForensics++(c23)
FFD [31] (2024)	FaceForensics++(c23)
RECCE [2] (2022)	FaceForensics++(c23)
UCF [30] (2023)	FaceForensics++(c23)
SPSL [19] (2021)	FaceForensics++(c23)
SRM [21] (2021)	FaceForensics++(c23)
F3Net [25] (2020)	FaceForensics++(c23)

Deepfake Detectors. Ten classical/advanced deepfake models were evaluated in the experiments (Table 4). The experiments engaged the pre-trained models from [30], which were encapsulated in callable application programming interfaces in order to conduct the evaluations.

Datasets. As mentioned in Section 3, the platform incorporated deepfake samples produced by seven deepfake generation methods, including Deepfake, Face2-Face, FaceSwap, NeuralTextures, Celeb-DF-V2 [18], StyleGAN and StarGAN [4]. The accuracy testing dataset comprised samples generated by Deepfake, Face2-Face and FaceSwap. The robustness testing set comprised four interference testing datasets generated in real time based on the accuracy testing dataset. The generalization testing dataset comprised samples from NeuralTextures, Celeb-DF-V2 and StarGAN.

The deepfake attack testing dataset comprised samples from StyleGAN. For adversarial sample attacks, an adversarial attack testing dataset was created using seven adversarial sample generation algorithms – CW, GenAP, DeepFool, PGD, FGSM, SemanticAdv and MI-FGSM. The NES algorithm was used for real-time adversarial attacks. The real samples in the testing datasets were drawn from FaceForensics++ [26] and Celeb-DF-V2, with a portion of the samples selected for performance testing.

In summary, for each detector, the total testing samples amounted to around 9,000 with a real-to-fake sample ratio of approximately 1:1. Based on experience and the attention levels, the λ-parameters were set as: $\lambda_1 = 0.4$, $\lambda_2 = 0.2$, $\lambda_3 = 0.2$, $\lambda_4 = 0.3$, $\lambda_5 = 0.3$, $\lambda_6 = 0.2$ and $\lambda_7 = 0.2$.

Evaluation Metrics. Traditional machine learning metrics were employed as the basic metrics – accuracy (acc), area under the curve (auc), precision (pre), recall (rec), F1-score (f1) and false positive rate (fpr). These metrics were used to evaluate the detection, security and efficiency of deepfake detectors.

4.2 Evaluation Method Effectiveness

Table 4 shows the ten deepfake detectors employed in the evaluation along with their release dates and training datasets (FaceForensics++(c23)). Table 5 shows the tertiary metric results corresponding to the primary detection metric. Table 6 shows the tertiary metric results corresponding to the primary security and efficiency metrics.

Table 7 shows the overall detection evaluation results (secondary and primary metrics). Table 8 shows the overall security evaluation results (secondary and primary metrics). The results demonstrate that the proposed quantitative evaluation system for deepfake detectors is feasible.

An attractive feature of the quantitative evaluation system is that it employs a bottom-up approach, capturing the local features as well as the overall comprehensive capabilities of deepfake detectors.

For example, consider the tertiary metric scores corresponding to the primary detection metric for the UCF deepfake detector (Table 5). Its tertiary metric scores – accuracy of 96.39%, area under the curve of 99.66%, recall of 93.74% and F1-score of 96.30% – are better than the scores of the other deepfake detectors. As a result, its secondary metric score – accuracy of 97.35% – is the best compared with the other detectors (Table 7). However, because the

Table 5. Tertiary metric scores for the detection metric.

Detector	**Tertiary Metrics**										
	acc	**auc**	**prec**	**rec**	**f1**	**fpr**	**dev_n**	**dev_b**	**dev_c**	**dev_r**	**fdr**
MesoInception	67.70%	85.02%	92.79%	38.60%	54.52%	3.08%	5.55%	12.02%	12.92%	9.43%	51.74%
Xception	93.28%	99.54%	99.54%	87.00%	92.85%	0.40%	6.19%	33.17%	9.03%	8.64%	85.38%
EfficientB4	94.98%	99.26%	97.87%	92%	94.85%	2.01%	5.97%	27.94%	10.19%	8.01%	88.21%
Capsule	82.95%	95.52%	93.19%	71.20%	80.73%	5.23%	3.87%	16.97%	12.68%	5.43%	76.97%
FFD	86.46%	99.18%	99.46%	73.40%	84.46%	0.40%	4.75%	34.37%	6.29%	5.65%	76.46%
RECCE	94.18%	99.08%	97.84%	90.40%	93.97%	2.01%	6.90%	35.39%	11.98%	9.35%	86.01%
UCF	96.39%	99.66%	98.94%	93.79%	96.30%	1.01%	5.46%	33.20%	7.71%	6.92%	87.58%
SPSL	71.11%	98.40%	99.53%	42.60%	59.66%	0.20%	1.43%	9.01%	3.66%	3.84%	55.83%
SRM	89.57%	98.56%	99.50%	79.60%	88.44%	0.40%	5.38%	17.79%	9.69%	7.79%	83.00%
F3Net	50.75%	52.68%	50.62%	73.80%	60.05%	72.43%	0.57%	2.24%	2.18%	2.18%	4.94%

Table 6. Tertiary metric scores for the security and efficiency metrics.

Detector	Tertiary Metrics									
	$\mathbf{det_s}$	**asr**	**flag**	**query**	**drop**	$\mathbf{dev_a}$	**rt**	**ait**	**mu**	**thr**
MesoInception	41.59	6.64	0	1,200	13.86	20.82	18.85	1.24	1534	0.05
Xception	79.16	9.46	0	1,200	0.47	17.80	18.85	1.24	1527	0.05
EfficientB4	78.16	18.71	0	1200	-0.02	18.21	19.71	1.31	1510	0.05
Capsule	77.14	15.07	0	1,200	0.12	21.10	18.65	1.21	1585	0.05
FFD	68.09	14.39	0	1,200	0.10	20.07	16.18	1.06	1574	0.06
RECCE	77.66	14.54	0	1,200	0.38	18.12	21.02	1.38	1661	0.05
UCF	68.47	10.78	0	1,200	-0.06	21.47	19.54	1.29	1568	0.05
SPSL	54.06	7.28	0	1,200	0.01	23.95	19.31	1.27	1520	0.05
SRM	79.60	12.93	0	1,200	5.17	20.65	18.92	1.25	1638	0.05
F3Net	56.08	1.22	1	1,200	1.67	18.88	15.95	1.05	1551	0.06

Table 7. Overall detection evaluation results.

Detector	Secondary Metrics			Primary
	Accuracy	**Robustness**	**Generalization**	**Detection**
MesoInception	72.60%	86.25%	51.74%	72.60%
Xception	95.30%	85.04%	85.38%	89.28%
EfficientB4	96.16%	86.45%	88.21%	91.04%
Capsule	85.89%	88.66%	76.97%	82.88%
FFD	90.43%	85.58%	76.46%	83.93%
RECCE	95.58%	83.36%	86.01%	89.31%
UCF	97.35%	86.31%	87.58%	91.23%
SPSL	78.52%	94.29%	55.83%	72.60%
SRM	92.55%	89.02%	83.00%	88.02%
F3Net	52.58%	95.28%	60.79%	64.40%

UCF deepfake detector is more affected by interference, its secondary robustness metric score of 86.31% is at a moderate level. Its secondary generalization metric score of 87.58% ranks second, demonstrating that it has good generalization ability. Its primary detection metric score of 91.23% demonstrates that it has the best detection performance.

The evaluation outcomes generally align with previous research. For example, according to Yan et al. [30], the UCF deepfake detector has superior accuracy and generalization abilities, and exceptional detection capabilities. This underscores the practicality and efficacy of the quantitative evaluation system.

4.3 Detection Evaluation Results

The tertiary metric scores corresponding to the primary detection metric in Table 5 show that the ten deepfake detectors exhibit varying sensitivity to the four

Table 8. Overall security evaluation results.

Detector	Secondary Metrics				Primary
	Anti Deepfake Sample	Anti Adversarial Attack	Anti Real-Time	Fairness	Security
MesoInception	76.28	90.85	86.14	71.32	81.63
Xception	85.26	90.07	99.53	81.32	88.77
EfficientB4	82.40	80.54	100	81.06	85.09
Capsule	95.55	82.45	99.88	75.43	88.46
FFD	80.62	84.09	99.90	77.81	84.95
RECCE	82.64	84.79	99.62	81.04	86.36
UCF	71.10	88.93	100	77.95	83.6
SPSL	90.61	90.73	99.99	69.50	88.30
SRM	90.00	86.03	94.83	77.69	87.31
F3Net	93.39	97.68	100	64.09	90.14

types of interference. Notably, the detectors exhibit significant vulnerabilities to blur conditions, with an average deviation of 22.21%. This underscores the importance of evaluating the robustness of deepfake detectors.

Analysis of the overall scores indicates that when the accuracy scores are low, the robustness scores are higher. This indicates that disturbances do not significantly impact detection accuracy. However, high accuracy is not only a fundamental requirement for deepfake detectors, but it is also a prerequisite for discussing their robustness. It is noteworthy that, since none of the detectors achieved an accuracy score above 90% and they are all susceptible to disturbances, they have limited robustness.

All the deepfake detectors considered in the evaluation demonstrate poor generalization, highlighting the challenge to effective deepfake detection. The average score of 75.2% in Table 7 underscores this observation and indicates the effectiveness of the proposed evaluation system.

The evaluation results emphasize that, while attempting to enhance deepfake detection accuracy, it is crucial to simultaneously work on improving the robustness and generalization capabilities. Indeed, all the aspects of detection performance must be considered to ensure that deepfake detectors meet the stringent demands to be successful in real-world applications.

4.4 Security Evaluation Results

An attractive feature of the evaluation system (platform and metrics) is the ability to conduct security assessments of deepfake detectors. Rigorous security testing identified certain levels of success by adversarial sample attacks. Table 6 shows that the EfficientB4 deepfake detector has the highest susceptibility to adversarial sample attacks, with an attack success rate near 19%. The other deepfake detectors in the evaluation were also successfully targeted by adversarial samples. Consequently, all of the detectors are exposed to the risk of compromise by adversarial samples.

According to the age deviation (dev_a) scores presented in Table 6, the deepfake detectors exhibit age bias that poses a security risk. The security risk is further underscored by the fairness scores in Table 8, indicating the need for heightened attention.

In the face of real-time adversarial attacks, the accuracy scores of nine deepfake detectors were largely unaffected and not one of them was exploited successfully. However, the costs of the attacks were comparatively high. Hence, the deepfake detectors are at minimal risk of security threats in real-time adversarial attack scenarios.

Clearly, the security characteristics of deepfake detectors must not be ignored. As such, the evaluation platform and metrics developed in this research are valuable for identifying potential security risks in deepfake detectors.

4.5 Discussion

The experimental results demonstrate the utility of the evaluation platform and the effectiveness of the evaluation metrics. In particular, common weaknesses were identified in the deepfake detectors that could be exploited by adversaries. It is also vital that researchers consider characteristics such as robustness and generalization in real-world deployments of deepfake detectors.

This research has yielded insights and tools for evaluating the detection and security characteristics of deepfake detectors. The automated evaluation platform greatly simplifies the assessment process, making it more accessible and efficient to evaluate deepfake detector performance. Since the ten deepfake detection models are encapsulated in application programming interfaces (APIs) and deployed on a local-area network (LAN) server, the differences in their efficiency metric scores were relatively minor.

5 Conclusions

The evaluation platform developed in this research automates the evaluation of deepfake detectors in a black-box manner, effectively reducing manual testing and analysis in the face of interference and adversarial attacks. The multidimensional quantitative evaluation system provides comprehensive assessments of deepfake detectors along three dimensions – detection, security and efficiency. Extensive experiments and evaluations involving ten state-of-the-art deepfake detectors demonstrate the usability of the platform and the effectiveness of the evaluation system. The evaluation also provides insights into the shortcomings of the deepfake detectors and their potential security risks.

Future research will explore interpretable evaluations of deepfake detectors. Also, it will conduct evaluations of deepfake detection systems used in real-world environments.

Acknowledgement

This research was supported by the National Key R&D Program of China under Grant no. 2021YFF0602104.

References

1. D. Afchar, V. Nozick, J. Yamagishi and I. Echizen, Mesonet: A compact facial video forgery detection network, *Proceedings of the IEEE International Workshop on Information Forensics and Security*, 2018.
2. J. Cao, C. Ma, T. Yao, S. Chen, S. Ding and X. Yang, End-to-end reconstruction-classification learning for face forgery detection, *Proceedings of the IEEE/CVF Conference on Computer Vision and Pattern Recognition*, pp. 4103–4112, 2022.
3. N. Carlini and D. Wagner, Towards evaluating the robustness of neural networks, *Proceedings of the IEEE Symposium on Security and Privacy*, pp. 39–57, 2017.
4. Y. Choi, M. Choi, M. Kim, J. Ha, S. Kim and J. Choo, StarGAN: Unified generative adversarial networks for multi-domain image-to-image translation, *Proceedings of the IEEE/CVF Conference on Computer Vision and Pattern Recognition*, pp. 8789–8797, 2018.
5. F. Chollet, Xception: Deep learning with depthwise separable convolutions, *Proceedings of the IEEE Conference on Computer Vision and Pattern Recognition*, pp. 1800–1807, 2017.
6. J. Deng, C. Lin, P. Hu, C. Shen, Q. Wang, Q. Li and Q. Li, Towards benchmarking and evaluating deepfake detection, *IEEE Transactions on Dependable and Secure Computing*, vol. 21(6), pp. 5112–5127, 2024.
7. B. Dolhansky, J. Bitton, B. Pflaum, J. Lu, R. Howes, M. Wang and C. Ferrer, The DeepFake Detection Challenge (DFDC) Dataset, arXiv: 2006.07397v4 (`arxiv.org/abs/2006.07397v4`), 2020.
8. T. Fawcett, An introduction to ROC analysis, *Pattern Recognition Letters*, vol. 27(8), pp. 861–874, 2006.
9. I. Goodfellow, J. Pouget-Abadie, M. Mirza, B. Xu, D. Warde-Farley, S. Ozair, A. Courville and Y. Bengio, Generative adversarial networks, *Communications of the ACM*, vol. 63(11), pp. 139–144, 2020.
10. L. Guarnera, O. Giudice and S. Battiato, Deepfake detection by analyzing convolutional traces, *Proceedings of the IEEE/CVF Conference on Computer Vision and Pattern Recognition Workshops*, pp. 2841–2850, 2020.
11. D. Guera and E. Delp, Deepfake video detection using recurrent neural networks, *Proceedings of the Fifteenth IEEE International Conference on Advanced Video and Signal Based Surveillance*, 2018.
12. J. Ho, A. Jain and P. Abbeel, Denoising diffusion probabilistic models, *Proceedings of the Thirty-Fourth International Conference on Neural Information Processing Systems*, article no. 574, pp. 6840–6851, 2020.
13. S. Hussain, P. Neekhara, M. Jere, F. Koushanfar and J. McAuley, Adversarial deepfakes: Evaluating vulnerability of deepfake detectors to adversarial examples, *Proceedings of the IEEE Winter Conference on Applications of Computer Vision*, pp. 3347–3356, 2021.
14. T. Karras, S. Laine and T. Aila, A style-based generator architecture for generative adversarial networks, *Proceedings of the IEEE/CVF Conference on Computer Vision and Pattern Recognition*, pp. 4396–4405, 2019.

15. D. Kingma and M. Welling, Auto-Encoding Variational Bayes, arXiv: 1312.6114v11 (`arxiv.org/abs/1312.6114v11`), 2022.
16. Y. Li, M. Chang and S. Lyu, *In ictu oculi*: Exposing AI-created fake videos by detecting eye blinking, *Proceedings of the IEEE International Workshop on Information Forensics and Security*, 2018.
17. Y. Li and S. Lyu, Exposing deepfake videos by detecting face warping artifacts, *Proceedings of the IEEE/CVF International Conference on Computer Vision and Pattern Recognition Workshops*, pp. 46–52, 2019.
18. Y. Li, X. Yang, P. Sun, H. Qi and S. Lyu, Celeb-DF: A large-scale challenging dataset for deepfake forensics, *Proceedings of the IEEE/CVF Conference on Computer Vision and Pattern Recognition*, pp. 3204–3213, 2020.
19. H. Liu, X. Li, W. Zhou, Y. Chen, Y. He, H. Xue, W. Zhang and N. Yu, Spatial-phase shallow learning: Rethinking face forgery detection in the frequency domain, *Proceedings of the IEEE/CVF Conference on Computer Vision and Pattern Recognition*, pp. 772–781, 2021.
20. K. Liu, I. Perov, D. Gao, N. Chervoniy, W. Zhou and W. Zhang, Deepfacelab: Integrated, flexible and extensible face-swapping framework, *Pattern Recognition*, vol. 141, article no. 109628, 2023.
21. Y. Luo, Y. Zhang, J. Yan and W. Liu, Generalizing face forgery detection with high-frequency features, *Proceedings of the IEEE/CVF Conference on Computer Vision and Pattern Recognition*, pp. 16312–16321, 2021.
22. Y. Mirsky and W. Lee, The creation and detection of deepfakes: A survey, *ACM Computing Surveys*, vol. 54(1), article no. 7, 2021.
23. H. Nguyen, J. Yamagishi and I. Echizen, Capsule-forensics: Using capsule networks to detect forged images and videos, *Proceedings of the IEEE International Conference on Acoustics, Speech and Signal Processing*, pp. 2307–2311, 2019.
24. A. Nichol and P. Dhariwal, Improved denoising diffusion probabilistic models, *Proceedings of the Thirty-Eighth International Conference on Machine Learning*, pp. 8162–8171, 2021.
25. Y. Qian, G. Yin, L. Sheng, Z. Chen and J. Shao, Thinking in frequency: Face forgery detection by mining frequency-aware clues, *Proceedings of the European Conference on Computer Vision*, pp. 86–103, 2020.
26. A. Rossler, D. Cozzolino, L. Verdoliva, C. Riess, J. Thies and M. Niessner, FaceForensics++: Learning to detect manipulated facial images, *Proceedings of the IEEE/CVF International Conference on Computer Vision*, 2019.
27. T. To, H. Luong, N. Nguyen, T. Nguyen, M. Tran and T. Do, Deepfake detection using EfficientNet: Working towards dense sampling and frame selection, *Proceedings of the RIVF International Conference on Computing and Communication Technologies*, pp. 612–617, 2022.
28. R. Tolosana, R. Vera-Rodriguez, J. Fierrez, A. Morales and J. Ortega-Garcia, Deepfakes and beyond: A survey of face manipulation and fake detection, *Information Fusion*, vol. 64, pp. 131–148, 2020.
29. L. Wang, X. Meng, D. Li, X. Zhang, S. Ji and S. Guo, DEEPFAKER: A unified evaluation platform for facial deepfake and detection models, *ACM Transactions on Privacy and Security*, vol. 27(1), article no. 10, 2024.
30. Z. Yan, Y. Zhang, Y. Fan and B. Wu, UCF: Uncovering common features for generalizable deepfake detection, *Proceedings of the IEEE/CVF International Conference on Computer Vision*, pp. 22355–22366, 2023.
31. D. Zhang, J. Chen, X. Liao, F. Li, J. Chen and G. Yang, Face forgery detection via multi-feature fusion and local enhancement, *IEEE Transactions on Circuits and Systems for Video Technology*, vol. 34(9), pp. 8972–8977, 2024.

Leveraging Security Vulnerabilities in Proactive Dashcam Forensics

Vishal Srivastava[1], Pulkit Garg[1], and Gaurav Gupta[2]

[1] Indian Institute of Technology Jodhpur, Karwar, India
[2] Ministry of Electronics and Information Technology, New Delhi, India
gauravg@gov.in

Abstract. Dashboard cameras are becoming increasingly prevalent in vehicles, offering valuable sources of evidence in a wide range of investigations. This chapter describes a novel dashcam forensics methodology that shifts from reactive evidence extraction to proactive evidence extraction without physical access. Common security vulnerabilities existing across dashcam models such as weak default passwords, exploitable operating systems and outdated services, and insecure communications protocols are leveraged for evidence extraction. The effectiveness of the methodology is demonstrated by gaining remote root access to popular dashcam models, enabling the acquisition of configuration data, recordings and even real-time video streams. The proactive methodology offers significant advantages to law enforcement agencies, enabling expedited data retrieval in time-sensitive investigations while preserving evidence integrity.

Keywords: Dashcam · Security Vulnerabilities · Proactive Forensics · Workflow

1 Introduction

A dashcam is an in-vehicle recording system typically mounted on the dashboard or windshield that continuously captures video and audio footage. Initially driven by concerns about road safety and personal protection, dashcams have experienced a significant surge worldwide [3]. Declining hardware costs and the proliferation of advanced features, such as Global Positioning System (GPS) tracking, motion detection, parking mode recording and cloud connectivity, have made dashcams appealing and more accessible to a broad audience.

The initial popularity of dashcams stemmed from their ability to provide irrefutable evidence in traffic incidents, protecting drivers from fraudulent claims and helping settle insurance disputes. However, the value of dashcam recordings quickly transcended their initial applications. In particular, law enforcement agencies have recognized the immense forensic potential of dashcam recordings [10], utilizing them to reconstruct accident scenes, verify witness statements and identify suspects in criminal activities [11]. Dashcams – with their unblinking gaze – often capture critical details that human witnesses may overlook or

Published by Springer Nature Switzerland AG 2026
E. Kurkowski and S. Shenoi (Eds.): DigitalForensics 2025, IFIP AICT 762, pp. 43–57, 2026.
https://doi.org/10.1007/978-3-032-09802-3_3

misinterpret. They provide objective lenses to capture the events leading up to, during and after incidents, offering crucial insights into vehicle movements, driver behavior, road conditions and environmental factors.

Dashcam forensics has primarily focused on reactive methodologies, relying on physical access to devices and their storage media in order to extract and examine evidence. Lallie [10] has conducted a detailed analysis of several dashcam models, identifying the types and locations of various forensic artifacts in the devices and their storage media. Lee et al. [13] built on this work by classifying metadata across 14 dashcam models from 11 manufacturers, highlighting the diversity of the data structures and potential challenges for evidence extraction and analysis.

While these pioneering studies of dashcam forensics have been valuable, their reliance on physical access can be problematic in time-sensitive investigations. Delays in obtaining warrants, accessing seized vehicles and analyzing large tranches of evidence have led to massive backlogs in law enforcement investigations.

This chapter proposes a paradigm shift in dashcam forensics – moving from a reactive mindset to a proactive mindset – to support law enforcement activities. Imagine a kidnapping scenario where a vehicle dashcam silently records everything as the criminal speeds away. In such a time-sensitive situation, waiting to gain physical access to the vehicle could have dire consequences. What is needed is a proactive methodology that can extract dashcam evidence in real time and "over the air." Of course, such "evidence" that is collected proactively could be contested in court proceedings and excluded from consideration. Still, it would be immensely valuable in critical incidents such as kidnappings, urgent manhunts and more.

The proposed proactive methodology leverages common security vulnerabilities in dashcam models such as weak default passwords, exploitable operating systems and services, and insecure communications protocols to facilitate the rapid and remote extraction of configuration data, recordings and real-time video streams. The methodology addresses a significant challenge cited by Lallie [11] related to the cumbersome manual extraction of dashcam evidence. In fact, the methodology is perfectly applicable to extract evidence from vehicles seized lawfully in traditional criminal investigations.

2 Dashcam Technology

Dashcams have become increasingly ubiquitous as they have transformed from simple recording devices to complex, interconnected systems. Understanding the underlying technology and functionalities is crucial to developing effective digital forensic techniques.

2.1 Storage

Dashcams rely on removable storage media such as SD cards and microSD cards. The memory cards host standard filesystems such as FAT32 and exFAT, allowing for easy data access and transfer. New dashcam models increasingly incorporate onboard embedded memory. For example, eMMC (embedded MultiMediaCard) chips soldered on dashcam circuit boards offer greater reliability and resistance to data corruption, especially in sudden power loss situations.

The choice of storage media and filesystem significantly impacts digital forensics. Removable storage media allow for straightforward data acquisition whereas onboard memory may require a specialized chip-off technique relying on expensive equipment. The increasing complexity of filesystems necessitates specialized forensic expertise and tools to access and analyze the stored data.

2.2 Network Connectivity

Early dashcams were isolated devices, their data accessible only through physical interactions. However, wireless communications technologies have endowed dashcams with networking capabilities, enabling features such as cloud storage, GPS tracking, smartphone integration and real-time video streaming:

- **Wi-Fi:** Wi-Fi connectivity enables dashcams to connect to local networks and smartphones, enabling wireless data transfer and remote viewing of recordings. The connectivity is welcomed by users, but it can be exploited for proactive forensic access.
- **Bluetooth:** Bluetooth enables communications with smartphones and other devices, facilitating features such as hands-free calling and audio streaming. From a forensic perspective, Bluetooth connections reveal information about paired devices and interaction history.
- **GPS:** GPS modules have become a standard feature in most dashcams, enabling precise location and time tracking. The geospatial data, embedded in National Marine Electronics Association (NMEA) files and video watermarks, is invaluable in forensic investigations, allowing for route mapping, location verification and timeline reconstruction.

The network connectivity of dashcams expands forensic opportunities by providing new avenues for data acquisition and analysis. However, digital forensic practitioners must consider the security implications of connected dashcams, address potential privacy concerns and leverage methods for accessing and analyzing data stored remotely or in the cloud.

2.3 Operating Systems

Dashcams rely on operating systems to support their functions and features. Early dashcams relied on simple, proprietary operating systems with limited functionality. Modern dashcams employ sophisticated operating systems:

- **Proprietary Operating Systems:** Many dashcams, especially those from smaller manufacturers, utilize proprietary operating systems developed for their hardware. These systems often lack standard interfaces and documentation, posing forensic challenges and requiring reverse engineering and specialized tools to access and analyze data.

- **Embedded Linux Operating Systems:** Embedded Linux is gaining popularity as a dashcam operating system due to its flexibility, open-source nature and software support. Familiarity with the operating system makes it easier for digital forensic practitioners to extract and analyze relevant data.
- **Android Automotive Operating Systems:** As mobile technologies are integrated in vehicles, Android Automotive operating systems are becoming viable for dashcams. Designed for popular Android platforms, the operating systems offer a wealth of features and connectivity options. However, analyzing such full-fledged mobile operating system can be formidable.
- **Real-Time Operating Systems:** Vehicles with integrated dashcam systems incorporate real-time operating systems (RTOSs) that support device functions while prioritizing real-time performance and reliability. These operating systems present challenges to digital forensic practitioners due to their specialized filesystems and limited documentation, requiring advanced techniques such as reverse engineering to extract data. Fortunately, real-time operating systems are rarely encountered in externally-mounted dashcams.

The choice of operating system significantly impacts forensic processes. Proprietary operating systems require specialized expertise and tools whereas common operating systems such as Embedded Linux and Android Automotive offer some degree of familiarity and are supported by a wide range of forensic tools.

2.4 Companion Applications Support

Dashcams often come with companion smartphone applications for Android and iOS devices. The companion apps support rich user interactions wirelessly through Wi-Fi and/or Bluetooth. From a forensic standpoint, companion apps are valuable sources of evidence, offering insights into user behavior, device settings and data access patterns.

Key features supported by dashcam companion apps include:

- **Live View:** This feature enables users to remotely see real-time dashcam video streams on their smartphones. The feature is particularly useful for adjusting camera angles, ensuring proper recording and monitoring vehicle surroundings. From a forensic perspective, access logs and timestamps associated with live view sessions provide valuable contextual information.
- **Remote Capture:** This feature enables users to remotely capture dashcam photos and videos. It also expands recording capabilities beyond the automatic modes, allowing the targeted capture of specific events. The remotely-captured files may reveal user intent and could constitute valuable evidence.
- **GPS Tracking and Route History:** Several companion apps are integrated in the GPS modules of dashcams, displaying vehicle locations in real-time on a map. The apps often store route history, providing detailed logs of vehicle journeys. The stored data can be crucial in forensic investigations, verifying locations, establishing timelines and revealing travel patterns and destinations of interest.

- **File Management and Album Access:** Companion apps make it convenient to manage dashcam recordings, enabling users to browse, download and delete files wirelessly. The apps often present recordings in an album view organized by date, time or recording mode. The file access history related to downloads, deletions and timestamps is valuable because it could reveal attempts to conceal or manipulate evidence.
- **Device Settings and Configuration:** Companion apps allow users to configure various dashcam settings, such as recording resolution, audio settings, G-sensor sensitivity and loop recording duration, and enabling or disabling features such as GPS logging, speed recording and watermarking. Accessing and analyzing the dashcam settings via companion apps can provide valuable insights into device capabilities and user recording preferences.

2.5 Recording Features and Modes

Dashcams offer various recording features and modes designed to capture important moments of journeys. Understanding these features can help interpret the recorded footage and extract relevant information.

- **Loop Recording:** Dashcams utilize loop recording to continuously record footage. Loop recording ensures that dashcams always capture recent events, but it also means that older footage may be overwritten (and lost) unless it is protected or manually saved periodically.
- **G-Sensor-Activated Recording:** Most dashcams incorporate a G-sensor (accelerometer) that triggers event recording when a sudden change in motion is detected. These recordings are typically protected from overwriting to preserve evidence of accidents and other significant events.
- **Parking Mode:** Dashcams often provide a parking mode that is activated when a vehicle is parked and the ignition is turned off. The mode typically utilizes motion detection or impact detection to trigger recording, the goal being to capture events that occur while the vehicle is unattended.
- **Time-Lapse Recording:** Some dashcams offer a time-lapse recording mode that captures images at set intervals, creating condensed videos of journeys. The mode is useful for monitoring over long periods of time as well as for capturing events that unfold slowly.

The available recording features and modes vary depending on the dashcam model. Digital forensic practitioners need to understand dashcam recording features and modes to interpret the recorded footage and extract relevant information for their investigations.

3 Forensic Artifacts in Dashcams

Dashcams hold surprising amounts of information [11]. Beyond the primary video and audio recordings, substantial data is contained in their filesystems, configuration files and video footage. These forensic artifacts provide rich contexts for understanding the events captured by dashcams.

3.1 Video and Audio Recordings

The most obvious forensic artifacts are dashcam video and audio recordings. The recordings provide visual and auditory accounts of events leading up to, during and after incidents. The video footage can be used to reconstruct accident scenes, identify vehicles and individuals involved, and analyze driver behavior. The audio recordings can capture conversations in the vehicle, potentially revealing incriminating statements and providing insights into the motives behind incidents.

3.2 Metadata

Vast amounts of metadata are embedded in dashcam recordings and filesystems. Users are typically unaware of the metadata but it is of significant value in forensic investigations.

- **Geospatial Data:** Dashcams equipped with GPS modules record precise location-time information alongside video footage. The data is typically stored as NMEA files with latitude and longitude coordinates, timestamps synchronized with GPS satellites, ground speed and direction of travel. This data enables digital forensic practitioners to map vehicle routes, verify locations and establish timelines.
- **Temporal Data:** Timestamps are embedded throughout dashcam filesystems, providing chronological records of events. Filenames often incorporate date-time data, indicating when recordings were initiated. Directory structures may reflect recording modes (e.g., normal driving, parking mode and event recording) and file creation dates. Additionally, EXIF metadata embedded in video files pinpoint the exact moments that frames were captured.
- **Speed Data:** Dashcams often embed vehicle speed data in location data. Speed data can be found in video watermarks, and EXIF metadata in video files and NMEA files. This data is vital to accident reconstruction, determining if speed was a factor and refuting/confirming driver claims.

3.3 Watermarks

Many dashcams embed watermarks directly in video frames. The watermarks typically include date-time information, speed travelled, GPS coordinates, and device model and serial number. This information is useful for verifying the integrity of footage and establishing the contexts of recordings.

3.4 Configuration Files

Dashcams store system settings and user preferences in configuration files, providing insights into device capabilities and the circumstances under which footage was captured. The configuration files may reveal recording resolution, audio settings, G-sensor sensitivity, loop recording duration and whether features such as GPS logging, speed recording and watermarking were enabled.

3.5 System Logs

Dashcam system logs document various operational events and user interactions. The logs record power on/off times, SD card insertions and removals, manual recording initiations, G-sensor triggered events and GPS connectivity status. Analysis of the log data provides valuable insights into dashcam usage history and user behavior, and helps corroborate or contradict witness statements.

Dashcams are far more than simple recorders of video and audio. They are complex digital devices that capture a wealth of information. By understanding and analyzing the full range of forensic artifacts in dashcam data, digital forensic practitioners can gain better understandings of events, increasing their ability to reconstruct incidents and verify facts.

4 Related Work

Early research in dashcam forensics focused on identifying and characterizing the diverse forensic artifacts contained in the devices. Lallie [10] conducted a preliminary analysis of seven dashcam models, revealing a wealth of information beyond the primary video and audio recordings. The study highlighted the significance of geospatial data embedded in NMEA files, temporal data in files and directory structures, speed data, watermarks, configuration settings and system logs. The research established the forensic potential of dashcam data.

In subsequent work, Lallie [11] analyzed metadata in 14 dashcam models from 11 manufacturers. The research revealed the diversity of data structures and formats used by manufacturers and highlighted the need for standardized methodologies and specialized tools for forensic analysis. The proposed metadata-driven approach, incorporating a normalized database schema and prototype open-source tool, sought to facilitate comprehensive and efficient analysis of dashcam data.

Daraghmi and Shawahna [4] have focused on the extraction and analysis of textual and auditory evidence from dashcam recordings. Their framework leveraged optical character recognition (OCR) and speech-to-text conversion to extract textual metadata and transcribe auditory warnings, enabling the automated analysis of these often-overlooked forms of evidence.

Recognizing the lack of standardized procedures for dashcam investigations, Lallie [11] proposed a set of forensic investigation guidelines. The guidelines, which encompass evidence preservation, acquisition, examination, analysis and reporting, ensure the integrity of dashcam evidence and provide a framework for conducting forensically-sound investigations.

The practical value of dashcam footage in real-world investigations has been demonstrated in several case studies. Giovannini et al. [5] illustrated the crucial role of dashcam evidence in a fatal vehicle-pedestrian crash investigation, revealing that the incident initially assumed to be accidental was actually a suicide. The case study highlighted the role of dashcams as objective witnesses and their potential to prevent miscarriages of justice.

The increased integration of dashcams within vehicle systems has introduced new challenges for forensic analysis. Lee et al. [12] explored the complexities of analyzing built-in dashcams with real-time operating systems. Their research demonstrated the need for advanced techniques such as reverse engineering to overcome the challenges posed by dedicated filesystems and limited documentation about real-time operating systems.

The social and ethical implications of dashcam data extraction and sharing have also been a focus of research. Kim et al. [9] investigated cross-national differences in motives and privacy concerns related to dashcam video sharing. Their findings highlighted the importance of balancing investigative needs with privacy rights and developing policies that ensure responsible and ethical data handling practices. Kim and colleagues also addressed privacy concerns associated with sharing dashcam footage by proposing ViewMap, a system that facilitates anonymous sharing while preserving user privacy through line-of-sight-based linking and path confusion techniques. The DashcamTalk Forum [16] has discussed the exploitation of vulnerabilities in dashcam services to gain unauthorized access to dashcam data.

Existing research has demonstrated the forensic potential of dashcams and has developed forensic methodologies for analyzing dashcam data. However, the methodologies involve reactive forensic analysis that requires physical access to dashcams and their storage media. Missing are proactive methodologies that actively leverage security vulnerabilities to advance dashcam forensic investigations.

5 Dashcam Security Analysis

A security analysis of various dashcam models has revealed security flaws that could be exploited by malicious actors or leveraged by law enforcement for proactive forensic access. The vulnerabilities include weak default passwords, exploitable operating systems and services, unencrypted storage and insecure streaming protocols. Three common dashcams available from Amazon India were investigated – Phillips Go Sure 30001 [15], CP-Plus AD H2B W [2] and 70mai A510 [1].

5.1 Passwords

Analysis conducted in this research revealed a common trend of weak or default passwords in the dashcam models. The devices utilize guessable passwords for their Wi-Fi access points. The vulnerability enables the interception of data, modification of settings and potentially control of the devices that compromises user privacy and the integrity of recordings. For example, the 70mai A510 dashcam does not enforce a password change during the initial setup.

The use of default passwords for sensitive services such as `ftp` (File Transfer Protocol) and `telnet` enable full access to the filesystem, potentially leading to remote code execution and complete system compromise. In fact, the default passwords are available in user manuals or online.

5.2 Operating Systems

The dashcams utilize outdated or poorly maintained operating systems riddled with known vulnerabilities. Vulnerable services such as `telnet`, `httpd` and `http` provide unauthorized access, potentially leading to root privileges and complete device control. This opens the door to malicious activities such as data detection and modification, installation of malware, even repurposing dashcams for nefarious activities like surveillance or participation in botnets.

5.3 Communications

Dashcams are increasingly reliant on wireless communications protocols such as Wi-Fi and Bluetooth for connectivity and data transfer. The lack of security in the protocol implementations exposes the devices to eavesdropping and man-in-the-middle attacks. Data transmitted over unencrypted Wi-Fi networks can be easily intercepted, revealing sensitive information such as GPS coordinates, user credentials and even video footage.

Real-time streaming protocols such as RTSP (Real-Time Streaming Protocol) are also vulnerable. Analysis revealed instances of dashcams using default RTSP ports without authentication mechanisms. As a result, simply knowing the device IP addresses and default ports enables access to the live video streams without authorization, essentially turning the dashcams into surveillance tools.

5.4 Storage

The analysis revealed that stored data, primarily on SD cards, is not encrypted. The sensitive data includes video recordings, GPS logs and configuration settings.

5.5 Additional Concerns

The analysis uncovered additional security concerns:

- **Firmware Updates:** Infrequent or non-existent firmware updates leave dashcams vulnerable to newly-discovered exploits, perpetuating security risks and leaving users with limited or no options for addressing them.
- **Data Storage:** Inadequate security measures for protecting data stored on the devices or in the cloud create opportunities for unauthorized access and data modification, jeopardizing evidence integrity and user privacy.
- **Companion Application Communications:** Data transmission over insecure connections, especially with companion applications, exposes sensitive information to interception. Analysis revealed that some of the dashcams use unencrypted channels for data transfer to companion applications.
- **Physical Security:** The lack of physical security features makes the dashcams easy targets for tampering and unauthorized access to storage media, increasing the risk of data compromise. In fact, SD cards can be replaced without requiring any authorization, enabling data to be modified or deleted, and malware to be implanted on the devices.

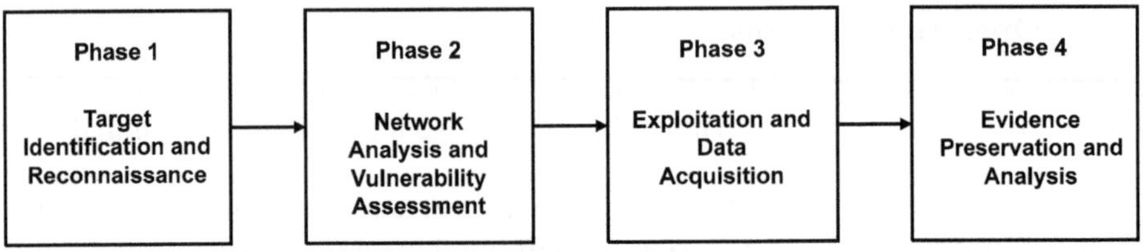

Fig. 1. Proactive dashcam forensics methodology.

6 Proactive Dashcam Forensics Methodology

The proactive forensics methodology capitalizes on dashcam security weaknesses to acquire valuable data, including recordings, configuration settings, system logs and real-time video streams, without requiring physical access to a device. The methodology is developed based on the analysis of three dashcam models. However, it is presented in a generalized manner by describing principles and techniques that are applicable to a broad range of dashcam models. The proactive forensics methodology focuses on maintaining evidence integrity, chain of custody and legal admissibility.

Figure 1 shows the proactive dashcam forensics methodology. The methodology comprises four phases:

- **Target Identification and Reconnaissance:** This phase involves identifying a targeted dashcam, gathering information about its make and model, and identifying its vulnerabilities. Open-source intelligence (OSINT) techniques, online forums and vulnerability databases are valuable resources during this phase.
- **Network Analysis and Vulnerability Assessment:** This phase focuses on analyzing dashcam network communications and identifying vulnerabilities that can be exploited to gain remote access. Tools such as Nmap [14] can be used to scan for open ports and identify running services. Vulnerability scanners and exploit databases can assist in pinpointing exploitable weaknesses.
- **Exploitation and Data Acquisition:** This phase involves exploiting the identified vulnerabilities to gain access to dashcam data. The techniques include exploiting weak default passwords and insecure communications protocols as well as leveraging known operating system exploits. Tools such as Hydra [8], Directory Buster [7] and Aircrack-Ng [6] can be used for initial exploitation.
- **Evidence Preservation and Analysis:** This phase focuses on ensuring the integrity and admissibility of the acquired data. A forensic imaging tool can be used to create a bit-for-bit copy of the dashcam storage media and targeted data extraction techniques can be employed to acquire specific directories and directories. Chain of custody procedures must be followed meticulously throughout this process.

7 70mai A510 Dashcam Exploitation Case Study

This section describes the application of the proactive forensics methodology on the 70mai A510 dashcam [1]: Proactive forensic analysis of the 70mai A510 dashcam demonstrated a complete security compromise that enabled remote access via `telnet` and `ftp` without authentication. The lack of RSTP authentication facilitated access to live video footage.

Target Identification and Reconnaissance. The 70mai A510 dashcam broadcasts a default Wi-Fi access point with an SSID specific to the model. The default password is "12345678" and there is no initial option to change it, which is a security risk. Moreover, the default credentials are the same for all devices of the brand.

The dashcam operates on a default IP address of `192.168.0.1`. This address was used to scan and enumerate the available services.

Network Analysis and Vulnerability Assessment. The default Wi-Fi credentials were used to connect to the dashcam network without any additional authentication. Port scanning and service identification using Nmap revealed the following open ports and running services on the dashcam:

- Port 21: `ftp`
- Port 23: `telnet`
- Port 80: `http`
- Port 554: `rtsp`

These services are potential attack vectors for unauthorized access. A Dirbuster scan revealed that an `http` service was running on port 80. However, the directory listing was disabled and no significant vulnerabilities in the service were identified.

Exploitation and Data Acquisition. The dashcam streams live video via `rtsp` on port 554. No authentication was required to access the stream, which enabled live video feed to be retrieved using a VLC media player with the URL `rtsp://192.168.0.1:554`.

Using brute-force tools, it was determined that `ftp` and `telnet` allow access using the default username "root" with an empty password. This provided full access to the dashcam filesystem, enabling video recordings, configuration files and other sensitive data to be downloaded. Since `telnet` authentication was disabled, logging in as "root" without a password granted complete control of the device. This enabled the modification of system files, unauthorized remote access and even potential firmware manipulation.

Evidence Preservation and Analysis. Upon obtaining root access, a forensic image of device storage was created to preserve the evidence. Using a forensically-sound extraction method, critical files, including video recordings, were retrieved. The process was documented meticulously to ensure the integrity of the evidence. Proper chain of custody was maintained to ensure that the acquired evidence would be legally admissible. Every step, including tool usage, timestamps and personnel involved, was documented carefully.

8 Proactive Forensics Results

This section describes the results obtained using the proactive forensics methodology on three dashcam models – 70mai A510 [1], CP PLUS AD H2B W [2] and Philips GS 3001 [15]. The results demonstrate the feasibility of exploiting security vulnerabilities to gain remote forensic access to dashcam data.

Tables 1 and 2 summarize the results obtained for the three dashcam models. The proactive forensics methodology was successfully applied to compromise various aspects of the three dashcam models and gain the highest (root) privilege access to the devices remotely. All the files stored on the dashcams were accessed. Additionally, RSTP live streams were obtained without any authentication, authorization, companion application use or physical access to the devices.

9 Conclusions

This chapter has presented a novel proactive forensic methodology for remotely accessing and acquiring data from dashcams by leveraging inherent security vulnerabilities. Security analyses of three commercially available dashcam models exposed vulnerabilities such as weak default passwords, exploitable operating systems and outdated services, and insecure communications protocols These vulnerabilities were leveraged to gain remote root access to popular dashcam models, enabling the acquisition of configuration data, recordings and real-time video streams.

As far as pure data extraction from dashcams is concerned, the methodology is advantageous because the remote access technique eliminates the need to seize a vehicle or break into it to obtain the dashcam. Additionally, it would not be necessary to apply invasive techniques such as desoldering chips and using chip programmers to extract data directly from the chips.

It is important to note that the methodology may not meet the legal standards for evidence collection. Absent a court order or other approvals, exploiting dashcam vulnerabilities and remotely extracting data over the air would be problematic – the method could be contested in court proceedings and the extracted evidence could be excluded from consideration. Nevertheless, the capabilities could be invaluable in critical incidents such as kidnappings and manhunts where swift access to potential life-saving information is vital.

The ease with which dashcam vulnerabilities were identified and exploited raises security concerns about the security of commercially available dashcams.

Table 1. Results of proactive forensics on three dashcam models.

Step	70mai A510 Dashcam	CP PLUS AD H2B W Dashcam	Philips GS 3001 Dashcam
Reconnaissance	1. Default Wi-Fi access point password (12345678) 2. No initial option to change default password for brand	1. Default WiFi access point password (CpadH2BW) 2. Default password for the model 3. Default Wi-Fi access point always on	1. Default Wi-Fi access point password (12345678) 2. Default password in user manual 3. Default Wi-Fi access point always on
Network Break-In	1. Connected to dashcam using discovered credentials	1. Connected to dashcam using discovered credentials	1. Connected to dashcam using discovered credentials
Dashcam IP Address Access	1. Default IP address (`192.168.0.1`)	1. Default IP address (`192.72.1.1`)	1. Default IP address (`192.168.42.1`)
Running Services Identification Using Nmap	1. 21 `ftp` 2. 23 `telnet` 3. 80 `http` 4. 554 `rtsp`	1. 23/tcp `telnet` 2. 80/tcp `thttpd` 3. 554/tcp `rtspd`	1. 443/tcp `tcpwrapped` 2. 80/tcp `http HFS` 3. 554/tcp `rtspd` 4. 3333/tcp `arcservice`
Credential Access by Exploiting Services via Brute Force Tools	1. 21 `ftp` Username (`root`) Password (Empty) 2. 23 `telnet` Username (`root`) Password (Empty) 3. 80 `http` Not accessible (continued)	1. 23 `telnet` Username (`root`) Password (Empty) 2. 80 `http` Various endpoints 3. 554 `rtsp` Unable to obtain live stream	1. 80 `http` Discussed in text 2. 554 `rtsp` Live stream URL without authentication (`rtsp://192.168.42.1:554/xxx.mov`)

Table 2. Results of proactive forensics on three dashcam models (continued).

Step	**70mai A510 Dashcam**	**CP PLUS AD H2B W Dashcam**	**Philips GS 3001 Dashcam**
Credential Access by Exploiting Services via Brute Force Tools	4. `554 rtsp` Live stream URL without authentication (`rtsp://192.168.0.1:554`)		
HTTP Access by Exploiting Services via Dirbuster Tool	1. Running web service Directory listing disabled and no major dashcam system files exposed	1. HTTP server (`http://192.72.1.1`) All dashcam system files exposed	1. HTTP server (`192.168.42.1:80`) 2. `554 rtsp` All dashcam system files exposed (upload, download, deletion)
Conclusion	Complete security compromise: Root access via **`telnet`** and **`ftp`** bypassed authentication without any authorization	Complete security compromise: Root access via **`telnet`** bypassed authentication without any authorization to remotely access entire dashcam filesystem	Complete security compromise: Root access via the web bypassed authentication without any authorization to remotely access entire dashcam filesystem (upload, download, delete files)

Also of concern is that malicious actors could engage in anti-forensics activity to hinder forensic investigations by manipulating or destroying dashcam evidence using the same vectors leveraged by the proposed methodology.

Future research will focus on developing proactive forensics methodologies for Internet-of-Things devices. Additionally, it will investigate protocols for conducting proactive forensics that will meet evidence admissibility criteria.

References

1. 70mai, Dash Cam A510, Shanghai, China (www.70mai.com/a510), 2025.
2. Aditya Infotech (CP PLUS), CP-AD-H2B-W CarKam, Noida, India (www.cpplusworld.com/cp-ad-h2b-w), 2025.
3. D. Ashra, Technology takes the wheel: Unveiling the drivers of car dashcam adoption, *International Journal of Innovation and Technology Management*, vol. 21(3), article no. 2450024, 2024.
4. Y. Daraghmi and I. Shawahna, Digital forensic analysis of vehicular video sensors: Dashcams as a case, *Sensors*, vol. 23(17), article no. 7548, 2023.
5. E. Giovannini, A. Giorgetti, G. Pelletti, A. Giusti, M. Garagnani, J. Pascali, S. Pelotti and P. Fais, Importance of dashboard camera (Dash Cam) analysis in fatal vehicle–pedestrian crash reconstruction, *Forensic Science, Medicine and Pathology*, vol. 17(3), pp. 379–387, 2021.
6. Kali.org, Aircrack-Ng (www.kali.org/tools/aircrack-ng), 2025.
7. Kali.org, Dirbuster (www.kali.org/tools/dirbuster), 2025.
8. Kali.org, Hydra (www.kali.org/tools/hydra), 2025.
9. M. Kim, J. Lim, H. Yu, K. Kim, Y. Kim and S. Lee, ViewMap: Sharing private in-vehicle dashcam videos, *Proceedings of the Fourteenth USENIX Symposium on Networked Systems Design and Implementation*, pp. 163–176, 2017.
10. H. Lallie, Dashcam forensics: A preliminary analysis of seven dashcam devices, *Forensic Science International: Digital Investigation*, vol. 33, article no. 200910, 2020.
11. H. Lallie, Dashcam forensic investigation guidelines, *Forensic Science International: Digital Investigation*, vol. 45(S), article no. 301558, 2023.
12. J. Lee, B. Hyeon, O. Jeon and N. Park, Analysis of real-time operating system filesystems: Built-in cameras from vehicles, *Forensic Science International: Digital Investigation*, vol. 44(S), article no. 301500, 2023.
13. K. Lee, J. Choi, J. Park and S. Lee, Your car is recording: Metadata-driven dashcam analysis system, *Forensic Science International: Digital Investigation*, vol. 38(S), article no. 301131, 2021.
14. Nmap.org, NMap: The network mapper – Free security scanner (nmap.org), 2025.
15. Philips, GoSure 3000 series – GoSure 3001, Gurugram, India (www.philips.co.in/c-p/LUMGS300X1_20/gosure-3000-series-gosure-3001), 2025
16. Porske, A500s Preliminary Hacking, *DashcamTalk Forum* (dashcamtalk.com/forum/threads/a500s-preliminary-hacking.46763), 2025.

Large Language Model Applications

Enhancing Digital Evidence Collection and Analysis Using Built-In Instant Messaging Solutions and Large Language Models

Yi-Anson Lam, Kam-Pui Chow, and Siu-Ming Yiu

University of Hong Kong, Hong Kong, China
yiansonlam@connect.hku.hk

Abstract. Digital evidence is typically extracted and preserved using specialized forensic tools. However, advancements in technology have contributed to the development of messaging platforms such as Signal and Telegram for which existing forensic tools often fall short. Developing new forensic tools is time-consuming and resource intensive.
This chapter addresses the challenges by employing quick-fix digital evidence collection methods that leverage built-in functions provided by instant messaging platforms. To enhance the digital forensic examination workflow, analytical tasks are offloaded to large language models using application programming interfaces provided by a large language model platform. The use of large language models significantly improves the efficiency of digital evidence processing. A triage screening methodology that provides executive summary reports is described. The methodology enhances the overall digital evidence collection workflow, ensuring that critical evidence and insights are not overlooked while maintaining rigorous standards of admissibility.

Keywords: Instant Messaging · Evidence Collection · Evidence Analysis · Large Language Models · Evidence Admissibility

1 Introduction

The proliferation of digital devices has significantly increased the volume of digital evidence and digital forensic collection and analysis efforts. As technology continues to advance, forensic tools for extracting and preserving digital evidence are becoming inadequate and inefficient. Developing new forensic tools to address the gaps is time-consuming and resource-intensive, creating a pressing need for alternative solutions.

This chapter seeks to address these challenges by proposing quick-fix methods for digital evidence collection that utilize built-in functions provided by emerging apps. Large language models (LLMs) are employed in the digital forensic examination workflow to streamline the analysis of digital forensic evidence, helping improve the efficiency of investigations.

Four digital evidence collection methods are proposed – one universal primary method and three secondary methods tailored for popular instant messaging

Published by Springer Nature Switzerland AG 2026
E. Kurkowski and S. Shenoi (Eds.): DigitalForensics 2025, IFIP AICT 762, pp. 61–76, 2026.
https://doi.org/10.1007/978-3-032-09802-3_4

(IM) applications. The evidence collection methods leverage built-in functions provided by instant messaging platforms to facilitate the extraction of digital content that traditional forensic tools do not support. Large language models are leveraged to offload digital evidence analysis, enabling digital forensic practitioners to quickly grasp the significance of device data and determine whether conventional extraction processes and in-depth analyses are still necessary. Since maintaining the chain of custody is crucial to rendering digital evidence admissible in legal proceedings, the general court stance regarding evidence admissibility is examined. The focus is on how courts perceive the integrity and reliability of the proposed workflow, especially in the context of fast screen capture and in-app data extraction.

2 Related Work

Various tools, frameworks and legal judgments have sought to address the challenges posed by the increased reliance on digital evidence in legal proceedings. Perkins [13] provides foundational insights into the role of digital evidence in legal investigations, emphasizing the importance of reliable tools to ensure evidence admissibility. Carrier [1] explored the abstraction layers in digital forensic tools motivated by the need to handle data in a manageable format instead of merely using tools to parse as much data as possible from digital devices; the work contributed to the segregation of various forensic examination and analysis processes.

The authenticity of computer-generated outputs in criminal matters has been a long-standing focus. Kurzban [7] emphasized the importance of digital forensics keeping up with the rapidly evolving technical environment. Losavio et al. [8] conducted a gap analysis on judicial experiences, shedding light on perceptions of digital evidence.

Garfinkel [3] explored future directions for digital forensics research, emphasizing the need for adaptability in response to technological advancements. Holt et al. [4] provided an in-depth understanding of the evolution of digital forensics in the context of cyber crime. Kaira et al. [5] discussed the Supreme Court of India's judgments on the admissibility of digital evidence, highlighting the implications of Section 65B of the Indian Evidence Act requiring certificates to safeguard the credibility of digital evidence. Solicitors have examined the role of messaging platforms such as WhatsApp in evidence collection in the context of Hong Kong judicial system [14].

KPMG Services [6] has outlined the certification requirements under the Evidence Act of Singapore, focusing on the legal framework for digital evidence admissibility. Moussa [10] has analyzed the authenticity of digital evidence, emphasizing its role in forensic investigations. Vasani and Kannan [18] examined the Indian Supreme Court's interpretation of Section 65B in the landmark Arjun v. Kailash case where the court clarified the mandatory requirements for certifying secondary digital evidence, albeit not for original evidence; this case is central to digital evidence admissibility in India and may well shape admissibility in other Asian-Pacific countries.

Blockchain technology has emerged as a promising approach for ensuring the integrity of digital evidence [17]. Pagani [11] highlights the importance of memory forensics and the analysis of encrypted communications. Other advancements in digital forensics include the classification and evaluation of forensic tools [12], extraction of memory artifacts from applications such as Telegram [2], applications of ChatGPT in digital forensic investigations [15] and integration of artifical intelligence tools for automated evidence retrieval [19]. Michelet and Breitinger [9] recently examined the use of large language models such as ChatGPT and Llama for producing digital forensic reports.

While previous research has focused extensively on digital forensic techniques and tools, gaps exist with regard to emerging platforms such as Signal, WhatsApp and Telegram. This research leverages built-in app functionalities to expedite evidence collection, eliminating the need to develop new forensic tools. By integrating large language models in the digital forensic examination workflow, an automated triage screening methodology is presented that provides executive summary reports on digital evidence. The method, which enables digital forensic practitioners to prioritize casework while ensuring admissibility in court, strikes a balance between efficiency and rigorous forensic standards, offering a scalable solution to address the growing demand for digital evidence processing.

3 Proposed Evidence Collection Methods

The proposed methods for rapid evidence collection from instant messaging apps address challenges faced by traditional forensic tools. These methods reduce backlogs, resolve unsupported data extraction problems and ensure transparency. Designed to be user-friendly, repeatable and applicable across diverse smartphone models, the methods enhance digital evidence collection.

The two-tiered approach comprises primary preservation and secondary extraction. The primary method involves direct screen capture that is applicable to most smartphones. The secondary method focusing on specific apps leverages their built-in export and/or database extraction functions. Both methods require the smartphones to be powered on.

The methods expedite data extraction, completing the process within the typical 24–36-hour detention window, faster than traditional forensic tools. Witnesses are required to be present during the extraction process to ensure integrity and transparency.

The preservation process begins with logging into a new session via a QR code or verification code from a smartphone, following which relevant content is captured on a second device. Witnesses present during this process include the offender or legal representative, digital forensic practitioner who conducts the capture, law enforcement officer who seized the device and an independent witness such as a first responder or supervisor not involved in the investigation. The digital forensic professional is responsible for documenting each step contemporaneously.

Given the volatile nature of digital evidence, especially for active app sessions, precautions must be taken to prevent remote wiping, such by enabling the airplane mode on the smartphone. In an urgent case where witnesses are unavailable, the live screen capture process must be videorecorded to preserve evidence integrity.

3.1 Primary Method

The primary method involving live screen capture is a simple, universal solution applicable to all smartphones regardless of make, model and operating system. The method involves three steps:

- **Step 1:** Use the original smartphone to scan a QR code in order to log into a second device.
- **Step 2:** Log into the same app account on the second device.
- **Step 3:** Capture digital content from the second device using a digital camera or built-in screenshot function.

This method involving live screen capture of the second device ensures that the original smartphone remains unaltered to maintain integrity. The captured content is preserved for analysis on the second device. The process must be fully documented by the digital forensic practitioner and witnessed by other parties.

The method is ideal when digital evidence is tied to cases with clear dates such as criminal intimidation, child pornography and voyeurism. However, the method is inadequate for cases such as deception and money laundering that come with large datasets containing data collected over extended periods of time.

3.2 Secondary Methods

Secondary methods involving user-level extraction are suitable for collecting evidence over longer time periods. The methods allow for the extraction of stored data, potentially all the way back to the app installation date, depending, of course, on the app extraction limits. They are particularly useful in cases such as deception and social unrest where evidence spans multiple conversations rather than isolated incidents.

Because traditional forensic tools often do not support data extraction from apps such as Signal, WhatsApp and Telegram, alternative user-level extraction methods were developed.

Signal. In the case of Signal, a digital forensic practitioner can employ common open-source tools such as Visual Studio or DB Browser to view the SQLite database. However, since Signal data is encrypted, the DB Browser for SQLite database is used to enable the decryption process before viewing the results.

Upon logging into the Signal Desktop, the database is found in Windows under the path `C:\Users\AppData\Roaming\Signal\sql`. The decryption key is located in the `config.json` file in the same path. Decryption is accomplished by copying and pasting the key and applying it as a raw key in the pop-up SQLCipher encryption window that requests key input. Following this operation, the digital forensic practitioner can access all the data files, including the text messages. To export to a human-readable version, it is necessary to go to the drop-down menu under File, select Export and then choose the Tables to JSON option. This displays the data in a table format with rows and columns of specific content, including time, sender number, messages, etc. The exported text messages are then verified using the Signal graphical user interface that displays the same text messages.

WhatsApp. In the case of WhatsApp, the SQLite database can also be retrieved and accessed. However, unlike the direct access technique for Signal, the smartphone has to be rooted in order to access and read the WhatsApp SQLite database. The rooting technique is not ideal because it alters the smartphone status prior to evidence extraction.

A better method is to leverage the built-in export function of WhatsApp without having to root the smartphone. This is done by tapping the button at the WhatsApp setting in the mobile version to select Chats and then Chat History. After clicking the Export Chat option under Chat History, a pop-up message requests whether to include media in the exported data. Depending on the case and the required digital content, the digital forensic practitioner could choose between the Without Media and Include Media options to export data. The main concerns with this method are the relevance of the exported data and its size. If media records relevant to the case exist, the digital forensic practitioner should select the Include Media option, which increases the amount of exported data.

The next step is to choose how WhatsApp should send the exported data. The options include sending the data to a Google Drive or via Bluetooth, Gmail or other instant messaging apps such as WhatsApp and Telegram. To avoid problems associated with cross platform transmission, WhatsApp is suggested as the medium for sending exported data. A spare smartphone should be readied as the container and a designated WhatsApp account on the device should be created to receive a copy of the exported data. If the Include Media option was selected, text messages in the TXT and multimedia formats are sent to the receiver's WhatsApp account. Upon opening the TXT document, the unencrypted messages can be read. It is also possible to send the exported data via Bluetooth to the local drive of a laptop or smartphone. The exported text messages and JPG images are then verified using the WhatsApp graphical user interface that displays the same text messages.

Telegram. Telegram provides the highest level of security of the three instant messaging applications. The SQLite database contains encrypted data, but un-

Table 1. Comparison of large language model features (1: worst; 5: best).

LLM	Developer	Reasoning	Speed	Conscientiousness
ChatGPT 4o	OpenAI	3	2	4
Claude 3	Anthropic	3	2	5
DeepSeek v3	DeepSeek	3	2	5

like Signal, the decryption key could not be located even when the smartphone was rooted. The only method for extracting Telegram data is to use the built-in export function in its Desktop version. As in the case of WhatsApp, the built-in export function of Telegram supports data extraction.

In the case of Telegram, after logging into the Telegram Desktop on the second device, it is required to click the three-dots icon in the top right corner and select Export Chat History. In the Chat Export Settings, the item types to be exported must be selected; the choices are Photos, Videos, Voice Messages, Video Messages, Stickers, GIFs and Files. The size limit for each export is 4,000 MB. The default export format is HTML, with the designated download path at `C:\Users\Downloads\Telegram Desktop`. Upon clicking the export button to confirm, the data is exported to the specified path. The exported text messages and photos must be verified against the Telegram graphical user interface to confirm that the same contents are displayed.

4 Large Language Model Integration

Large language models were explored as a triage tool to screen data extracted from instant messaging applications obtained via app extraction methods or conventional digital forensic tools. A sample in the Excel table format was exported from a conventional forensic analysis tool. A Python script was employed to interact with various large language models using Poe, a widely recognized large language model platform. The paid version of Poe, which requires an application programming interface (API) token for access, was leveraged to facilitate the use of large language models. The outputs generated by the large language models were subsequently analyzed.

Three key criteria – reasoning, speed and conscientiousness – were considered to evaluate the performance of three prominent large language models. The three models – ChatGPT 4o, Claude 3 and Deepseek v3 – have demonstrated notable levels of precision and accuracy in summarizations that align with the primary objective of enhancing the overall workflow of digital forensic investigations. Table 1 presents a comparison of the three large language models [16].

Inaccuracy and hallucinations are significant concerns when using large language models. Consequently, such models should not be used to automatically generate executive summary reports intended for judicial proceedings. However, the models can provide valuable insights into the significance of instant messag-

```
def poe_query(content):
    api_key = "Mnhog4fjiA_[redacted]"

    query = (
        "Please generate a report based on the following text that includes: "
        "(i) a summary of the basic information of the instant messaging chat groups, "
        "(ii) an identification of the topics of discussion within the chats; "
        "(iii) an assessment of the overall sentiment of the conversations. "
        "Here's the content: " + content[0:500]
    )
```

Fig. 1. Large language model prompt.

ing chats, assisting digital forensic practitioners in evaluating the relevance of the extracted data. This methodology has the potential to significantly reduce the risk of overlooking crucial digital evidence obtained from other devices associated with a case. By prioritizing and streamlining the analysis process, a digital forensic practitioner can conduct a more effective and focused examination of digital forensic data.

In an experiment, a raw Excel file was created by exporting content from a Telegram chat group using a forensic tool. The Excel file contained 966 rows of data from a synthetic riot case, each row corresponding to a message sent in the chat group. The raw evidence, characterized by its lack of direction and focus, was cumbersome and difficult to interpret. Targeted prompts were crafted to instruct the large language models on summarizing the instant messaging content. The objective was to streamline the process for digital forensic practitioners who are typically interested in quickly understanding the implications of the evidentiary data. Essentially, the large language models would serve as triage tools, enabling practitioners to assess and determine the directions of their investigations, and whether to dig deeper or halt the investigations based on the value of the chat conversations.

Figure 1 shows the prompt issued to the large language models. The specific requests were:

- Summarize the basic information of the instant messaging chat group, including the list of participants.
- Identify the topics of discussion in the chats.
- Assess the overall sentiment of the conversations.

Note that the prompt was designed not to ask the large language models to make judgments about criminality, just to facilitate the investigation.

5 Large Language Model Reports

This section describes the executive summary reports about the chat group produced by the three large language models.

ChatGPT 4o Report.

Chat Group Information.
Participant List: *The chat group had 20 participants, including named and unnamed members. The participants had a mix of identifiable names, nicknames and anonymous IDs. Example aliases or nicknames included XXX48862 Ho./., XXX098015, XXX418804 Ken, XXX477034 Happy TT, XXX930778 Fuckgov16, XXX31216 Milk Tea Less Sweet, XXX70395 Happy Healer, XXX391798 Big Cloth Lui, XXX62241 Pp, XXX254928 Yellow and Blue (Owner) and XXX631853 Stephen.*
Activity Timeline: *The chats spanned from October 13, 2019 to November 18, 2019, with frequent daily interactions, including real-time updates.*
Communications Structure: *The chats used informal and colloquial language, with heavy usage of Cantonese (written in Chinese characters and Romanized Cantonese), occasional English and slang. Media attachments included photos, videos, stickers, voice messages and file links.*
Discussion Topics.
The chats primarily focused on the following topics:
Protests and Activism: *Discussions about the Hong Kong protests of 2019, including logistics, planning and updates.*
Safety Concerns and Police Activity: *Frequent mentions of police activity and methods for avoiding detection.*
Internal Group Dynamics: *Frustrations, disputes and camaraderie among group members.*
Casual Conversations: *Personal topics, jokes and banter.*
Technical and Logistical Coordination: *Telegram channels, voice messages and file sharing for planning.*
Incidents and Conflict: *Clashes with police, injuries and loss of supplies.*
Sentiment Analysis.
The sentiments included:
Negative Sentiment: *Anger and frustration directed at external entities and group members.*
Humor and Camaraderie: *Jokes and lighthearted comments to maintain morale.*
Determination and Unity: *Strong focus on achieving goals and staying organized.*

Claude 3 Report.

Chat Group Information.
Participant List: *The chat group had 20 participants. Example nicknames and user names were Happy Healer (user name: XXX370395), Happy TT (user name: XXX477034) and Kan (user name: XXX333842).*
Discussion Topics.
The chats primarily focused on the following topics:
Planning and Logistics: *Locations, gathering points, routes and timings.*

Obtaining and Distributing Supplies: *Supplies items such as included masks, helmets and gloves.*
Encounters and Clashes with Police: *Tactics and updates on police movements.*
Communications: *Telegram channels and forums.*
News and Updates: *Protest violence, arrests and injuries.*
Casual Conversations and Humor: *Interactions and jokes among members.*
Example Quote.
"Don't go discussing 'fantasies' on the streets. Police will screw you up. They are listening actively on the streets. Some crazy ones even pretend to be your friends to mess with you."
Sentiment Analysis.
Mix of anger, frustration, camaraderie and support. Members demonstrated solidarity. However, towards the end, tensions and disagreements emerged in the group.

DeepSeek v3 Report.

Chat Group Information.
Participant List: *The chat group had diverse participants with nicknames such a Happy Healer, Lv Bu · Qi Yu and Yellow and Blue (Owner).*
Activity Timeline: *The chats spanned from October 13, 2019 to November 18, 2019.*
Communications Structure: *The chats, conducted primarily in Cantonese, included text, voice, videos and stickers, with some messages deleted.*
Discussion Topics.
The chats primarily focused on the following topics:
Planning and Coordination: *Meeting times and locations, often using coded language.*
Incidents and Concerns: *Mentions of surveillance, arrests and missing members.*
Violence and Tactics: *Threats of violence and use of fire or explosives.*
Humor and Internal Disputes: *Jokes and arguments within the group.*
Political Context: *References to protests and specific locations.*
Safety and Secrecy: *Efforts to avoid detection and delete messages.*
Sentiment Analysis.
Mix of serious and urgent discussions about potentially illegal activities. The tone shifted between serious and humorous, with a strong emphasis on secrecy and avoiding detection.

Table 2 compares the key aspects of the chat group identified by the three large language models.

6 Evaluation

This section discusses the evaluation results and the recommended large language model.

Table 2. Comparison of key aspects of the chat group.

Aspect	ChatGPT 4o	Claude 3	DeepSeek v3
Participants	20 participants, aliases, IDs	20 participants, key members identified	Diverse participants, aliases, nicknames
Activity Timeline	Oct. 13, 2019 to Nov. 18, 2019	Not specified	Oct. 13, 2019 to Nov. 18, 2019
Topics	Protests, logistics, safety, internal incidents, casual conversations	Protests, logistics, police clashes, casual conversations	Planning, incidents, political context, safety, internal disputes
Sentiment	Mixed: Anger, humor, determination	Mixed: Camaraderie, frustration, tension	Mixed: Serious discussions with humor and secrecy
Chat Style	Informal, colloquial Cantonese with slang	Coded language, direct messages	Coded language, secrecy emphasis

6.1 Large Language Model Results

A survey involving 30 digital forensic professionals revealed that 47% of the respondents preferred the DeepSeek v3 results whereas 33% favored the ChatGPT 4o results and 20% preferred the Claude 3 results. Although DeepSeek v3 was the most preferred model, many respondents noted that the ChatGPT 4o and Claude 3 results could effectively complement the forensic investigation by providing additional perspectives and nuanced details.

DeepSeek v3. DeepSeek v3 was chosen as the most preferred option due to its strong focus on forensic details that are crucial in digital forensic investigations:

- **Planning and Coordination:** The model results highlight meeting times, locations and the use of coded language, which are critical to understanding the structure and intent of the chat group.
- **Safety and Secrecy:** The model results mention efforts to avoid detection and delete messages, offering essential clues for evidence recovery and preservation.
- **Political Context:** The model results incorporate details about sensitive topics, such as protests and specific locations (e.g., Campus A and Campus B), providing essential contextual information to digital forensic practitioners.

The largest group of respondents (47%) emphasized that DeepSeek v3 provided the most actionable insights for a forensic investigation, particularly in identifying high-risk behaviors and reconstructing events.

ChatGPT 4o. ChatGPT 4o was noted for its structured and detailed overview, making it a strong complement to DeepSeek v3:

- **Participant Information:** The model results provide rich details about aliases, nicknames and participant structures, which assist in identifying key individuals in the chat group.
- **Sentiment Analysis:** The model results provide a nuanced breakdown of emotions, such as anger, humor and determination, which can help assess group dynamics.

A total of 33% of survey respondents preferred ChatGPT 4o. They cited the model for its clarity and attention to participant details as valuable complements to DeepSeek v3.

Claude 3. Claude 3 was recognized for its concise summaries and unique elements that complemented the forensic analysis:

- **Direct Quotes:** The model results include quotes from group chats, such as warnings about police surveillance, adding a layer of context that is missing in the other results.
- **Sentiment Analysis:** The model results highlight camaraderie and internal tensions, useful for assessing the cohesion and disagreements within the chat group.

Overall, 20% of respondents valued Claude 3 for its brevity and inclusion of critical elements. However, it was noted that its results were less comprehensive than those provided by DeepSeek v3 and ChatGPT 4o.

Combining Model Strengths. While DeepSeek v3 was the most preferred model, several survey respondents mentioned that the outputs of ChatGPT 4o and Claude 3 could be effectively combined with DeepSeek v3 to provide a more robust forensic analysis. ChatGPT 4o added depth in the participant analysis and sentiment breakdown whereas Claude 3 provided concise summaries and unique contextual elements such as direct quotes.

6.2 Large Language Model Recommendations

DeepSeek v3, which provided detailed, forensically-relevant outputs, is the most suitable large language model for digital forensic analysis. However, ChatGPT 4o and Claude 3 complement DeepSeek v3 by excelling in areas such as participant identification, sentiment analysis and concise contextual interpretation. Leveraging the strengths of all three large language models could provide a more comprehensive and robust framework for forensic investigations. DeepSeek v3 demonstrated a notable advantage in analyzing conversations conducted in Chinese, giving it an edge in language-specific cases.

It is important to note that this study did not seek to identify the best large language model; instead, it attempted to explore model capabilities for research purposes. Further evaluations should be conducted to assess model performance on specific datasets and contexts. Of course, limitations such as server congestion caused by high traffic can impact the speed, stability and overall performance of large language models. These factors underscore the importance of continuous research and evaluation in the rapidly evolving technical area of large language models.

7 Digital Forensic Requirements

The U.S. National Institute of Standards and Technology (NIST) has specified requirements for imaging tools in digital investigations. These include: (i) full duplication or imaging of the original disk/partition; (ii) no alterations to the original disk; (iii) verification of disk image integrity; (iv) logging of errors during imaging and (v) accurate, comprehensive documentation.

This research has identified four additional requirements for digital evidence preservation methods that do not employ proprietary tools: (i) direct data visualization or acquisition from the same account; (ii) no modifications to the original data; (iii) integrity verification of outputs against the originals and (iv) comprehensive logging, documentation and witnessing of digital forensic processes for transparency.

Requirements for digital evidence admissibility in court proceedings vary by country. One is the free proof system used by France and Germany, where judges decide admissibility without prerequisite proof. Another is the restricted law system in the United States and United Kingdom, where evidence must meet strict reliability standards before admission, including proving the accuracy and proper functioning of digital devices.

Despite varying global requirements, common preferences include valid legal authority, clear visualization, expert witness validation and prioritization of original outputs as direct evidence. Based on these criteria, the results of the methods described in this chapter would have greater likelihood of acceptance compared with black-box forensic tools whose operations are obscure and could be unreliable.

8 Digital Evidence Extraction Workflow Evaluation

The conventional digital forensic examination workflow does not appear to be a viable solution for handling the overwhelming investigative caseloads. The processes involved are time-consuming and the resulting backlogs run contrary to the famous quote – "Justice delayed is justice denied." Clearly, time is a mission-critical factor in the digital forensic examination workflow.

The methods proposed in this chapter reduce the evidence acquisition time while enhancing the efficiency of evidence collection and analysis. Specifically, the time required for examinations could be reduced significantly. Figure 2 compares the conventional digital forensic examination workflow and the proposed offloaded digital forensic examination workflow proceeding to a full examination,

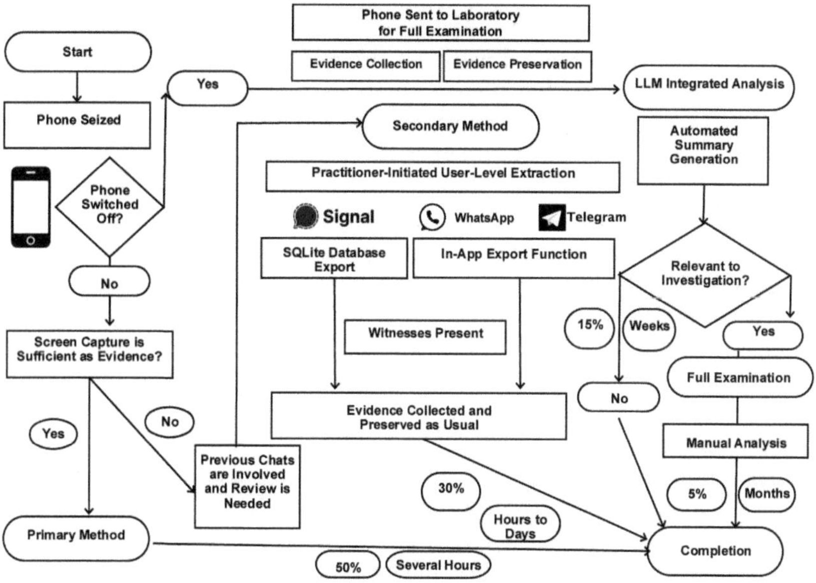

(a) Conventional digital forensic examination workflow.

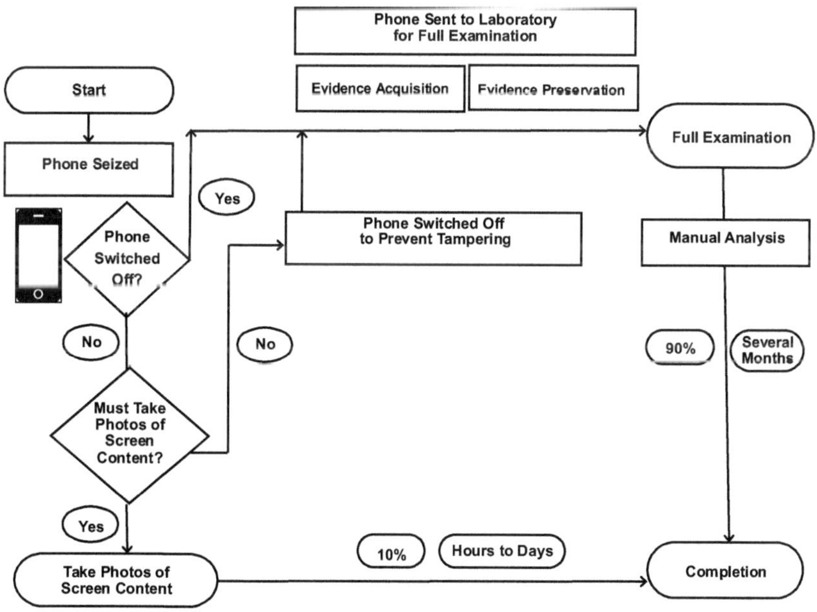

(b) Offloaded digital forensic examination workflow.

Fig. 2. Comparison of digital forensic examination workflows.

along with the time required after offloading or diversion. In the conventional workflow, around 90% of digital devices are submitted for full examination. The enhancements in the proposed workflow are estimated to reduce the number of digital devices submitted for full examinations to just 5%.

The proposed methods are simple enough to be performed by digital forensic practitioners without specialized expertise. Conventional forensic tools demand technical skills and extensive training that render them less accessible. This is particularly challenging in regions where law enforcement personnel are transitioned to conduct digital forensic investigations with limited training. Simplified workflows reduce the reliance on certified experts and ease courtroom presentations where circumstantial evidence often suffices.

Judges often lack the technical knowledge to interpret complex forensic evidence, leading to delays and difficulties in delivering informed judgments. The proposed live screen capture method simplifies evidence presentation by replicating the graphical user interface of the original digital device. The direct visualization minimizes the reliance on expert witnesses and reduces the need for deep technical explanations in court proceedings.

Proprietary digital forensic tools operate as black-box systems, which makes it difficult to assess their reliability. In contrast, the proposed methods prioritize transparency and adhere to open-source principles, ensuring that the processes are replicable and auditable. The transparency improves their admissibility compared with proprietary tools.

The proposed methods address gaps in conventional forensic tools, such as unsupported instant messaging applications and cloud-based data. Live screen captures are particularly effective for volatile data during arrests when digital devices are active, yielding better results than subsequent laboratory-based acquisitions. Screen captures also help alleviate backlogs by enabling quicker data collection.

Large language models streamline digital forensic investigations by rapidly analyzing and summarizing large datasets, enabling digital forensic practitioners to identify critical evidence and prioritize resources. The proposed hybrid workflow integrates large language models with conventional digital forensic tools, increasing efficiency and accelerating investigations while maintaining thoroughness.

9 Limitations

The proposed methods assume that subjects will willingly disclose passwords and PINs, which cannot be guaranteed. While password-cracking tools can address this issue, they may introduce delays and additional complexities. Furthermore, the reliance on Internet connectivity for live screen captures, data exports and database decryption (e.g., with Signal Desktop) can pose challenges, particularly in environments with unstable or restricted networks. To mitigate these risks, future workflows could incorporate closed network setups to maintain evidence integrity and operational reliability.

Privacy is another significant limitation, particularly when leveraging large language models in digital forensic investigations. Using third-party application programming interfaces for large language model processing may expose sensitive evidence to external systems, raising significant privacy and security concerns. To address this issue, an on-premises setup for large language models is recommended so that all data processing occurs within a secure and controlled local environment. This complies with privacy regulations and reduces the risks posed by unauthorized access and data breaches.

However, on-premises large language model solutions introduce challenges due to their computational requirements. Large language models require high-performance graphics processing units especially when handling large datasets. An adequate computing infrastructure is critical to maintaining the speed and accuracy of large-language-model-driven analyses. This can pose barriers to law enforcement agencies with limited budgets and technical expertise. Therefore, careful consideration must be given to designing scalable, cost-effective solutions for deploying on-premises large language model solutions.

10 Conclusions

The triage screening methodology described in this chapter leverages built-in functions provided by instant messaging platforms such as Signal, WhatsApp and Telegram for evidence collection. The methodology offloads analytical tasks to large language models, streamlining digital evidence processing and ensuring that critical evidence and insights are not overlooked. It enables digital forensic practitioners to prioritize casework while ensuring admissibility in court, striking a balance between efficiency and rigorous forensic standards.

References

1. B. Carrier, Defining digital forensic examination and analysis tools using abstraction layers, *International Journal of Digital Evidence*, vol. 1(4), 2003.
2. P. Fernandez-Alvarez and R. Rodríguez, Extraction and analysis of retrievable memory artifacts from the Windows Telegram Desktop application, *Forensic Science International: Digital Investigation*, vol. 40(S), article no. 301342, 2022.
3. S. Garfinkel, Digital forensics research: The next 10 years, *Digital Investigation*, vol. 7(S), pp. S64–S73, 2010.
4. T. Holt, A. Bossler and K. Seigfried-Spellar, Chapter 14: Evolution of digital forensics, in *Cybercrime and Digital Forensics*, Routledge, London, United Kingdom, 2022.
5. T. Kaira, A. Anand and B. Dhawan, The Supreme Court of India redefines admissibility of electronic evidence in India, *Digital Evidence and Electronic Signature Law Review*, vol. 12, pp. 33–37, 2015.
6. KPMG Services, Evidence Act Certification, Singapore (`assets.kpmg.com/content/dam/kpmg/sg/pdf/2017/12/Evidence-Act-certification-brochure.pdf`), 2024.

7. S. Kurzban, Authentication of computer-generated evidence in the United States federal courts, *IDEA: The Journal of Law and Technology*, vol. 35(4), pp. 437–461, 1995.
8. M. Losavio, J. Adams, and M. Rogers, Gap analysis: Judicial experience and perception of electronic evidence, *Journal of Digital Forensic Practice*, vol. 1(1), pp. 13–17, 2006.
9. G. Michelet and F. Breitinger, ChatGPT, Llama, can you write my report? An experiment on assisted digital forensics reports written using (local) large language models, *Forensic Science International: Digital Investigation*, vol. 48(S), article no. 301683, 2024.
10. A. Moussa, Electronic evidence and its authenticity in forensic evidence, *Egyptian Journal of Forensic Sciences*, vol. 11, article no. 20, 2021.
11. F. Pagani, Advances in Forensic Investigations of Volatile Memory (in French), Doctoral Dissertation, Doctoral School of Computer Science, Telecommunications and Electronics, Sorbonne University, Paris, France, 2019.
12. A. Parveen, Z. Khan and S. Ahmad, Classification and evaluation of digital forensic tools, *TELKOMNIKA – Telecommunication, Computing, Electronics and Control*, vol. 18(6), pp. 3096–3106, 2020.
13. S. Perkins, Computer Forensic Software in a Corporate Environment, Global Information Assurance Certification Paper, SANS Institute, Bethesda, Maryland (`www.giac.org/paper/gsec/3082/computer-forensic-software-corporate-environment/105122`), 2003.
14. Robertsons Solicitors, Text message evidence in Hong Kong, Hong Kong, China (`robertsonshk.com/en/news/text-message-evidence-in-hong-kong`), June 18, 2015.
15. M. Scanlon, F. Breitinger, C. Hargreaves, J. Hilgert and J. Sheppard, ChatGPT for digital forensic investigation: The good, the bad and the unknown, *Forensic Science International: Digital Investigation*, vol. 46(S), article no. 301609, 2023.
16. D. Shah, ChatGPT vs DeepSeek vs Claude – Which LLM fits your needs? *Portkey Blog* (`portkey.ai/blog/chatgpt-vs-deepseek-vs-clarity`), February 1, 2025.
17. D. Sharma and Sakshi, Blockchain-based digital forensics investigation, *International Journal of Science and Research*, vol. 12(1), pp. 558–560, 2023.
18. B. Vasani and V. Kannan, Supreme Court on the admissibility of electronic evidence under Section 65B of the Evidence Act, *India Corporate Law Blog* (`corporate.cyrilamarchandblogs.com/2021/01/supreme-court-on-the-admissibility-of-electronic-evidence-under-section-65b-of-the-evidence-act`), January 27, 2021.
19. R. Yadav, AI-driven digital forensics, *International Journal of Scientific Research and Engineering Trends*, vol. 10(4), pp. 1673–1681, 2024.

Chat Log Analysis Using Large Language Models

Yueheng Mao[1,2], Min Yu[1,2], Pengbo Zhang[1,2], Kam-Pui Chow[3], Jianguo Jiang[1,2], Gang Li[4], Xiang Meng[1], and Weiqing Huang[1]

[1] Chinese Academy of Sciences, Beijing, China
[2] University of Chinese Academy of Sciences, Beijing, China
yumin@iie.ac.cn
[3] University of Hong Kong, Hong Kong, China
[4] Deakin University, Burwood, Australia

Abstract. Digital forensic analyses that are conducted manually using forensic tools can be laborious and error prone. The situation is exacerbated given the large volumes of digital evidence that have to be processed and analyzed. Large language models developed by state-of-the-art artificial intelligence research can be engaged to reduce the workloads of digital forensic practitioners.
This chapter describes a framework that leverages large language models to automate chat log forensics. A novel metric is specified for assessing the forensic effectiveness of large language models from three key perspectives: factual evidence, criminal motive and subject relationships. The experimental results demonstrate the utility and performance of the framework in chat log investigations.

Keywords: Chat Log Analysis · Large Language Models · Automation

1 Introduction

Advances in computing and networking technologies are increasing the scope and magnitude of cyber crimes and the associated investigations [20]. All digital activities are bound to leave traces [11, 12] and the digital evidence can be collected legally [14]. Bentham, a distinguished British jurist, said that evidence is the cornerstone of justice [9]. It follows that digital evidence is the cornerstone of cyber crime justice.

Digital forensics involves the identification, preservation, analysis and presentation of digital evidence in legal proceedings [1]. Digital forensic practitioners currently engage forensic tools for evidence acquisition but are required to conduct a number of manual technical analyses. Indeed, the complete analysis of digital data in large cases may take months or even years. As technology evolves and the volume of data grows exponentially, advanced tools and techniques are needed to efficiently process, analyze and interpret digital evidence.

The emergence of the transformer architecture in 2017 has given rise to the development of large language models [24]. After extensive research, modern large language models such as ChatGPT [7, 18] hold promise for automating the

Published by Springer Nature Switzerland AG 2026
E. Kurkowski and S. Shenoi (Eds.): DigitalForensics 2025, IFIP AICT 762, pp. 77–94, 2026.
https://doi.org/10.1007/978-3-032-09802-3_5

analysis of digital data [21]. Large language models are attractive options for generating scripts, summarizing evidence, acquiring knowledge and conducting multilingual analysis, sentiment analysis and subject relationships analysis [4].

Chat logs are important repositories of evidence in cyber crime investigations because they provide direct evidence relevant to the cases at hand. However, chat logs are voluminous and current manual chat log analysis techniques are tedious, time-consuming and prone to error. This chapter describes a framework that leverages large language models to automate chat log forensics. A novel metric is specified for assessing the forensic effectiveness of large language models from three key perspectives: factual evidence, criminal motive and subject relationships. Experimental results demonstrate the utility and performance of the large language model based framework in chat log investigations.

2 Background and Related Work

This section discusses digital forensics and chat log investigations, along with large language models and their applications in digital forensics.

2.1 Digital Forensics and Chat Log Investigations

Digital forensics involves criminal and other investigations, computer science and jurisprudence. The principal task in a cyber crime investigation is to reconstruct the case using digital data and answer the six 5W1H questions – the who, what, where, when, why and how of the case [6]. Digital forensics seeks to provide evidence for the administration of justice by proffering digital evidence obtained via computer-based investigations and analyses. It is commonly defined as the process of applying computing principles and methods and their related sciences and technologies to obtain computer-related evidence that proves or disproves objective facts [8].

Chat logs are important repositories of evidence in cyber crime investigations because they often provide direct evidence relevant to the cases at hand. Chat logs are considered to be relatively reliable evidence because they are obtained directly from the communications devices of subjects. The authenticity and reliability of chat logs are further enhanced when corroborated by other evidentiary sources.

Since chat logs capture conversations involving subjects, they are important to inferring their motives and intentions and may contain background information about the offenses, personal motives and interests, attitudes towards targets and victims, etc. Also, they can reveal the relationships between the subjects of investigations.

Forensic analyses of chat logs are typically conducted manually using forensic tools. However, the logs are often large and distributed in nature, rendering their analyses laborious and error prone. The situation is exacerbated due to the large volumes of logs that have to be processed and analyzed. A promising solution is to employ large language models developed by state-of-the-art artificial intelligence research to reduce the workloads of digital forensic practitioners engaged in chat log investigations.

2.2 Large Language Models and Applications

The application of artificial intelligence models in digital forensics has mainly involved data classification and identification in malware forensics, network forensics, computer system forensics, device forensics and evidence chain construction. Advances in large language models have opened the door to new opportunities in the digital forensics domain.

Large language models are artificial intelligence models, often with tens of billions or more parameters, that undergo unsupervised training using large amounts of unlabeled text. The ChatGPT chatbot developed by OpenAI [22] employs the GPT-3.5 and GPT-4 large language model architectures. Developed using reinforcement learning, ChatGPT can engage in natural and smooth conversations in numerous scenarios. Other large language models similar to ChatGPT include Gemini developed by Google [5], GLM developed by Smart Spectrum [3], Claude developed by Anthropic, SparkDesk developed by Xunfei, Wenxin Yiyi developed by Baidu, and Tongyi Qianwen developed by Aliyun.

Researchers have begun to train increasing large language models to explore their performance limits. Although the large language models engage similar architectures and pre-training as smaller language models, they exhibit advanced capabilities, especially with regard to solving complex tasks – a characteristic called "emergent ability" [25]. Analogous to the phenomenon of phase transition in physics, emergent ability manifests itself as a rapid increase in model performance over random levels as scale increases; this is often referred to as a qualitative change arising from a quantitative change.

Researchers have explored the possibility of using large language models for digital forensics. Scanlon et al. [21] discuss the advantages and disadvantages of using ChatGPT in digital forensic investigations. They highlight limitations due to the quality of the training data as well as the high degree of specialization. Despite the fact that ChatGPT's responses can be unprofessional and unreliable, Scanlon and colleagues opine that large language models can be applied in several digital forensic scenarios. Michelet and Breitinger [16] have investigated the feasibility of producing digital forensic reports using large language models, observing that digital forensic practitioners can leverage the models in the report writing process given professional proofreading and corrections. Dinis-Oliveira and Azevedo [2] note that ChatGPT and other artificial intelligence tools still have limitations and raise some legal and ethical concerns.

Other researchers have proposed methods that employ large language models in digital forensics. Oh et al. [17] proposed a ransomware classification method using a large language model and the Volatility Framework for memory forensics. Wickramasekara and Scanlon [26] developed an inheritance framework using AutoGen and a large language model that reduces investigation workloads. Jia et al. [10] applied a large language model to detect deepfakes. Umeike [23] employed predictive supervised learning algorithms for crime prediction that assists law enforcement in making tactical decisions to improve policing strategies and policies.

3 Proposed Framework

This section describes the proposed framework that leverages large language models to automate chat log forensics. A novel metric named BLEUDF is specified for assessing the forensic effectiveness of large language models.

3.1 Chat Log Analysis

Chat logs can be input to a large language model for automated analysis. In this work, chat logs are analyzed in three dimensions – factual evidence, criminal motive and subject relationships:

- **Factual Evidence:** Factual evidence is the most essential element in a case investigation because it directly describes the circumstances related to the criminal activity. Analyzing factual evidence involves investigating the facts pertaining to the criminal act and specifying what the suspect did, including the when, where and how.
- **Criminal Motive:** The criminal motive helps understand the various actions and events involved in the case, along with the reasons and logic behind the criminal behavior. Clarifying the criminal motive helps in the overall analysis of the case.
- **Subject Relationships:** The subjects in a case include the suspects, victims and witnesses, as well as casual participants. It is important to clarify the relationships and dynamics of all the subjects involved in the case.

Large language models can identify key information such as times, locations and transactions from a large number of unordered chat logs. For example, given chat logs pertaining to a financial fraud case, a large language model can quickly identify and sort crucial clues such the times and amounts of financial transactions.

However, inherent limitations in the training data may cause large language models to inaccurately analyze chat logs in certain scenarios. For instance, in a criminal case involving many technical terms, a large language model may misinterpret the meanings of the terms, contributing to unfair judgments about certain subjects.

3.2 BLEUDF Index

The Bilingual Evaluation Understudy (BLEU) metric evaluates the quality of machine-generated translations against reference translations based on the degrees of matching n-grams [19]. Motivated by the BLEU metric, the proposed

Table 1. BLEUDF variables.

Variable	**Symbol**	**Description**
Suspect	S	Relevant subjects
Behavior	B	Criminal behavior
Location	L	Location
Time	T	Time
Motive	Mo	Criminal motive
Method	Me	Criminal methods

Bilingual Evaluation Understudy for Digital Forensics (BLEUDF) index evaluates the accuracy of large language model outputs based on the matching of n-grams.

The 5W1H principle involving the six questions (elements) – who, what, when, where, why and how – is central to digital evidence. Accordingly, six variables conveying the six elements of digital evidence are employed to compute the BLEUDF metric (Table 1).

Chat log analysis results provided by large language models are expected to vary. Therefore, the accurate analysis and output of keywords are especially important. Additionally, the weights of the six elements in the chat log analysis results are expected to be different. To better assess the completeness and reasonableness of the results, it is necessary to have different (and adjustable) weights for the different elements.

The composite element value E is computed as:

$$E = \frac{1}{n}(\alpha \sum (S + L + T) + \beta \sum (B + Me) + \gamma \sum Mo)$$

where n is the number of matches to keywords in the output, α, β and γ are adjustment factors that are given different weights depending on the situation subject to the constraint that $\alpha + \beta + \gamma = 1$. Note that S, L and T correspond to basic evidence and can be given a lower weight α. Since B and Me represent evidence that is directly relevant to a case, they are given a higher weight β. Mo is important but may be more difficult to prove, so it is given a medium weight γ.

The analysis results output by different large language models are compared using standard digital evidence element keywords. The proportion of the output results accounted for in the keyword list is used to compute the BLEUDF evaluation index:

$$\text{BLEUDF} = E * exp(\frac{1}{n} \sum_{n=1}^{N} P_n)$$

where P_n is the n-gram based accuracy expressed as:

$$P_n = \frac{\sum_{\text{n-gram} \in \text{yCounterClip(n-gram)}}}{\sum_{\text{n-gram} \in \text{yCounter(n-gram)}}}$$

The BLEUDF evaluation index is used to assess the forensic effectiveness of a large language model. From among the manually-extracted keywords, the factors related to suspect, time and location collectively have weight α, the factors related to behavior and method collectively have weight β and the factors related to motive have weight γ. The BLEUDF computation involves an n-gram operation with the manually-extracted keywords through the statements outputted by the large language model. The final value in the range $[0, 1]$. The greater the BLEUDF value, the better the large language model analysis of the case.

3.3 AutoDF Framework

The AutoDF digital forensics framework leverages large language models to automate the forensic analysis of chat logs. The framework increases the efficiency of chat log examination and analysis, and accelerates the forensic process while ensuring accuracy.

Figure 1 shows the AutoDF framework. The framework integrates several large language models that are selected based on multiple factors. First, models with a wide range of knowledge coverage and strong language understanding capabilities are preferred. For example, models trained on diverse datasets, including legal- and forensic-related text, are more likely to be included. Second, in addition to their BLEUDF scores, the adaptability of large language models to different types of chat log data is considered. Some large language models may perform better on structured chat logs whereas other models are better suited to unstructured or multilingual chat logs.

4 Experiments

This section provides details about the experiments, including the dataset used, the data processing and analysis, and the evaluation methods.

4.1 Dataset

To protect the privacy of subjects, it was not possible to use chat logs from real cases in the experiments. Therefore, chat logs extracted from simulated cases in digital forensics competitions were employed. The competition organizers have provided guarantees about the integrity of the prosecution materials and digital data, information, procedures and evidence, enabling complete simulated cases to be used without raising issues related to privacy and legality. Additionally, the simulated cases are rich in content, covering civil, economic and criminal offenses.

The chat logs used in the experiments were drawn from a Meiya Cup 2023 competition case [15]. In October 2023, the Hong Kong police received a report of a murder in the New Territories. The deceased individual's name was Li Zhetu. His cell phone indicated that he was in regular contact with a woman named

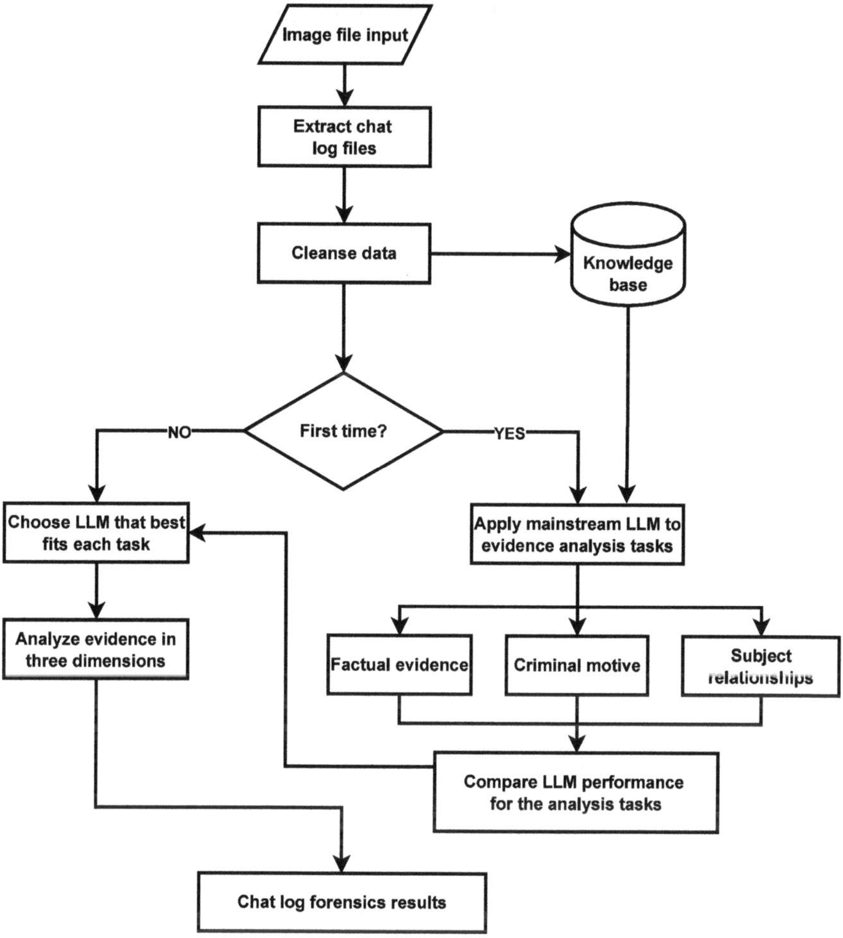

Fig. 1. AutoDF framework.

Peggy Li and three men named Benz, Peter and Leo. The police suspected that they were involved in the case. The investigation revealed an anonymous subject who belonged to a fraudulent organization was involved and that Peggy Li was a close female friend of the deceased.

4.2 Data Processing

Chat logs in the case were exported using Magnet Axiom Examine (version 5.4.0.26185) [13], a comprehensive judicial analysis software tool. (The tool was not used to extract the chat logs.) Evidence was preserved in various formats, most of it in the E01 image file format. The evidence included a collection of files and cell phone backup files.

Table 2. Chat log data.

Sender	Timestamp	Message
Li Zhetu	2023/9/7 3:28:52	"Hello, are you Peggy?"
Peggy Li	2023/9/7 3:29:28	"Are you Chris?"
Li Zhetu	2023/9/7 3:29:36	"Yes."
Li Zhetu	2023/9/7 3:45:54	"What else do you usually do besides drones?"
Peggy Li	2023/9/7 7:33:58	"Nothing special, because I'm busy with work."
Li Zhetu	2023/9/7 7:38:49	"What kind of work do you do?"
Peggy Li	2023/9/7 7:40:34	"My job is accounting."
Li Zhetu	2023/9/7 7:41:23	"Wow, that's really busy."
Peggy Li	2023/9/7 7:43:31	"Yeah, no way. That's why I'm going to play with drones as soon as I get a break."
Li Zhetu	2023/9/7 7:44:03	"I'd love to go drone flying with you."
Peggy Li	2023/9/7 7:44:17	"Yeah, I'll ask you out if I have time."
Li Zhetu	2023/9/7 7:44:35	"A word is a definite."
Peggy Li	2023/9/7 7:44:51	"What about you? And what do you do for a living?"
Li Zhetu	2023/9/7 7:45:06	"I work in interior design."
Peggy Li	2023/9/7 7:45:30	"Do I get a discount for decorating with you?"

The extracted chat logs were subjected to data cleansing and text pre-processing. To ensure that important information was not excluded, the chat logs were unredacted. However, the text format was standardized.

Data cleansing involves processing data to ensure its quality and usability before performing any analysis. It is especially important for chat logs because they usually have several formatting issues. The data cleansing operations performed included the deletion of duplicates, handling of special characters (e.g., converting emoticons to corresponding words), deletion of stop words and standardization of text (e.g., deleting redundant spaces and converting upper case letters to lower case letters and vice versa). The operations ensured that the chat logs were more standardized, accurate and usable, providing a reliable dataset for subsequent analysis and modeling.

Chat records were extracted from all the relevant software, including WhatsApp, WeChat and Telegram. Although chat records from multiple platforms were collected, the analysis of chat content had little to do with the specific chat software. Initially, hundreds of thousands of original chat records were extracted. After performing the data cleansing operations, only 8,000 useful chat records remained. The extracted chat records collectively had more than ten dimensions.

Table 2 shows sample chat log data. Note that Sender corresponds to the sender of the message. Timestamp indicates when the message was sent; its format is -UTC+08:00 (yyyy/M/d). The timestamps provide a chronology that is crucial to analyzing the case.

4.3 Analysis and Results

This section discusses the analysis of factual evidence, criminal motive and subject relationships, the analysis of multilingual chat logs, and the evaluation of the AutoDF framework.

Factual Evidence Analysis. Engineering prompts for the large language models involved several considerations. Specifically, the prompts had to cover various forensic task requirements such as extracting factual evidence, analyzing the criminal motive and identifying subject relationships. First, a set of basic prompts related to different types of criminal activities was created. The prompt content was continuously tested and adjusted based on the large language model outputs, and iterative optimization was performed. Finally, prompts involving multiple rounds of interaction were created to simulate conversations with digital forensic practitioners.

The following prompt was submitted to seven large language models to define the roles and specify the analysis task:

> *You are an expert in digital forensics. Something has happened and I need your help to understand the whole thing. I'm going to provide you with several conversations between the suspects. You need to carefully analyze these conversations. As a digital forensics expert, your job is to solve several important problems and find evidence of crimes. If you can analyze these chat logs accurately, it will play a crucial role in solving this case.*
> *Please conduct a criminal factual behavioral analysis of the following chat logs to analyze the illegal and criminal things done by each character through the chat logs, mainly what someone did at what time and by what means.*

The SparkDesk model listed the factual evidence of five subjects for subsequent analysis. By contrast, the GPT-4o large language model produced the following output:

> *Based on the chat logs provided, I will analyze the potentially illegal and criminal activities undertaken by the characters. Here is the breakdown of the activities, along with times, methods and sequences of events.*
>
> *<u>Criminal Activity:</u>*
> *This conversation reveals the fraudulent scheme carried out by Li Zhetu and Benz. They are engaging in a cryptocurrency investment scam, where they receive funds from a woman under the pretext of investing in a project. They offer large returns in the form of BHB tokens, which are likely worthless or part of a pyramid scheme. When the woman suspects fraud and asks for her money back, Benz instructs Li Zhetu to ignore her, indicating their intent to defraud her.*

Timeline and Methods:
September 7, 2023: Li Zhetu engages in casual conversations about drones and investments, showing an interest in cryptocurrency. This sets the stage for his later criminal activity.
September 15, 2023 (3:34:27): Li Zhetu discloses that he has obtained HKD 200,000 from a woman for investment. He contacts Benz, who introduces him to a suspicious cryptocurrency project.
September 15, 2023 (3:50:53): Benz offers a deal to exchange HKD 200,000 for 20 million BHB tokens, signaling the start of the scam. Benz provides links to cryptocurrency exchanges for Li Zhetu to perform the transactions.
September 19, 2023 (2:21:23): Li Zhetu informs Benz that the same woman is willing to invest an additional HKD 300,000, further deepening the fraudulent activity.
September 19, 2023 (7:36:19): The woman asks for her money back, suspecting that she has been defrauded. Benz advises Li Zhetu to ignore her, confirming the scam.
September 19, 2023 (7:42:09): Li Zhetu acknowledges that the woman realizes they are scamming her, demonstrating their intent to deceive.

Fraudulent Investment Scheme:
Li Zhetu and Benz solicited money from a woman, promising cryptocurrency investments but had no intention of providing real returns. This constitutes fraud.

Cryptocurrency Manipulation:
Benz's offer of 20 million BHB tokens for HKD 200,000 is likely part of a pump-and-dump scheme or involves worthless cryptocurrency. They manipulate and exploit the woman's trust to steal her money.

Conclusions:
Li Zhetu and Benz are involved in a cryptocurrency investment scam, where they fraudulently obtain large sums of money from a female victim. Despite the victim's requests to withdraw her funds, they intentionally ignore her, showing clear criminal intent. This case involves fraud, deceit and illegal financial activity via cryptocurrency platforms. The conversations serve as direct evidence of the conspiracy and the fraudulent methods used to exploit the victim.

Clearly, GPT-4o is able to describe and analyze the five subjects involved in the chat logs and construct a complete timeline of the crime. Also, it has a clear perception of the behavioral facts of both sides of the conversations.

Table 3 compares the factual evidence results for seven large language models. The best results are indicated in bold font. The GPT-4o and Gemini models yielded the best analysis results. They have high BLEUDF values as well as quick response times that are important for chat log analysis. The other large language models were not good enough for analyzing factual evidence; in fact, they produced some analysis errors.

Table 3. Factual evidence analysis results.

Model	BLEUDF Index	Response Time
GLM-4	0.52899	10.75 s
ChatGPT 3.5	0.67709	15.26 s
GPT-4o	**0.91591**	12.60 s
Gemini	0.74487	**1.35 s**
Claude-3	0.51723	10.63 s
WenXinYiYan	0.32196	27.52 s
TongYiQianWen	0.37311	36.59 s

Large language models can provide additional assistance to digital forensic practitioners by reasoning about the factual evidence. The following prompt was submitted to demonstrate the capability:

If Li Zhetu is the victim, your next step as a digital forensics expert would be to determine what evidence can be found in Li Zhetu's evidence samples based on the information above.

The SparkDesk model mentioned emails and computer repair records in its response. By contrast, GPT-4o provided the following output:

Email Communications:
If they communicated via email, the email may contain evidence such as investment plans, profit reports and attachments that could include investment contracts, screenshots of transfer records or other related documents.
Computer Repair Records:
If Li Zhetu retained technical documents, remote assistance logs and system state comparisons before and after the repair on his computer, which Peggy Li assisted with, these could prove that Peggy Li indeed provided computer repair help and whether there was any unauthorized access or data tampering during this process.

Based on the reasoning conducted by the large language models, evidence was discovered in the chat log files that Peggy Li had used a Kali Linux system to download a file about virtual currency from Li Zhetu's computer and the date of this activity was after the date that the computer was repaired. Therefore, there was reason to suspect that Peggy Li had been involved in fraud and other criminal activities with Li Zhetu as the victim.

Additionally, in the storage path of a Thunderbird mailbox, an email that Li Zhetu had sent to Benz was discovered. The email attachment contained a list of friends who invested in virtual currencies, which is consistent with the reasoning of the large language model that Li Zhetu had an investment circle. These results demonstrate that large language models can reason soundly about factual evidence.

Table 4. Criminal motive analysis results.

Model	BLEUDF Index	Response Time
GLM-4	0.52311	14.14 s
ChatGPT 3.5	0.67709	16.76 s
GPT-4o	**0.95766**	11.58 s
Gemini	0.87591	**2.52 s**
Claude-3	0.38064	12.53 s
WenXinYiYan	0.36045	31.71 s

Criminal Motive Analysis. Inferring the criminal motives of suspects is a complex task. Rich experience is required in order to accurately analyze criminal motives. The following prompt was input to six large language models to evaluate their ability to analyze the suspects' criminal motives:

Next, as an expert in digital forensics, you need to analyze the behavioral motives of these characters, mainly through the behaviors involved in these tasks, to infer the motives and purposes of their crimes.

Table 4 compares the criminal motive analysis results for six large language models. The best results are indicated in bold font. GPT-4o and Gemini model outperform the other models by wide margins. Their analyses are more accurate and the response times are much better.

Subject Relationships Analysis. The following prompt was input to the GPT-4o model to assess its ability to infer the subjects' character traits and relationships:

Finally, you, as the digital forensics expert, you need to draw a table describing the web of relationships between the various characters in the chat logs, including descriptions of the characters' roles, a compendium of their relationships and descriptions of the behavioral characteristics of the characters.

Table 5 shows the subject relationships analysis provided by GPT-4o. Figure 2 shows a network diagram of the subject relationships generated by GPT-4o.

Figure 3 shows a more complex network diagram of the subject relationships generated by Gemini.

Multilingual Chat Log Analysis. To explore the feasibility of handling multilingual data, additional experiments were conducted using a dataset containing chat logs in multiple languages – Simplified Chinese, Traditional Chinese and English. Common language translation tools were used to uniformly translate the multilingual chat logs to English. The English translations were input to the large language models for analysis.

Table 5. Subject relationships analysis generated by GPT-4o.

Subject	Role	Relationships	Behavioral Characteristics
Li Zhetu	*Central figure in scam; intermediary.*	*Friend of Peggy Li and Golddee. Partner of Benz in the fraudulent cryptocurrency scheme.*	*Opportunistic and eager to gain financial profit. Shows interest in cryptocurrency and tech. Deceptive, as seen when he facilitates the scam. Passive, but follows Benz's instructions on how to manage the fraud.*
Peggy Li	*Casual friend; uninvolved in the crime.*	*Friend of Li Zhetu; shares common interest in drones.*	*Casual and friendly, with no involvement in illegal activities. Enthusiastic about drones.*
Golddee	*Friend in tech/drone community; uninvolved.*	*Friend of Li Zhetu through the tech/drone community.*	*Focused on tech and drone flying. Has no connection to criminal activity, purely tech-related interactions.*
Benz	*Mastermind of the scam; manipulative partner.*	*Partner of Li Zhetu in the crypto-currency fraud scheme.*	*Manipulative, confident and experienced in fraudulent schemes. Guides Li Zhetu through the process of defrauding investors. Dismissive of legal and ethical considerations, advising to ignore the victim's concerns.*
Unidentified Female	*Investor and victim of the scam.*	*Financially involved with Li Zhetu and Benz as the target of their cryptocurrency scheme.*	*Trusting and initially unaware of the scam. Provided HKD 200,000, later realizing that she is being defrauded. Requests a refund, showing her suspicions and growing awareness of the fraud.*

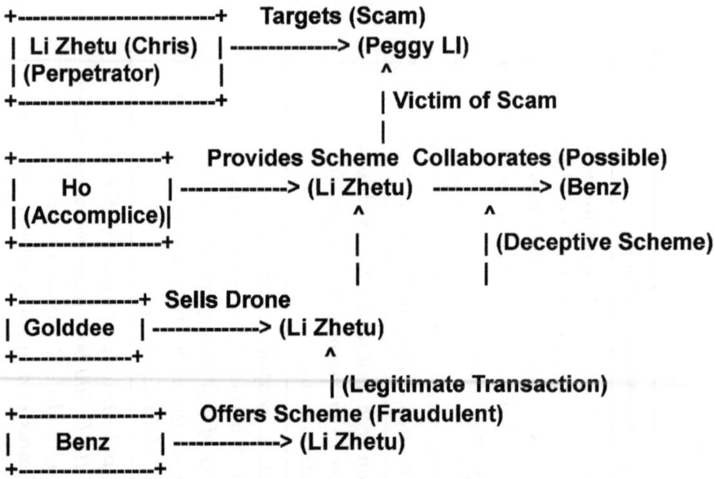

Fig. 2. Network diagram of subject relationships generated by GPT-4o.

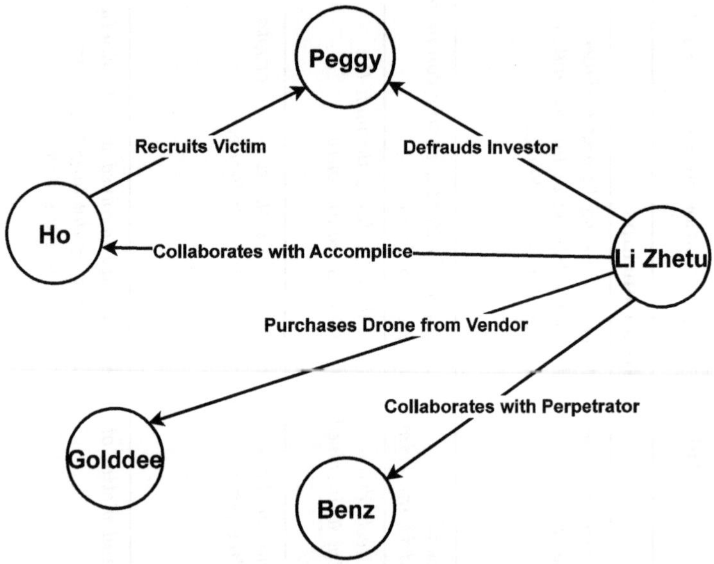

Fig. 3. Network diagram of subject relationships generated by Gemini.

Table 6 shows the multilingual assessment results. The best results are indicated in bold font.

The mainstream large language models – GPT-4o and Gemini – could identify factual evidence, infer the criminal motive and construct the subject relationships network relatively well. In the case of GPT-4o, the BLEUDF index

Table 6. Multilingual chat log analysis results.

Model	Language	BLEUDF Index	Analysis Time
GPT-4o	Simplified Chinese	0.8614	12.85 s
	Traditional Chinese	0.8349	13.41 s
	English	**0.9032**	**10.15 s**
Gemini	Simplified Chinese	0.8156	2.72 s
	Traditional Chinese	0.8431	2.98 s
	English	**0.8825**	**2.49 s**

decreased slightly when processing multilingual chat logs compared with pure English chat logs. The BLEUDF index still remained at a relatively high level and GPT-4o could accurately analyze key information about criminal activities such as the time, location and *modus operandi.*

The results indicate that, combined with effective language translation preprocessing, large language models can analyze chat logs with multilingual data. However, it was observed that the translation to English causes some information loss that affects the accuracy of the results. Future work will focus on further optimizing the translation strategy and the ability of large language models to analyze multilingual data.

AutoDF Evaluation. Additional experiments were conducted to compare the performance of the AutoDF framework with that of human digital forensic practitioners. Approximately 8,000 chat logs were passed to the AutoDF framework and to five digital forensic practitioners for analysis.

Table 7. AutoDF versus human digital forensic practitioner comparison.

Method	BLEUDF Index	Analysis Time
AutoDF	0.8624	**2 m 18 s**
Practitioners	**0.8916**	16m 35 s

Table 7 compares the performance of the AutoDF framework against that of the five digital forensic practitioners. The best results are indicated in bold font. The average performance of the five digital forensic practitioners was slightly better than the AutoDF performance in terms of accuracy as measured by the BLEUDF index. However, the analysis time of two minutes and 18 seconds required by AutoDF to perform chat log analysis was significantly better than the average time of 16 minutes and 35 seconds required by the digital forensic practitioners.

The practicality of using large language models is clear. Time is of the essence in real-world digital forensic investigations. Large language models and the AutoDF framework are very effective at automating the processing and analysis of chat logs, enabling digital forensic practitioners to obtain evidence in a timely manner while eliminating human error. Massive chat logs can be handled rapidly and the analysis results can help practitioners identify potential suspects and reconstruct the criminal activity accurately, providing strong support in criminal investigations.

5 Discussion

Seven large language models were employed to analyze chat logs and their performance was evaluated in three dimensions – factual evidence, criminal motive and subject relationships. The research results demonstrate that large language models offer clear advantages when analyzing chat logs compared with traditional methods. Manual methods may miss some subtle clues in large volumes of chat logs due to human limitations. However, large language models can effectively analyze chat log data from multiple perspectives and provide more comprehensive and detailed analysis results. In addition, the AutoDF framework greatly improves the efficiency of digital forensic analysis compared with traditional methods.

The research results demonstrate that most of the current large language models can analyze subject behavior in a large dataset of chat records, and can differentiate between normal behavior and criminal behavior. The large language models can effectively analyze criminal motives and glean clues pertaining to criminal activities, which would be very useful to digital forensic practitioners. The models are relatively good at discerning the characteristics of subjects and their relationships, but their ability to generate network diagrams of subject relationships needs improvement. Overall, GPT-4o and Gemini produced the best results of the seven large language models employed in the research.

However, this work has some limitations. Although large language models show great potential for chat log analysis, their performance depends greatly on the quality of training data. Large language model training data that lacks relevant forensic knowledge or contains biases would yield inaccurate analysis results. Additionally, the AutoDF framework currently processes chat logs from common communications apps; it is not effective at handling special-purpose or encrypted chat applications.

6 Conclusions

Large language models can be leveraged effectively to automate chat log analysis, clearly identifying the factual evidence, inferring criminal motives and discerning the relationships between subjects. The experimental results demonstrate the speed and accuracy of automated chat log analysis, helping reduce the workloads of digital forensic practitioners as well as human error. Of course, several open legal and ethical issues remain to be resolved before large language models can be applied to streamline real-world criminal investigations.

References

1. H. Arshad, A. Bin Jantan and O. Abiodun, Digital forensics: Review of issues in scientific validation of digital evidence, *Journal of Information Processing Systems*, vol. 14(2), pp. 346–376, 2018.
2. R. Dinis-Oliveira and R. Azevedo, ChatGPT in forensic sciences: A new Pandora's box with advantages and challenges to pay attention, *Forensic Sciences Research*, vol. 8(4), pp. 275–279, 2023.
3. Z. Du, Y. Qian, X. Liu, M. Ding, J. Qiu, Z. Yang and J. Tang, GLM: General Language Model Pretraining with Autoregressive Blank Infilling, arXiv: 2103.10360v2 (`arxiv.org/abs/2103.10360v2`), 2021.
4. D. Dunsin, M. Ghanem, K. Ouazzane and V. Vassilev, A comprehensive analysis of the role of artificial intelligence and machine learning in modern digital forensics and incident response, *Forensic Science International: Digital Investigation*, vol. 48, article no. 301675, 2024.
5. Gemini Team Google, Gemini: A Family of Highly Capable Multimodal Models, arXiv:2312.11805v1 (`arxiv.org/abs/2312.11805v1`), 2024.
6. J. Han, J. Kim and S. Lee, 5W1H-Based Expression for the Effective Sharing of Information in Digital Forensic Investigations, arXiv: 2010.15711v1 (`arxiv.org/abs/2010.15711v1`), 2020.
7. H. Henseler and H. van Beek, ChatGPT as a copilot for investigating digital evidence, *Proceedings of the Third International Workshop on Artificial Intelligence and Intelligent Assistance for Legal Professionals in the Digital Workplace*, pp. 58–69, 2023.
8. M. Hewling, Digital Forensics: An Integrated Approach for the Investigation of Cyber/Computer Related Crimes, Ph.D. Thesis, Department of Computing, University of Bedfordshire, Luton, United Kingdom, 2013.
9. J. Israel, Cornerstones of the judicial process, *Kansas Journal of Law and Public Policy*, vol. 2, pp. 5–30, 1993.
10. S. Jia, R. Lyu, K. Zhao, Y. Chen, Z. Yan, Y. Ju, C. Hu, X. Li, B. Wui and S. Lyu, Can ChatGPT detect deepfakes? A study of using multimodal large language models for media forensics, *Proceedings of the IEEE/CVF Conference on Computer Vision and Pattern Recognition Workshops*, pp. 4324–4333, 2024.
11. V. Kalokyri, A. Borgida, A. Marian and D. Vianna, Integration and exploration of connected personal digital traces, *Proceedings of the ExploreDB'17 Conference*, article no. 3, 2017.
12. A. Kasper and E. Laurits, Challenges in collecting digital evidence: A legal perspective, in *The Future of Law and eTechnologies*, T. Kerikmae and A. Rull (Eds.), Springer, Cham, Switzerland, pp. 195–233, 2016.
13. Magnet Forensics, Introduction to Magnet AXIOM, Waterloo, Canada (`www.magnetforensics.com/resources/introduction-magnet-axiom`), 2025.
14. A. Marcella and R. Greenfield, *Cyber Forensics: A Field Manual for Collecting, Examining, and Preserving Evidence of Computer Crimes*, Auerbach Publications, New York, New York, 2008.

15. Meiya Pico, Meiya Cup 2023 Competition, Xiamen, China (meiyacup.com), 2023.
16. G. Michelet and F. Breitinger, ChatGPT, Llama, can you write my report? An experiment on assisted digital forensics reports written using (local) large language models, *Forensic Science International: Digital Investigation*, vol. 48(S), article no. 301683, 2024.
17. D. Oh, D. Kim and H. Kim, volGPT: Evaluation on triaging a ransomware process in memory forensics with a large language model, *Forensic Science International: Digital Investigation*, vol. 49(S), article no. 301756, 2024.
18. L. Ouyang, J. Wu, X. Jiang, D. Almeida, C. Wainwright, P. Mishkin, C. Zhang, S. Agarwal, K. Slama, A. Ray, J. Schulman, J. Hilton, F. Kelton, L. Miller, M. Simens, A. Askell, P. Welinder, P. Christiano, J. Leike and R. Lowe, Training language models to follow instructions with human feedback, *Proceedings of the Thirty Sixth International Conference on Neural Information Processing Systems*, pp. 27730–27744, 2022.
19. K. Papineni, S. Roukos, T. Ward and W. Zhu, BLEU: A method for the automatic evaluation of machine translation, *Proceedings of the Fortieth Annual Meeting of the Association for Computational Linguistics*, pp. 311–318, 2002.
20. M. Pollitt, A history of digital forensics, in *Advances in Digital Forensics VI*, K. Chow and S. Shenoi (Eds.), Springer, Berlin Heidelberg, Germany, pp. 3–15, 2010.
21. M. Scanlon, F. Breitinger, C. Hargreaves, J. Hilgert and J. Sheppard, ChatGPT for digital forensic investigation: The good, the bad and the unknown, *Forensic Science International: Digital Investigation*, vol. 46(S), article no. 301609, 2023.
22. V. Taecharungroj, "What can ChatGPT do?" Analyzing early reactions to the innovative AI chatbot on Twitter, *Big Data and Cognitive Computing*, vol. 7, article no. 35, 2023.
23. R. Umeike, Comparative crime analysis and prediction using machine learning algorithms: Assessing the tools and addressing the threats, *Proceedings of the Thirty-Fifth International Conference on Tools with Artificial Intelligence*, pp. 135–142, 2023.
24. A. Vaswani, N. Shazeer, N. Parmar, J. Uszkoreit, L. Jones, A. Gomez, Ł. Kaiser and I. Polosukhin, Attention is all you need, *Proceedngs of the Thirty-First International Conference on Neural Information Processing Systems*, pp. 6000–6010, 2017.
25. J. Wei, Y. Tay, R. Bommasani, C. Raffel, B. Zoph, S. Borgeaud, D. Yogatama, M. Bosma, D. Zhou, D. Metzler, E. Chi, T. Hashimoto, O. Vinyals, P. Liang, J. Dean and W. Fedus, Emergent Abilities of Large Language Models, arXiv: 2206.07682v2 (arxiv.org/abs/2206.07682v2), 2022.
26. A. Wickramasekara and M. Scanlon, A framework for integrated digital forensic investigation employing AutoGen AI agents, *Proceedings of the Twelfth International Symposium on Digital Forensics and Security*, 2024.

Explanatory Phishing Message Detection Using Persuasion Structure

Cheuk-Yu Ip, Yi-Anson Lam, and Siu-Ming Yiu

University of Hong Kong, Hong Kong, China
lesterip@connect.hku.hk

Abstract. The last decade has seen phishing scams increasingly leveraging text and instant messages instead of email as attack vectors. Due to fewer diagnostic cues available in text and instant messages and the use of short URLs, generative artificial intelligence and advanced baiting techniques by scammers, the effectiveness of conventional phishing scam detection approaches based on sender information, domain name, image, content and context is being challenged.
This chapter describes a novel approach for identifying Chinese phishing text and instant messages based on the persuasion structure in scam plots and explaining to potential scam victims why the text and instant messages are deemed deceptive. A compact phishing content dataset was constructed to cover three common types of phishing scams encountered in Hong Kong, following which the MacBERT large language model was employed to identify persuasion features. The resulting model yields 92.5% overall accuracy in text/instant message corpus classification and 95.7% accuracy in scam detection. Additional testing demonstrates that the model generalizes well to a global English phishing text message dataset, reflecting the universality of scam detection based on persuasion structure.

Keywords: Phishing Scams · Hong Kong · Text Messages · Instant Messages · Scam Detection · Persuasion Structure · Large Language Model

1 Introduction

Phishing is the practice of leveraging email, text/instant messages, phone calls or QR codes to trick users into revealing sensitive information that may be used for nefarious purposes. The scams exploit and manipulate human psychology by inducing trust, urgency, fear, greed, sympathy, curiosity, etc. to dupe victims into taking actions such as revealing sensitive information or clicking a link that downloads malware. Although phishing scams typically seek to obtain victim information for financial gain, they are also executed to gain access to sensitive computing systems and even advance state-sponsored hacking campaigns.

Phishing scams are one of the most prevalent cyber crimes worldwide. The U.S. Federal Bureau of Investigation received more than 298,000 phishing complaints in 2023, amounting to more than 33% of the total complaints received [12].

Published by Springer Nature Switzerland AG 2026
E. Kurkowski and S. Shenoi (Eds.): DigitalForensics 2025, IFIP AICT 762, pp. 95–112, 2026.
https://doi.org/10.1007/978-3-032-09802-3_6

In Hong Kong, more than 8,600 cases of phishing scams, online account abuse and card-not-present cases were reported in 2023, resulting in a total loss of 25.6 million USD [17]. The reported loss does not include phishing email and text messages used as attack vectors for other criminal activities such as business email compromises, romance scams and job scams.

This research is motivated by the phenomenon that, due to advances in spam email filtering techniques, phishing scams are increasingly leveraging text and instant messages that provide few diagnostic or linguistic cues for scam detection. Meanwhile, scammers have been enhancing their baiting techniques and pretexts over time using QR codes [36] and artificially-generated content [25]. In recent years, email scams employing classical charity, lottery and inheritance pretexts accounted for an insignificant number of scams reported in Hong Kong. This is because the vast majority of scamming email are automatically identified and the pretexts are poorly adapted to local contexts. The principal phishing scams currently perpetrated in Hong Kong involve data phishing and account hijacking.

Data phishing scammers disseminate text/instant messages and email impersonating legitimate entities such as government agencies, utility companies, telecommunications service providers, online merchants and companies with customer loyalty programs. The pretexts, which involve outstanding payments, eligibility for refunds, service abnormalities and expiring loyalty points, dupe the recipients to clicking the provided links that take them to websites where they enter sensitive information such as credit card information and login credentials. The scammers proceed to perform unauthorized credit card transactions, misappropriate loyalty points and more.

Account hijacking involves two scams, text/instant messaging hijacking and impersonation, performed in sequence. In the first scam, text/instant messages impersonating providers such as WhatsApp and Telegram are sent to potential victims informing them that their accounts are abnormal and requesting them to click links to enter their registered phone numbers for verification and to input the verification codes that are subsequently sent to them. The verification codes are provided by genuine providers upon instructions provided by the scammers who have requested that the victim accounts are to be transferred (i.e., hijacked) to the scammers' devices.

Alternatively, text/instant messaging hijacking may be executed by search engine optimization poisoning. An example is a scammer setting up a phishing website that resembles the legitimate WhatsApp web login interface and placing ads that use "WhatsApp" and "web" as keywords. A search engine user who types the keywords is presented a link to the phishing website at the top of the search results. The phishing website has a QR code that tricks the user to fall victim to QRLJacking [16], which enables the scammer to log into the WhatsApp account of the victim via the web platform simultaneously. Upon gaining access to the text/instant messaging account, the scammer impersonates the text/instant messaging hijacking victim and uses social engineering tactics to convince the victim's contacts to provide financial assistance.

Regardless of the pretexts employed, scammers usually follow common persuasion strategies in attempting to dupe their victims. This chapter describes how phishing scams can be detected by identifying the common structure in persuasion strategies (persuasion structure) employed by scammers in their email and text/instant messages. The principal advantage of leveraging persuasion structure is that phishing scams can be detected even when scammers change their pretexts.

2 Related Work

This section describes related research on psychological perspectives, linguistic features and phishing detection techniques, along with explanatory approaches used in spam detection.

2.1 Psychological Perspectives

Research has consistently shown that the accuracy of humans detecting lies is only slightly above chance [2]. While non-verbal cues such as appearance, gesture and demeanor may be employed to detect deception [9], they are unreliable and may actually reduce the ability to detect deception [34]. By contrast, verbal cues are considered more reliable for detecting deception, especially in the case of phishing messages that contain verbal cues.

Scammers often invoke fear, threat, excitement or urgency to persuade victims to respond [32]. Human vulnerabilities such as greed, kindness, curiosity, trust and obedience to authority are also commonly exploited in social engineering attacks [18]. Most scammers tend to urge victims to respond quickly; insufficient time for thinking through the requests often causes victims to fall into heuristic processing [26]. Indeed, Vishwanath et al. [33] suggest that humans disproportionately focus on urgency cues in phishing email and often ignore other elements such as source, and grammatical and spelling errors.

Van der Heijden and Allodi [30] have employed the six principles of influence [7] – reciprocity, consistency, social proof, authority, liking and scarcity – to measure the cognitive triggers that influence the likelihood of potential phishing victims complying with scammer instructions. Their results indicate that consistency and scarcity manifest clear positive associations with successful phishing attacks. Butavicius et al. [6] argue that reciprocity, consistency and liking are more dependent on mutual and recurring relationships, and they maintain that authority and scarcity are the most effective phishing tactics.

Due to the transition of phishing vectors from email to text/instant messages, scammers tend to design short, precise content to fit into messages with limited space. Exploiting multiple human vulnerabilities and applying multiple principles of influence in single phishing messages is impractical. However, analysis of recent phishing messages in Hong Kong conducted in this research has revealed that greed, urgency, authority, scarcity and kindness are common message elements. Of course, most of these elements are also commonly incorporated in marketing campaigns and notification messages. Therefore, the mere existence of these elements in messages would not necessarily imply that they involve phishing. However, the elements could be phishing indicators.

2.2 Linguistic Features

Linguistic research suggests that scammers make more negative statements and complaints, are less forthcoming and less compelling [9], and employ more sense-based words such as seeing and touching [14]. Zhou et al. [37] have summarized 27 linguistic characteristics into nine constructs – quantity, complexity, uncertainty, non-immediacy, diversity, affect, specificity, expressiveness and informality – to systematically differentiate between deception and truth. Hauch et al. [15] have conducted a meta-analysis and consolidated 79 linguistic cues such as word quantity, word length, sentence length, writing errors, causation, emotions, first-person pronouns and swear words. Interpersonal deception theory developed by Buller and Burgoon [4] that focuses on face-to-face communications suggests that scammers tend to convey uncertainty and vagueness, withhold information, express non-immediacy and show insincerity.

This research posits that most of the linguistic features mentioned above are more commonly observed in synchronized face-to-face communications. However, in the case of asynchronous communications such as phishing, where messages are well-formulated and scammers can edit and fine-tune content between successive phishing attempts, scammers are more conscious about delivering content without deceptive cues. Additionally, phishing scams are mainly one-way communications where the scammers do not establish long-term interactions with potential victims. Since scammers have less cognitive loads, they are less likely to include obvious deceptive cues such as grammatical and spelling errors, and swear words.

Blommaert and Omoniyi [1], who analyzed the English competencies of advanced fee fraudsters in terms of writing styles and textual features, opine that the fraudsters demonstrate "grassroots literacy" such as inconsistent punctuation, spelling errors and unwarranted use of capitals. By contrast, preliminary research conducted in the present work has observed that phishing scams reported in Hong Kong are highly adapted to local contexts and demonstrate language proficiency, possibly attributed to grammar checking tools, language translators and generative content tools such as ChatGPT. Indeed, this research posits that advancements in phishing techniques and assistive tools will render phishing scams less linguistically specific.

2.3 Phishing Detection

This section discusses phishing detection based on websites, email headers and persuasion strategies.

Phishing Websites. Phishing websites often resemble legitimate websites or bear the logos of legitimate organizations to increase trustworthiness. Jain and Gupta [19] leveraged 19 features related to URLs and source code to achieve 99% accuracy in phishing website detection. Maroofi et al. [22] employed 38 features related to lexical characteristics of domain names, ranking and popularity, active and passive domain name system (DNS) information, website content, WHOIS and top-level domain information, transport layer security certificate, etc. to construct a machine learning system that yielded 97% phishing website detection accuracy.

The main drawback with using URLs is the difficulty of detecting compromised domains, where benign websites are commandeered by scammers to inject phishing content. Also, short URLs are commonly employed by scammers to hinder phishing URL detection. In the dataset created in this research, about 10% of the extracted phishing URLs have short URLs (e.g., `bit.ly` and `cutt.ly`) in which the domain names are legitimate *per se*. Thus, using short URLs to differentiate between benign and phishing URLs does not appear to be worthwhile. Unfortunately, mass phishing website detection based on website content and multiple features requires significant processing power and Internet bandwidth. To address these issues, this work has sought to assess the persuasion structure displayed in text content, which is applicable to discerning phishing tactics without having to identify phishing websites.

Email Headers. Over the years, various standards such as the Sender Policy Framework (SPF), DomainKeys Identified Mail and Domain-Based Message Authentication have been instituted to enhance the integrity of email systems [24]. Fernandez et al. [13] proposed the early detection of newly-registered suspicious domains using passive DNS data and SPF rules that identified 85% of spam domains before the initiation of spam campaigns. However, due to the shift of the phishing attack vector from email to text/instant messages, there is a pressing need to identify diagnostic cues other than email headers.

Persuasion Strategies. Edwards et al. [11] engaged bag-of-words, frequent terms and semantics, along with linguistic inquiry and word count (LIWC) features in an advanced fee scam baiting dataset to explore the persuasion cues of scammers in email conversations. Tsinganos et al. [28] trained a convolutional neural network on a chat-based social engineering corpus to achieve 71.6% accuracy at determining if chats contain persuasive payloads. These works suggest that scam classification based on persuasion strategy is feasible, possibly yielding high accuracy without the use of large language models (LLMs). Bustio-Martinez et al. [5] employed a random forest classifier to detect phishing messages by identifying principles of persuasion similar to the principles of influence [7] to attain an area under the curve of the receiver operating characteristic (AUC-ROC) metric value of 86%. Valecha et al. [29] leveraged a support vector machine to differentiate phishing email from genuine email by identifying the persuasion cues suggested by Cialdini [7], yielding 96.5% accuracy in determining whether or not email contained the cues.

2.4 Explanatory Approaches

Truth bias is a common human bias where individuals tend to believe messages are true when they do not have sufficient suspicion [21]. Vishwanath et al. [32] suggest that, when humans perceive higher risks online (i.e., higher cyber risk beliefs), they tend to raise suspicions about the veracity of phishing email. Bond et al. [3] opine that knowing the incentive that an individual has to lie could significantly improve lie detection. This research posits that alerting the public to suspected phishing attacks without explanation is undesirable because a black-box solution without properly elaborating the rationale is less effective at boosting their cyber risk beliefs.

An explainable approach during scam detection has been applied to various financial crimes such as unauthorized credit card transactions [35] and suspicious payments [31] by leveraging transaction times, amounts and patterns, etc. Koide et al. [20] have employed ChatGPT-4 to detect phishing email and provide explanations based on email headers and urgency cues in text content. Nguyen et al. [23] have engaged a deep learning approach to classify phishing email and identify the sentence most relevant to phishing. However, given the lack of metadata such as email headers and limited content space in the case of text/instant messages, detailed assessments based on sender information and identifying the sentence most relevant to phishing may be impractical. Therefore, this work has adopted a novel approach that engages the persuasive strategy of a text/instant message to explain why it is considered to be phishing.

3 Phishing Scam Detection Methodology

Explanatory phishing scam detection based on persuasion strategy is a multi-class classification problem. The proposed phishing scam detection methodology engages a three-step approach to classify messages as phishing scams. Figure 1 summarizes the three steps in the detection methodology.

3.1 Persuasion Feature Identification and Structure Building

Step 1 initiates by collecting phishing scam messages and conversations. Following this, common psychological features and linguistic cues are identified in the content. Note that cues such as monetary amounts and URLs have operational functions in instructing potential victims to take the intended actions instead of creating psychological effects. These features and cues form the basis of the persuasion structure. Similar features and linguistic cues are also extracted from benign messages such as genuine notification alerts and marketing campaigns. The most comprehensive persuasion structures found in each type of phishing

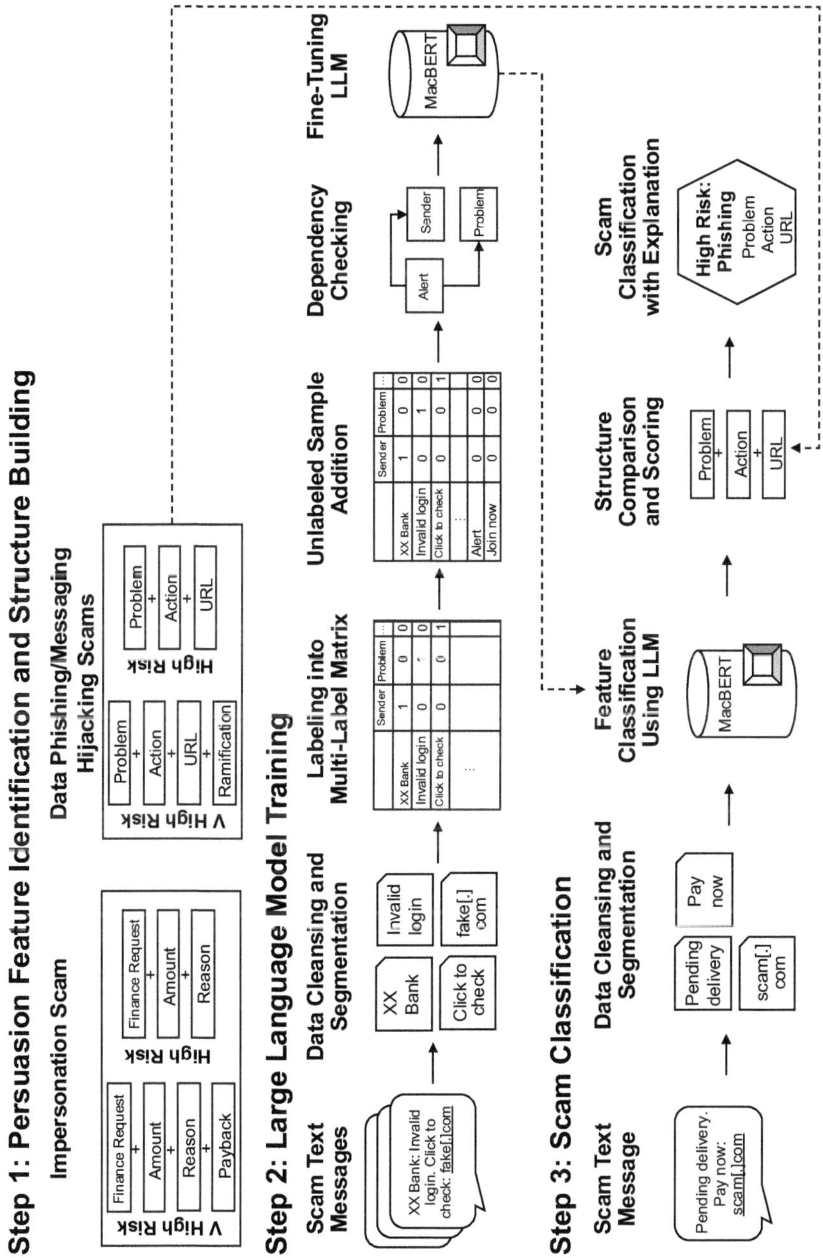

Fig. 1. Phishing scam detection methodology.

scam are assessed as having very high risk whereas less comprehensive persuasion structures are assessed as having high risk or moderate risk based on the numbers of features displayed. In the absence of identified persuasion structures in messages or after distinguished features normally encountered in benign messages (but rarely in phishing such as landline number) are determined to exist, the associated messages are classified as normally low risk.

3.2 Large Language Model Training

Step 2 initiates by removing the protocol portions (HTTP and HTTPS) of URLs in scam messages and retaining the remaining message parts. Each message is then split into text corpora by pause or end punctuation marks and the end-of-line character "\n." Next, each text corpus is manually labeled as a one-hot encoding matrix. The matrix contains features commonly identified in the pool of scam messages, including but not limited to the persuasion features identified in Step 1 (e.g., sender and greeting that occasionally exist, but are not determinative in scam classification). If a text corpus contains more than one feature, multiple labels are assigned (i.e., multiple values are assigned to the columns where the features exist). If a text corpus does not fit any feature, no label is assigned (i.e., all the columns have 0 values). Additional unlabeled samples extracted from benign messages are added to the matrix to reduce data imbalance. Rounds of dependency checks are conducted to remove features that have insignificant or adverse effects on feature classification accuracy (e.g., greeting). Finally, the labeled text corpora are used to fine-tune a pre-trained large language model.

This work has adopted the MacBERT large language model of Cui et al. [8] that replaces the original masked language model (MLM) task in RoBERTa with a masked language model as a correction (Mac) mechanism. MacBERT was determined to yield the best performance for Chinese content compared with the other Chinese large language models evaluated in this research.

3.3 Scam Classification

In Step 3, a text message in question undergoes the same data cleansing and segmentation process described in Step 2. The text corpora extracted from the messages are input to the large language model fine-tuned in Step 2 for feature identification. The identified features are compared against the persuasion structures pre-defined in Step 1, and the corresponding scam type and risk level are provided as outputs. The persuasion feature of each text corpus is identified and can be displayed to explain why the message is deemed deceptive.

4 Data Collection and Feature Pre-Processing

Data collection for testing started with a pool of more than 23,000 scam messages (mainly text and instant messages) that Hong Kong citizens received and

Table 1. Summary of datasets grouped by source.

Source	Type	Number of Messages	Text Corpora	Identifiable Features	Unlabeled Corpora
Law Enforcement	Text	600	2,282	2,735	211
Law Enforcement	Email	16	183	107	79
Open Sources	Text	93	287	357	39
Open Sources	Email	35	247	141	109
Benign	Text	76	229	183	75
Total		**820**	**3,228**	**3,523**	**513**

shared with a law enforcement agency between February 2024 and August 2024. After filtering the non-phishing-related data and removing duplicate messages (as well as messages with the same textual content but different URLs), a total of 616 messages remained. Additionally, 128 other distinct phishing scam messages received in Hong Kong between 2021 and August 2024 were collected from open sources such as media reports and press releases from victim organizations to enrich the collected data.

In order to balance the dataset, 76 benign text messages, mainly marketing campaign and notification messages, found in open sources were added. Because the phishing messages were in Chinese or English, all the English messages were translated to Chinese using the built-in translation function provided by Microsoft Office. The messages were then split into text corpora based on selected punctuation marks. A total of 3,228 text corpora were obtained.

The 3,228 text corpora were manually labeled by a trained research assistant. All content with personal identifiable information was removed. Also, 513 of the 3,228 corpora were not labeled due to the absence of matching features. The data phishing and text/instant messaging hijacking scams were found to share similar persuasion features – alert, sender, problem, action, purpose, ramification and URL. In contrast, impersonation scams had different persuasion features – finance request, amount, reason and payback.

Table 1 summarizes the datasets grouped by source. Table 2 shows the persuasion features and meanings, and provides sample corpora for messages used in data phishing and messaging hijacking scams. Table 3 shows the persuasion features and meanings, and provides sample corpora for messages used in impersonation scams.

Among the identified features, alert, sender, purpose and greeting existed only in some phishing messages. These features correspond to cues of urgency, authority and trust and, despite the limited size of text and instant messages, scammers implicitly incorporated the cues in the main message bodies. Therefore, these features were considered to be insignificant in the formulation of the persuasion strategy. Additionally, benign messages often contain inquiry landline numbers, but these were rarely encountered in phishing messages. After summarizing the features, the persuasion structures and corresponding risk levels were

Table 2. Persuasion features in data phishing and messaging hijacking scams.

Feature	Meaning	Sample Corpus (English)
Alert*	Sign of warning	"Official reminder"
Sender*	Name of purported sending organization	"DHL (WhatsApp)"
Problem	Existing issue/ potential benefit	"Parcel pending delivery" "Your account is at risk"
Action	Action required to address issue/obtain the benefit	"Please verify shipment fee of 2.7 USD" "Please login to URL"
Purpose*	Purpose of the action	"To avoid delay for security check"
Ramification	Consequence if no action taken	"Otherwise your account will be deactivated within 12 hours"
URL	URL directing to a phishing website	"`1ln.run/Z4LGk`" "`hk-vvhatsapp.com`"

*Feature less significant in phishing scam persuasion strategies.

Table 3. Persuasion features in impersonation scams.

Feature	Meaning	Sample Corpus (English)
Greeting*	Greeting to the recipient	"Daddy"
Finance	Request for financial assistance	"Please help transfer online"
Amount	Amount of financial request	"10,000 dollars"
Reason	Pretext for request	"My account reached the limit"
Payback	Promise to payback or return money	"Will return to you tomorrow"

*Feature less significant in impersonation scam persuasion strategies.

formulated according to the numbers of characteristics commonly displayed in phishing scams. Table 4 shows the features and risk levels in data phishing and messaging hijacking scams. Table 5 shows the features and risk levels in impersonation scams.

Dependency checking revealed that two labels, alert and greeting, were associated with a few phishing messages. Since insufficient samples could negatively impact training accuracy, the two labels were eliminated. Specifically, text corpora with the two labels were treated as unlabeled samples in the dataset. Additionally, although the feature sender was not determinative in scam classification, text corpora with the label often existed in the dataset. Since such a label improves feature classification accuracy, the feature was retained in the dataset. Table 6 summarizes the 11 persuasion features in phishing scam messages after dependency checking.

Table 4. Features and risk levels in data phishing and messaging hijacking scams.

Feature	Very High	High	Medium	Medium	Normally Low	High (Email)/ Low (Message)*
Problem	Present	Present	Present	Absent	Indifferent	Present
Action	Present	Present	Absent	Present	Indifferent	Present
Ramification	Present	Absent	Indifferent	Present	Indifferent	Indifferent
URL	Present	Present	Present	Present	Indifferent	Absent
Landline	Absent	Absent	Absent	Absent	Present	Absent

*For recipients unable to identify URL embedded in email graphics/texts.

Table 5. Features and risk levels in impersonation scams.

Feature	Very High	High	Medium	Medium*
Finance Request	Present	Present	Present	Present
Amount	Present	Present	Present	Absent
Reason	Present	Absent	Absent	Present
Payback	Present	Present	Absent	Indifferent

*Occurs in on-going scams where plots are unveiled before dialog completion.

Table 6. Summary of persuasion features in phishing scam messages.

Phishing Type	Feature	Number of Features
Data Phishing and Messaging Hijacking	Sender	296
	Problem	797
	Action	744
	Purpose	132
	Ramification	306
	URL	562
	Landline	62
Impersonation	Finance Request	208
	Amount	160
	Reason	111
	Payback	145
Total		**3,523**

5 Experiments and Results

The 820 text messages in the dataset were numbered serially and randomly split into 80% for training and 20% for testing. The large language model employed in the experiments was the MacBERT-large Chinese transformer model that comprises 24-layer transformer with 330 million parameters. The learning rate was set to 1e-5 and the batch size was set to 8. The loss function used was BCEWithLogitsLoss.

Repeated testing revealed that hyperparameter values for L1 (lasso) and L2 (ridge) regularization of 1e-5 and 5e-5, respectively, yielded optimal training performance and generalization ability. After three epochs of training using the

Table 7. Summary of the testing performance by persuasion feature.

Feature	TP	TN	FP	FN	Acc	Prec	Recall	F1
Sender	4,620	42,427	77	0	100%	98%	100%	99%
Problem	10,703	34,804	462	1,155	97%	96%	90%	93%
Action	10,934	35,728	231	231	99%	98%	98%	98%
Purpose	1,694	45,122	0	308	99%	100%	85%	92%
Ramification	4,312	42,196	539	77	99%	89%	98%	93%
URL	8,855	38,115	77	77	100%	99%	99%	99%
Landline	1,001	45,969	0	154	100%	100%	87%	93%
Finance Request	3,003	43,659	385	77	99%	89%	98%	93%
Amount	2,464	44,583	77	0	100%	97%	100%	98%
Reason	1,540	45,430	77	77	100%	95%	95%	95%
Payback	2,079	44,737	0	308	99%	100%	87%	93%
Average (Macro)					**99%**	**97%**	**94%**	**95%**

80% training dataset, the model yielded 99.6% training accuracy in classifying the 11 features.

Accuracy, precision, recall and F1-score were selected as the key performance indicators:

$$\text{Accuracy (Acc)} = \frac{\text{TP} + \text{TN}}{\text{TP} + \text{TN} + \text{FP} + \text{FN}} \times 100$$

$$\text{Precision (Prec)} = \frac{\text{TP}}{\text{TP} + \text{FP}} \times 100$$

$$\text{Recall (R)} = \frac{\text{TP}}{\text{TP} + \text{FN}} \times 100$$

$$\text{F1-Score (F1)} = \frac{2 \times \text{Precision} \times \text{Recall}}{\text{Precision} + \text{Recall}} \times 100$$

where TP denotes true positives, TN denotes true negatives, FP denotes false positives and FN denotes false negatives.

Model evaluation using the 20% testing dataset yielded an overall accuracy (exact match ratio) of 92.5% and overall accuracy (macro average precision) of 97%. Although the macro average accuracy by feature reached 99%, it is not considered a good indicator because FP and FN should also be considered in determining performance. Table 7 summarizes the testing performance by persuasion feature.

For the unlabeled text corpora, the accuracy (exact match ratio) reached 99.7%. Because each unlabeled corpus contains all zero values, the TP and FN values were zero. The precision, recall and F1-score were also zero values accordingly. Table 8 summarizes the testing performance of the unlabeled text corpora.

Table 8. Summary of testing performance of unlabeled text corpora.

Feature	TP	TN	FP	FN	Precision	Recall	F1-Score
Unlabeled	0	5,626	17	0	0%	0%	0%

Other Chinese large language models with comparable numbers of parameters such as GLM-Large-Chinese [10] (350 million parameters) and BERT-Base-Chinese developed by the HuggingFace Team (110 million parameters) were tested, but the performance in each case was poorer. Large language models with larger numbers of parameters such as Qwen 1.5 (4 billion parameters) and Qwen 2 (7 billion parameters) were examined, but their performance was not as good as MacBERT probably due to over-parameterization.

Table 9. Sample message with identified features for risk assessment.

Text Corpus (English)	Feature	Risk
"Your ID account is at risk"	Problem	High
"Please log in to `HK-apple.com` withing 24 hours to complete the verification"	Action, URL	
"Emergency lockout for your ID security"	Problem	

After classifying the features of the text corpora, the text corpora were grouped back to the original messages by serial number. The identified features of each message were grouped for comparison and scoring according to the predetermined criteria in Tables 4 and 5. Table 9 shows a sample message with all the identified features and the assessed risk level after the re-grouping.

The 20% text corpora in the testing dataset were grouped back to the original 164 text messages (149 phishing and 15 benign). Of the 149 phishing messages, 142 messages were correctly assessed as having very high risk to medium risk. The 15 benign messages were assessed as having normally low risk. The accuracy was computed to be 95% ($= \frac{157}{164} \times 100$).

The undetected phishing messages were analyzed. The detection failures – assessing their risk as normally low – occurred because the phishing messages were defective in that they had incomplete persuasion structures. These defective messages would be less effective in convincing potential victims to fall prey to their scams. Table 10 shows a sample phishing message classified as having normally low risk.

Table 10. Sample undetected phishing message.

Text Corpus (English)	Feature	Risk
"Warm reminder"	None	Normally Low
"Click here to verify `Telegrarn.cc` for protection of your account"	Action, URL Purpose	

6 Generalizability Assessment

This section discusses the generalizability of the model in classifying previously-unseen benign text messages collected in Hong Kong and the generalizability of the model in classifying scam messages from elsewhere in the world.

6.1 Benign Text Messages

Assessing the generalizability of the model in classifying unseen benign text messages in Hong Kong focused on marketing campaign and notification messages because their content structures and persuasion strategies are comparable to those in phishing scam messages. This is important because individuals overwhelmed by false positive scam message alerts would suffer alert fatigue, negatively impacting scam prevention.

One hundred benign marketing campaign and notification messages from Hong Kong different from those in the training and testing datasets were collected. The collected messages were split into 462 text corpora to create a testing dataset. All the text corpora were unlabeled to ensure complete blindness.

Table 11. Sample undetected phishing message.

Text Corpus (English)	Feature	Risk
"Citibank: Apple Pay service (last 4 digits of card number 3340) is no longer available"	Sender, Problem	High
"Please visit `citibank.com.hk` for more more information"	Action, URL	

The model trained using the 3,228 text corpora described in Section 4 was employed. Without reference to the accuracy at classifying the corpus, the predicted corpora were used for structure comparison and scoring. The scoring classified 92 messages as normally low risk, three as medium risk and five as high risk, yielding an accuracy of 0.92% for scam classification. A less than satisfactory result was obtained because some benign messages displayed the same persuasion features as phishing messages. In other words, the phishing messages highly impersonated the features of the benign notification messages. Table 11 shows an example of a message identified as false positive. In any case, despite the limited number of benign messages in the training samples, the model still generalized reasonably well to classify unseen benign messages.

6.2 Global Context

The generalizability of the model in classifying scam messages from elsewhere in the world was also assessed. Assuming that human nature is universal, the persuasion strategies used by scammers worldwide would be the same, although the pretexts may vary from location to location (e.g., bank name in a message).

This hypothesis was tested using the Smishing Dataset I [27], a phishing text message dataset from `Smishtank.com`. The dataset claims to provide a corpus of 1,090 smishing samples (1,062 samples were in fact found in the data file). All the samples were translated to Chinese using the built-in Microsoft Office functionality. Untranslated messages (e.g., "RS_TAX_REFUND_ID_#8OGZP7VEY9 [URL]," "H.ere's our l.ittle present f.or u [URL]"), messages with incomplete meaning (e.g., "Congratulations! [URL]") and text messages used as attack vectors in job scams, investment frauds, romance scams and e-shopping fraud were removed. A total of 640 messages remained for testing model generalizability.

The 640 messages were assigned unique message IDs and were split into 3,339 text corpora to create the testing dataset. All the text corpora in the dataset were unlabeled. Once again, the model trained using the 3,228 text corpora described in Section 4 was employed. The predicted persuasion features of the text corpora were grouped by message ID for risk level assessment. The model classified 79.8% of the messages as having very high risk, high risk or medium risk. This result shows that the model generalizes reasonably well to phishing messages from a different geographical location with a different culture.

7 Limitations

The limited number of phishing text message samples available for this research restricted the testing accuracy. Given that scammers disseminate text messages with the same content to thousands of recipients, unless they significantly change the wording in the texts to enhance the click rate or the public becomes cautious about scam plots, the scammers have little incentive to keep changing message content or pretexts substantially. As a result, collecting adequate numbers of phishing text message samples is challenging. Increasing the training dataset size by augmenting it with phishing text message samples from multiple countries could enable the model to classify more features in various pretexts and reduce the false positive rate.

Another limitation is that detection based on textual content is vulnerable to homograph attacks where scammers use fake URLs that look similar to legitimate URLS to trick users. Attacks that are effective in the English context involve alphabets being replaced with resembling non-ASCII characters, such as replacing the letter “a” with the Cyrillic letter “а.” In Chinese, look-alike characters, but with different meanings, could be used interchangeably by scammers. Adding such phishing message samples to the training dataset would enhance phishing text message detection.

8 Conclusions

This chapter has described a novel methodology for detecting Chinese phishing text and instant messages based on the persuasion structure in scam plots and explaining to potential scam victims why the text and instant messages are deemed deceptive. The methodology relying on persuasion structure draws on research in psychology, linguistics and cognitive science. The MacBERT large language model was employed to identify persuasion features related to three common types of phishing text scams encountered in Hong Kong – data phishing, text/instant messaging hijacking and impersonation. Despite the limited diagnostic cues embodied in phishing messages compared with phishing email, the trained model yielded a phishing text/instant message detection accuracy of 95.7%. Additional testing using an English text message dataset demonstrated that the trained model generalizes well to regions with other languages and cultures, reflecting the universality of scam detection based on persuasion structure.

Future research will focus on identifying persuasion strategies and scammer tactics for additional types of scams and leveraging them to increase the phishing detection coverage.

References

1. J. Blommaert and T. Omoniyi, Email fraud: Language, technology and the indexicals of globalization, *Social Semiotics*, vol. 16(4), pp. 573–605, 2006.
2. C. Bond, Jr. and B. DePaulo, Accuracy of deception judgments, *Personality and Social Psychology Review*, vol. 10(3), pp. 214–234, 2006.
3. C. Bond, Jr., A. Howard, J. Hutchison and J. Masip, Overlooking the obvious: Incentives to lie, *Basic and Applied Social Psychology*, vol. 35(2), pp. 212–221, 2013.
4. D. Buller and J. Burgoon, Interpersonal deception theory, *Communication Theory*, vol. 6(3), pp. 203–242, 1996.
5. L. Bustio-Martinez, V. Herrera-Semenets, J. Garcia-Mendoza, M. Avarez-Carmona, J. Gonzalez-Ordiano, L. Zuniga-Morales, J. Quiroz-Ibarra, P. Santander-Molina, J. van den Berg, Uncovering phishing attacks using principles of persuasion analysis, *Journal of Network and Computer Applications*, vol. 230, article no. 103964, 2024.
6. M. Butavicius, K. Parsons, M. Pattinson and A. McCormac, Breaching the human firewall: Social engineering in phishing and spear-phishing emails, *Proceedings of the Australasian Conference on Information Systems*, 2016.
7. R. Cialdini, *Influence: The Psychology of Persuasion*, HarperCollins, New York, New York, 2007.

8. Y. Cui, W. Che, T. Liu, B. Qin, S. Wang and G. Hu, Revisiting pre-trained models for Chinese natural language processing, in *Findings of the Association for Computational Linguistics*, T. Cohn, Y. He and Y. Liu (Eds.), Association for Computational Linguistics, Stroudsburg, Pennsylvania, pp. 657–668, 2020.
9. B. DePaulo, J. Lindsay, B. Malone, L. Muhlenbruck, K. Charlton and H. Cooper, Cues to deception, *Psychological Bulletin*, vol. 129(1), pp. 74–118, 2003.
10. Z. Du, Y. Qian, X. Liu, M. Ding, J. Qiu, Z. Yang and J. Tang, GLM: General language model pre-training with autoregressive blank infilling, *Proceedings of the Sixtieth Annual Meeting of the Association for Computational Linguistics,* vol. 1, pp. 320–335, 2022.
11. M. Edwards, C. Peersman and A. Rashid, Scamming the scammers: Towards automatic detection of persuasion in advance fee frauds, *Proceedings of the Twenty-Sixth International Conference on World Wide Web Companion*, pp. 1291–1299, 2017.
12. Federal Bureau of Investigation, Internet Crime Report 2023, Internet Crime Complaint Center, Washington, DC (`www.ic3.gov/AnnualReport/Reports/2023_IC3Report.pdf`), 2024.
13. S. Fernandez, M. Korczynski and A. Duda, Early detection of spam domains with passive DNS and SPF, *Proceedings of the Twenty-Third International Conference on Passive and Active Measurement*, pp. 30–49, 2022.
14. J. Hancock, L. Curry, S. Goorha and M. Woodworth, Lies in conversation: An examination of deception using automated linguistic analysis, *Proceedings of the Twenty-Sixth Annual Conference of the Cognitive Science Society*, pp. 534–539, 2004.
15. V. Hauch, I. Blandon-Gitlin, J. Masip and S. Sporer, Are computers effective lie detectors? A meta-analysis of linguistic cues to deception, *Personality and Social Psychology Review*, vol. 19(4), pp. 307–342, 2014.
16. R. Heartfield and G. Loukas, Protection against semantic social engineering attacks, in *Versatile Cybersecurity*, M. Conti, G. Somani and R. Poovendran (Eds.), Springer, Cham, Switzerland, pp. 99–140, 2018.
17. Hong Kong Police Force, Technology Crime Figures, Hong Kong, China (`cyberdefender.hk/statistics`), 2024.
18. D. House and M. Raja, Phishing: Message appraisal and the exploration of fear and self-confidence, *Behavior and Information Technology*, vol. 39(11), pp. 1204–1224, 2020.
19. A. Jain and B. Gupta, Towards detection of phishing websites on client-side using a machine learning based approach, *Telecommunication Systems*, vol. 68, pp. 687 700, 2018.
20. T. Koide, N. Fukushi, H. Nakano and D. Chiba, ChatSpamDetector: Leveraging Large Language Models for Effective Phishing Email Detection, arXiv: 2402.18093v2 (`arxiv.org/abs/2402.18093v2`), 2024.
21. T. Levine, H. Park and S. McCornack, Accuracy in detecting truths and lies: Documenting the "veracity effect," *Communication Monographs*, vol. 66(2), pp. 125–144, 1999.
22. S. Maroofi, M. Korczynski, C. Hesselman, B. Ampeau and A. Duda, COMAR: Classification of compromised versus maliciously registered domains, *Proceedings of the IEEE European Symposium on Security and Privacy*, pp. 607–623, 2020.
23. V. Nguyen, T. Wu, X. Yuan, M. Grobler, S. Nepal and C. Rudolph, An Innovative Information Theory Based Approach to Tackle and Enhance the Transparency in Phishing Detection, arXiv: 2402.17092v2 (`arxiv.org/abs/2402.17092v2`), 2024.
24. H. Orman, From whom? SMTP headers hold the clues, *IEEE Internet Computing*, vol. 22(1), pp. 87–95, 2018.

25. M. Schmitt and I. Flechais, Digital deception: Generative artificial intelligence in social engineering and phishing. *Artificial Intelligence Review*, vol. 57, article no. 324, 2024.
26. F. Stajano and P. Wilson, Understanding scam victims: Seven principles for systems security, *Communications of the ACM*, vol. 54(3), pp. 70–75, 2011.
27. D. Timko and M. Rahman, Smishing Dataset I: Phishing SMS dataset from Smishtank.com, *Proceedings of the Fourteenth ACM Conference on Data and Application Security and Privacy*, pp. 289–294, 2024.
28. N. Tsinganos, I. Mavridis and D. Gritzalis, Utilizing convolutional neural networks and word embeddings for early-stage recognition of persuasion in chat-based social engineering attacks, *IEEE Access*, vol. 10, pp. 108517–108529, 2022.
29. R. Valecha, P. Mandaokar and H. Rao, Phishing email detection using persuasion cues, *IEEE Transactions on Dependable and Secure Computing*, vol. 19(2), pp. 747–756, 2022.
30. A. van der Heijden and L. Allodi, Cognitive triaging of phishing attacks, *Proceedings of the Twenty-Eighth USENIX Security Symposium*, pp. 1309–1326, 2019.
31. S. Visbeek, E. Acar and F. den Hengst, Explainable fraud detection with deep symbolic classification, in *Explainable Artificial Intelligence*, L. Longo, S. Lapuschkin and C. Seifert (Eds.), Springer, Cham, Switzerland, pp. 350–373, 2024.
32. A. Vishwanath, B. Harrison and Y. Ng, Suspicion, cognition automaticity model of phishing susceptibility, *Communication Research*, vol. 45(8), pp. 1146–1166, 2016.
33. A. Vishwanath, T. Herath, R. Chen, J. Wang and H. Rao, Why do people get phished? Testing individual differences in phishing vulnerability within an integrated information processing model, *Decision Support Systems*, vol. 51(3), pp. 576–586, 2011.
34. R. Wiseman, The megalab truth test, *Nature*, vol. 373, p. 391, 1995.
35. Z. Xiao and J. Jiao and L. Zhang, Explainable fraud detection for few labeled time series data, *Security and Communication Networks*, vol. 2021, article no. 9941464, 2021.
36. K. Yong, K. Chiew and C. Tan, A survey of the QR code phishing: The current attacks and countermeasures, *Proceedings of the Seventh International Conference on Smart Computing and Communications*, 2019.
37. L. Zhou, J. Burgoon, J. Nunamaker and D. Twitchell, Automating linguistics based cues for detecting deception in text-based asynchronous computer-mediated communications, *Group Decision and Negotiation*, vol. 13, pp. 81–106, 2004.

Forensic Investigations

Counterfeit Handbag Detection Using Supervised Contrastive Learning

Yaotian Yang[1], Yu Yang[1], Jixin Zou[2], Linna Zhou[1], and Zhihao Li[2]

[1] Beijing University of Posts and Telecommunications, Beijing, China
yangyu@bupt.edu.cn
[2] Institute of Forensic Science, Beijing, China

Abstract. Traditional counterfeit handbag detection methods approach the problem as a direct image classification task. However, due to the very close similarity between genuine and counterfeit handbags, it is difficult to distinguish between the two types of handbags.
This chapter describes a two-stage universal detection framework. In the first contrastive learning stage, a Siamese network is employed to discover subtle differences between the two classes. In the second transfer learning stage, the previously-trained backbone network is frozen, following which a classifier is added to implement the transfer from contrastive learning to classification. To enhance discrimination, a multilevel feature selection module is incorporated to refine features and a dimension reduction pyramid pooling module is employed to fuse multiscale features. Experimental results demonstrate that the proposed framework achieves the highest precision of 99.1% on three testing datasets, outperforming existing mainstream methods.

Keywords: Counterfeit Detection · Handbags · Contrastive Learning · Siamese Network

1 Introduction

The thriving second-hand market has facilitated the proliferation of counterfeit products ranging from basic goods to luxury items [6]. A 2017 study noted that the international trade volume of counterfeit luxury goods reached 1.2 trillion dollars, causing significant societal impacts [12]. Due to continuous advancements in counterfeit technology and emergence of sophisticated imitation methods, traditional manual identification methods are unable to balance accuracy and efficiency, and cultivating human experts requires significant investments in materials and time [2].

Responding to these trends, researchers have developed various counterfeit detection mechanisms. Quick response (QR) codes track production processes to prevent counterfeiting [23]. Digital watermarking embeds information in electronic products to verify authenticity [24]. Chemical marking adds special chemicals to verify the source and authenticity of products [30]. However, these methods are inadequate for detecting counterfeit luxury handbags.

Published by Springer Nature Switzerland AG 2026
E. Kurkowski and S. Shenoi (Eds.): DigitalForensics 2025, IFIP AICT 762, pp. 115–129, 2026.
https://doi.org/10.1007/978-3-032-09802-3_7

Advances in deep learning technology, especially convolutional neural networks, have recently been applied to counterfeit detection [14, 15]. However, these methods, which treat counterfeit detection as an image classification task, have two limitations. First, due to the high similarity between genuine and counterfeit samples, directly classifying genuine and counterfeit samples is a challenging problem. Second, the methods cannot reliably identify genuine and counterfeit samples.

This chapter describes a two-stage universal detection framework that addresses the limitations. The first stage involves supervised contrastive learning, which enables a model to extract more discriminative features from data by comparing the similarities of input sample pairs. In the second stage, the parameters of the trained model are frozen and transfer learning is employed to render the model as a feature extractor. The rendered model is combined with a classifier to identify genuine and counterfeit samples.

A multilevel feature selection module is incorporated to enhance the discrimination ability of the model. The module captures feature maps output at different stages of feature extraction and employs encoders to generate the corresponding attention weights. The attention weights collectively influence the final feature map produced by the model, reinforcing the effective information and suppressing the ineffective information in the feature maps.

Improved pyramid pooling is also implemented. Pyramid pooling performs multiscale pooling on the same feature map using pooling kernels of different granularities and concatenates different feature vectors along the feature dimensions. However, traditional pyramid pooling produces high-dimensional feature vectors and simple concatenation does not effectively integrate the information contained in different feature vectors. To address this issue, a dimension reduction layer is improved after pyramid pooling, promoting the effective fusion of different scale features and facilitating additional processing in subsequent tasks.

2 Related Work

This section discusses relevant research in intelligent counterfeit detection, contrastive learning and transfer learning.

2.1 Intelligent Counterfeit Detection

Advances in machine learning have continually enhanced counterfeit detection. Sharma et al. [16] have applied deep learning techniques to analyze microscopic images to detect counterfeits. Alsallal et al. [1] have used a support vector machine and the k-nearest neighbor algorithm to identify counterfeit drugs. Kumar et al. [7] have developed a three-layer convolutional neural network to identify counterfeit currency. Teymournezhad et al. [18] have employed a deep neural network based on image processing and GoogLeNet for counterfeit currency detection. Desai et al. [5] have proposed a counterfeit currency recognition method based on generative adversarial networks (GANs). Their approach employs a generator to synthesize counterfeit currency and a discriminator to distinguish between genuine and counterfeit currency.

Research related to the detection of counterfeit handbags is relatively limited. Most methods typically treat detection an image classification problem, using models to extract image features and perform classification to determine authenticity. Due to the increasing sophistication of counterfeiting techniques, these methods do not effectively capture the subtle differences existing between genuine and counterfeit handbags, which limits their detection performance.

2.2 Contrastive Learning

Contrastive learning attempts to learn better representations by comparing the similarities and dissimilarities of genuine and counterfeit samples. It focuses more on exploring inherent data relationships to discover the underlying patterns.

Contrastive learning can be categorized as unsupervised contrastive learning, semi-supervised contrastive learning and supervised contrastive learning. Unsupervised contrastive learning [3, 17] does not rely on labeled data; instead, it constructs positive sample pairs via various data augmentations of a single image and negative sample pairs through data augmentations of different images. Supervised contrastive learning [8, 31] relies on labeled data to construct positive and negative sample pairs to guide the learning process. Semi-supervised contrastive learning [9, 27, 33] employs small amounts of labeled data to guide the learning process while leveraging large amounts of unlabeled data to improve model generalization ability.

Siamese network [4, 21] and triplet network [10, 13] architectures are widely adopted for contrastive learning. A Siamese architecture reinforces the similarity of a given category and the dissimilarity of different categories using paired samples as inputs. A triplet network introduces additional anchor samples to capture the relationships between samples. The advantage of contrastive learning lies in its ability to discover relationships between data by comparing the similarities and dissimilarities of contrastive samples. However, it cannot be directly used for image classification. Therefore, in this work, transfer learning is employed to transform the contrastive learning task to an image classification task.

2.3 Transfer Learning

Transfer learning [33] employs a pre-trained model to improve performance. Its principal learning strategies include model-based transfer learning, feature-based transfer learning, generative-adversarial-network-based transfer learning and relation-based transfer learning. These learning strategies effectively transfer the knowledge learned in one task to another related task, accelerating the learning process [27].

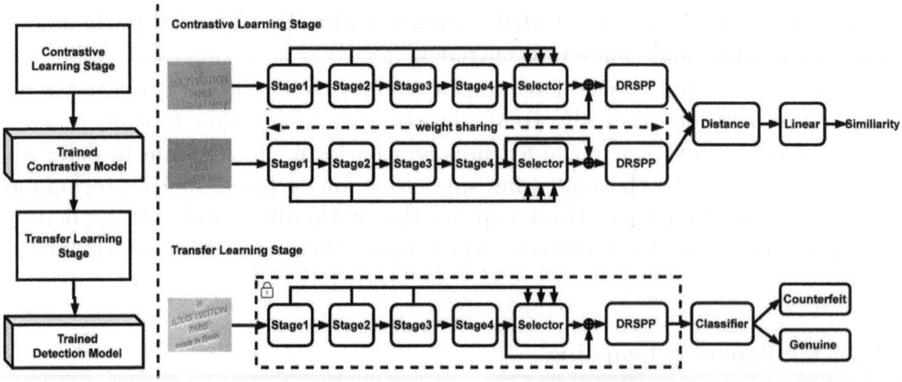

Fig. 1. Universal framework for counterfeit handbag detection.

3 Universal Detection Framework

Figure 1 shows the proposed two-stage universal framework for detecting counterfeit handbags. In the first contrastive learning stage, a Siamese network is designed to learn the similarities and dissimilarities between the data; this enhances the feature extraction capability of the backbone network. In the second transfer learning stage, the backbone network is frozen as a feature extractor and combined with a classifier to distinguish between input images of genuine and counterfeit handbags.

3.1 Discriminative Feature Learning

During the contrastive learning stage, the similarities between samples are modeled and feature representations that accurately reflect class differences are extracted. This process requires the construction of positive sample pairs and negative sample pairs. Positive sample pairs comprise samples with the same class label whereas negative sample pairs comprise samples belonging to different classes (different class labels).

The training dataset is denoted as $D = \{(x_i, y_i)\}_{i=1}^{S}$ where $x_i \in X$ is a sample, $y_i \in Y$ is its class label and S is the total number of samples. For any two samples, x_i and x_j, the set of positive sample pairs P and the set of negative sample pairs N are defined as:

$$P = \{((x_i, x_j), y) | \, x_i \neq x_j, y = 1\}$$
$$N = \{((x_i, x_j), y) | \, x_i \neq x_j, y = 0\}$$

When a positive sample pair is randomly selected from set P or a negative sample pair is randomly selected from set N and input to the model, the model outputs a similarity score for the sample pair to guide the learning of the discriminative features.

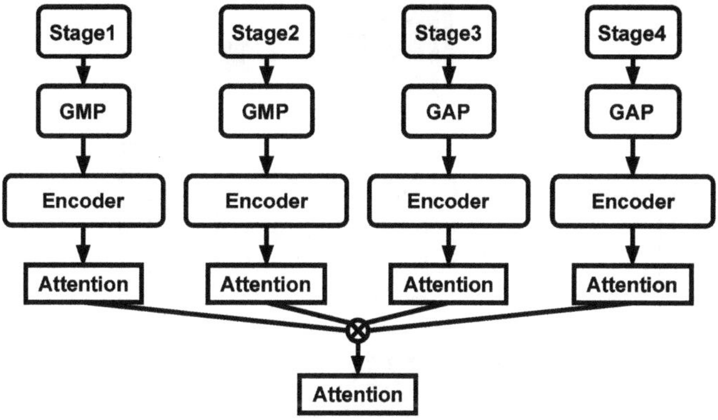

Fig. 2. Multilevel feature selection module.

The contrastive model architecture incorporates a Siamese network with shared weights. In a universal detection framework, any feature extraction model can be employed. The proposed framework leverages ResNet50 that has four stages. The first convolutional layer in ResNet50 employs a 7×7 kernel to process an input image with three channels (RGB). The subsequent layers use 3×3 kernels to extract features progressively. The deeper layers capture semantic information, ultimately producing 2,048 output channels, each representing a unique feature dimension that contributes to a comprehensive 2048-dimensional feature representation of the input image.

Existing attention mechanisms utilize features from the previous layer's output to compute attention weights, which fails to jointly leverage features from the outputs of the various stages [11, 29, 32]. To use this information, a multilevel feature selection (MFS) module is employed to retain feature maps from the four stages. The feature maps are utilized to compute channel attention weights, with each weight reflecting a unique feature selection strategy. The multiplication of the four attention weights facilitates collective decision-making that augments the salient features and diminishes the irrelevant features.

Figure 2 shows the multilevel feature selection module. Global max pooling is employed for the feature maps at the first two stages to emphasize image texture information. Global average pooling is employed for the feature maps in the last two stages to highlight semantic information. Each of the four sets of feature vectors is then input to a dedicated encoder comprising two linear layers. The encoders are designed to generate attention weights, which are subsequently multiplied to yield the decision outcome. Additionally, to mitigate information loss, a residual connection is incorporated in the architecture to ensure that the encoded information is preserved and effectively integrated in the subsequent model stages. This enhances the overall performance of the feature extraction process.

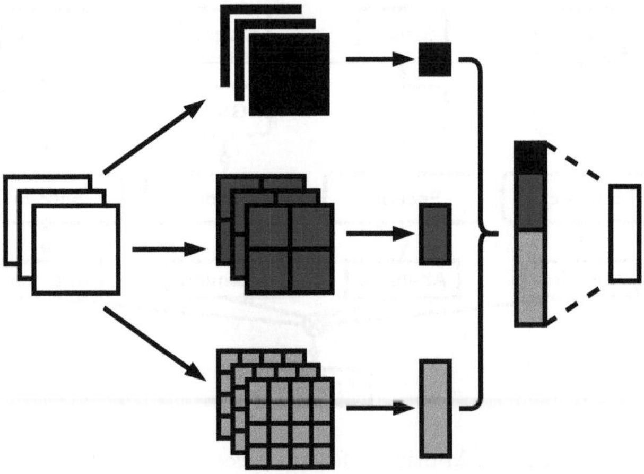

Fig. 3. Dimension reduction pyramid pooling module.

Previous research has demonstrated that pyramid pooling can enhance neural network performance. However, current studies do not adequately focus on the augmented vector dimensionality in the output of pyramid pooling; they also fail to integrate information across the diverse pooling levels sufficiently [22, 25, 26]. Therefore, after extracting high-dimensional features from the input images, a dimension reduction pyramid pooling (DRPP) module is employed to extract multiscale features and integrate multiscale information.

Figure 3 shows the dimension reduction pyramid pooling module. In the pyramid pooling portion, a series of operations are performed at different levels on each input feature map $F \in R^{w \times h \times d}$, where w and h are the width and height of the feature map, respectively, and d is the number of channels in the feature map. Pooling strategies are performed at three distinct scales, dividing the original feature maps into 4×4, 2×2 and 1×1 regions, respectively. Average pooling is applied to each independent region, following which the resulting feature maps from the three pooling operations are flattened and concatenated to obtain the output feature vector $\mathrm{V} \in R^n$, where n is the dimension of the feature vector.

The dimension reduction portion employs a linear transformation L with an output dimension smaller than the input dimension to reduce the feature vector dimension and promote feature fusion. The feature vector V' with reduced dimension is computed as:

$$\mathrm{V}' = L(\mathrm{V}) = \mathrm{W} \cdot \mathrm{V} + \mathrm{b}$$

where $\mathrm{W} \in R^{n \times m}$ is the weight matrix used for linear transformation and n and m are the input and output dimensions, respectively, and $\mathrm{b} \in R^m$ is the bias.

In order to effectively compare the feature vectors extracted from sample pairs, a distance metric function is introduced to quantify their similarities and dissimilarities. The function involves computing the differences between vector elements and squaring them to amplify the differences. The distance vector $\mathrm{D} \in R^m$ (m is the vector dimension) of a sample pair (V_i', V_j') is computed as:

$$\mathrm{D} = \mathrm{Distance}(V_i', V_j') = \left[(V_{i,1}' - V_{j,1}')^2, (V_{i,2}' - V_{j,2}')^2, \ldots, (V_{i,m}' - V_{j,m}')^2\right]$$

After quantifying the distances between sample pairs using the distance metric function, a linear transformation is applied to learn the similarities of sample pairs. The inputs to the linear layer are the distance vectors of the sample pairs and the output is a similarity value $s \in [0, 1]$:

$$s = \mathrm{linear}(\mathrm{D}) = \mathrm{W}^l \cdot \mathrm{D} + \mathrm{b}^l$$

where $\mathrm{D} \in R^m$ is the input distance vector, $\mathrm{W}^l \in R^{m \times 1}$ is the weight matrix of the linear transformation, $\mathrm{b}^l \in R^1$ is the bias and $s \in (0, 1)$.

Next, the binary cross-entropy loss (BCE) between the similarity values and the labels of the sample pairs are computed to evaluate model predictive accuracy. This is followed by model optimization and training. The final loss that guides the optimization of the model parameters is computed as:

$$\mathrm{Loss} = \mathrm{BCE}(\mathrm{s}, \mathrm{y}) = -(\mathrm{y} \cdot \log(\mathrm{sigmoid}(\mathrm{s})) + (1 - \mathrm{y}) \cdot \log(1 - \mathrm{sigmoid}(\mathrm{s})))$$

where s denotes the similarities of sample pairs and $\mathrm{y} \in \{0, 1\}$ denotes the labels of the sample pairs, and sigmoid(s) is computed as:

$$\mathrm{sigmoid}(s) = \frac{1}{1 + e^{-s}}$$

3.2 Task Transfer Learning

During the task transfer learning stage, the backbone network is frozen and is only used to extract features from input images; it is not involved in the training process. A single-layer classifier is incorporated after the backbone network to perform image classification. The classifier transforms the contrastive learning task to a classification task and utilizes the features extracted by the backbone network for image classification. The transformation better utilizes the features learned during the contrastive learning stage and enhances classification performance.

The output features of the backbone network c are computed as:

$$c = \mathrm{Classifier}(\mathrm{V}') = \mathrm{W}^c \cdot \mathrm{V}' + \mathrm{b}^c$$

where $\mathrm{W}^c \in R^{m \times k}$ denotes the weight coefficients of the classifier and k is the number of categories.

At this stage of training, since the backbone network is frozen, only a few fine-tuning steps are needed to update the parameters of the classifier before it is employed for counterfeit handbag detection.

4 Experiments and Results

This section describes the experimental setup, datasets and evaluation metrics, along with the comparative analysis, ablation analysis and visual analysis results.

4.1 Experimental Setup

The model was trained for 150 epochs during the contrastive learning stage and was trained for ten epochs during the transfer learning stage. The batch size was 12 (12×2 samples). The training process employed an SGD optimizer with an initial learning rate of 0.001, and a cosine annealing decay strategy with a decay period of 20 epochs and minimum learning rate of 0.0005.

Each dataset was divided into training, validation and testing datasets in an 8:1:1 ratio for experimentation, with the input image size set to 448×448. Only the training dataset was used for the contrastive learning stage. The validation and testing datasets were reserved for the final transfer learning stage.

4.2 Datasets

To validate the effectiveness of the counterfeit handbag detection framework, a dedicated superset of luxury handbag data covering three independent datasets – leather tag dataset, metal buckle dataset and metal round label dataset – was employed. The three datasets contained 3,095, 1,836 and 2,300 genuine/counterfeit samples, respectively. Figure 4 shows samples from the leather tag, metal buckle and metal round label datasets.

4.3 Evaluation Metrics

Three metrics, precision, recall and F1-score, were employed to evaluate the counterfeit handbag detection performance. The metrics are defined in terms of: (i) true positives (TP) – number of positive samples correctly predicted as positive; (ii) true negatives (TN) – number of negative samples correctly predicted as negative; (iii) false positives (FP) – number of negative samples incorrectly predicted as positive; and (iv) false negatives (FN) – number of positive samples incorrectly predicted as negative.

Precision (Pr) refers to the proportion of samples predicted as positive by a classifier that are truly positive. It measures the ability of a classifier to predict positive samples. Precision is computed as:

$$\text{Precision} = \frac{\text{TP}}{\text{TP+FP}}$$

Recall (Re) refers to the proportion of true positive samples predicted as positive by a classifier. It measures the ability of a classifier to identify positive samples. Recall is computed as:

(a) Leather tag dataset samples.

(b) Metal buckle dataset samples.

(c) Metal round label dataset samples.

Fig. 4. Dataset samples.

$$\text{Recall} = \frac{\text{TP}}{\text{TP+FN}}$$

The F1-score (F1), the harmonic mean of precision and recall, considers the precision and recall abilities of a classifier. It ranges from 0 to 1, with higher values indicating better classifier performance. The F1-score is computed as:

$$\text{F1-Score} = \frac{2 \times (\text{Precision} \times \text{Recall})}{\text{Precision+Recall}}$$

4.4 Comparative Analysis

Comparative experiments were conducted using four mainstream detection models and the proposed ContrastDetect model on the three datasets.

Table 1 shows the detection performance of the five models on counterfeit handbag samples. The best results for the evaluation metrics are highlighted in bold and the second-best results are underlined. For the leather tag dataset,

Table 1. Detection performance on counterfeit samples.

Model	Leather Tag Dataset			Metal Buckle Dataset			Metal Round Label Dataset		
	Pr	Re	F1	Pr	Re	F1	Pr	Re	F1
Swin Transformer [9]	98.2%	97.0%	97.6%	**98.9%**	94.6%	96.7%	**99.2%**	**98.5%**	**98.9%**
ECA-Net [19]	95.2%	95.2%	95.2%	87.4%	89.2%	88.3%	93.9%	92.5%	93.2%
MMAL-Net [28]	98.8%	97.6%	98.2%	98.9%	92.5%	95.6%	99.2%	94.7%	96.9%
CBAM [20]	68.6%	79.2%	73.5%	77.9%	79.6%	78.7%	79.9%	83.5%	81.6%
ContrastDetect	**99.4%**	**98.8%**	**99.1%**	95.8%	**97.8%**	**96.8%**	96.2%	95.5%	95.8%

ContrastDetect yielded the best results for all three evaluation metrics. For the metal buckle dataset, ContrastDetect yielded the best results for two of the three evaluation metrics. For the metal round label dataset, ContrastDetect yielded suboptimal, albeit second-best, results for two of the three metrics. Overall, ContrastDetect had the best results with five top scores and two second-best scores. The second-ranked performer, Swin Transformer, had four top scores and three second-best scores.

Table 2. Detection performance on genuine samples.

Model	Leather Tag Dataset			Metal Buckle Dataset			Metal Round Label Dataset		
	Pr	Re	F1	Pr	Re	F1	Pr	Re	F1
Swin Transformer [9]	96.7%	98.0%	97.3%	94.7%	**98.9%**	**96.8%**	**98.0%**	**99.0%**	**98.5%**
ECA-Net [19]	94.6%	94.6%	94.6%	88.8%	86.8%	87.8%	89.9%	91.8%	90.8%
MMAL-Net [28]	97.4%	98.7%	98.0%	92.8%	98.9%	95.7%	93.2%	99.0%	96.0%
CBAM [20]	71.5%	59.1%	64.7%	78.7%	76.9%	77.8%	75.8%	71.1%	73.4%
ContrastDetect	**98.7%**	**99.3%**	**99.0%**	**97.8%**	95.6%	96.7%	93.9%	94.8%	94.4%

Table 2 shows the detection performance of the five models on genuine handbag samples. Once again, the best results obtained for the evaluation metrics are highlighted in bold and the second-best results are underlined. For the leather tag dataset, ContrastDetect yielded the best results for all three evaluation metrics. For the metal buckle dataset, ContrastDetect yielded the best result for precision and the second-best result for the F1-score. However, for the metal round label dataset, ContrastDetect yielded suboptimal results, albeit one second-best result for precision. Overall, the Swin Transformer had the best results with five top scores and one second-best score. ContrastDetect was second-ranked performer with four top scores and two second-best scores.

The Swin Transformer model demonstrated superior performance on the metal round label dataset. However, it is important to compare the numbers of trained parameters employed by the five counterfeit handbag detection models (Table 3). The ContrastDetect parameter count of 0.41 million is much less than the parameter counts of the four other models, with Swin Transformer having the largest parameter count of 87.93 million. ContrastDetect has a sig-

Table 3. Trained model parameter counts.

Model	Trained Parameters
Swin Transformer	87.93 million
ECA-Net	23.51 million
MMAL-Net	24.38 million
CBAM	24.82 million
ContrastDetect	0.41 million

nificantly lower parameter count than the other models because its parameters were frozen during the second stage, which only required the training of the classifier component.

4.5 Ablation Analysis

Ablation experiments were conducted to validate the effectiveness of the multi-level feature selection module and dimension reduction pyramid pooling module. In the absence of public datasets for authenticating genuine and counterfeit handbags, which are extremely similar, handbag authentication is similar to a fine-grained classification problem. Therefore, a public fine-grained bird dataset comprising 200 extremely similar bird categories was employed in the experiments.

Table 4. Ablation analysis results.

Strategy	Accuracy (Two Categories)	Accuracy (200 Categories)
Base	100.0%	54.7%
Base + MFS	100.0%	68.2%
Base + DRPP	100.0%	65.9%
Base + DRPP + MFS	100.0%	71.9%

Table 4 shows the ablation analysis results using four strategies – the base model alone, followed by the base model with the multilevel feature selection (MFS) and dimension reduction pyramid pooling (DRPP) modules individually and in combination. When randomly selecting two bird categories to conduct the experiments, the accuracy of all four strategies reached 100%. When conducting experiments using all 200 bird categories, incorporating the DRPP module led to an accuracy improvement of 11.2% over the base model, and incorporating the MFS module contributed to an accuracy improvement of 13.5% over the base model. Incorporating both the modules with the base model yielded a remarkable 71.9% accuracy value, an improvement of 17.2% over the base model.

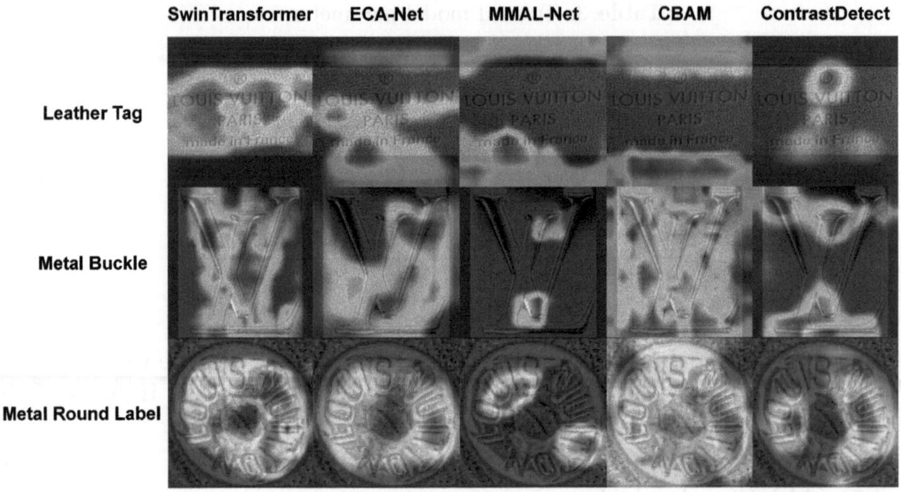

Fig. 5. Model attention areas.

4.6 Visual Analysis

To verify whether the models judge authenticity based on actual authentication points, the gradient-weighted class activation mapping technique was employed to visualize the attention areas of the models. Figure 5 shows the heatmaps generated by different models for the same sample. The highlighted attention areas of the ContrastDetect model align with the actual authentication regions, demonstrating a greater focus on detailed areas and rendering detection less susceptible to background interference.

To demonstrate the ability of the ContrastDetect model to extract discriminative features, dimensionality reduction analysis was conducted using t-distributed stochastic neighbor embedding (t-SNE) on the feature maps extracted from the backbone network. Figure 6 shows the feature visualizations. The circular dots in two distinct colors denote the genuine and counterfeit handbag samples, providing evidence that ContrastDetect can effectively extract discriminative features.

5 Conclusions

The proposed counterfeit handbag detection framework based on supervised contrastive learning addresses the challenging classification problem caused by the high similarity between counterfeit and genuine products in traditional intelligent counterfeit detection methods. By integrating contrastive learning and transfer learning, the detection framework effectively distinguishes between counterfeit and genuine samples. The integrated approach serves as a universal detection framework because the backbone network and classifier can be implemented using any existing methods, contributing to increased flexibility, scalability and applicability to counterfeit detection in diverse domains.

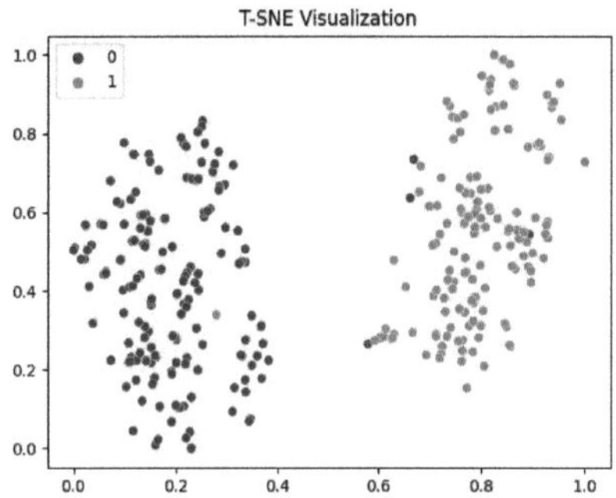

(a) Leather tag features.

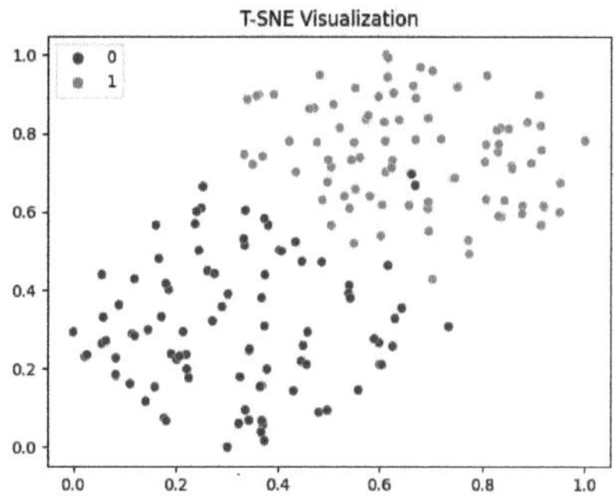

(b) Metal buckle features.

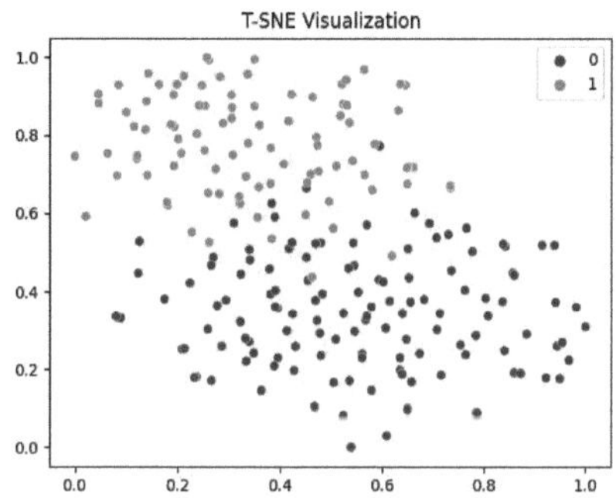

(c) Metal round label features.

Fig. 6. Feature visualizations.

Future research will explore applications in other domains. Also, it will integrate advanced feature extraction and classification techniques to enhance counterfeit detection performance and efficiency.

Acknowledgement

This research was supported by the National Key R&D Program of China under Grant no. 2022YFC3300803, Natural Science Foundation of China under Grant no. 62172053, 111 Project under Grant no. B21049 and Open Foundation of Guizhou Provincial Key Laboratory of Public Big Data under Grant no. 2018BDKFJJ019.

References

1. M. Alsallal, M. Sharif, B. Al-Ghzawi and S. al Mutoki, A machine learning technique to detect counterfeit medicine based on an x-ray fluorescence analyzer, *Proceedings of the International Conference on Computing, Electronics and Communications Engineering*, pp. 118–122, 2018.

2. V. Chand and C. Fei, Self-brand connection and intention to purchase a counterfeit luxury brand in emerging economies, *Journal of Consumer Behavior*, vol. 20(2), pp. 399–411, 2021.
3. X. Chen and K. He, Exploring simple Siamese representation learning, *Proceedings of the IEEE/CVF Conference on Computer Vision and Pattern Recognition*, pp. 15750–15758, 2021.
4. V. Dalai and K. Kadambari, Face identification using visible eye region via vanilla CNN and Siamese networks, *Proceedings of the Second International Conference on Advanced Computing and Innovative Technologies in Engineering*, pp. 2597–2600, 2022.
5. S. Desai, A. Rajadhyaksha, A. Shetty and S. Gharat, CNN based counterfeit Indian currency recognition using a generative adversarial network, *Proceedings of the International Conference on Artificial Intelligence and Smart Systems*, pp. 626–631, 2021.
6. S. Kalyoncuoglu and B. Sahin, Moderating the role of materialism in the effect of perceived value on purchase intention of counterfeits of luxury brands, *International Journal of Marketing Studies*, vol. 9(4), pp. 76–88, 2017.
7. S. Kumar, G. Singal, S. Sirikonda and R. Netravathi, A novel approach for detection of counterfeit Indian currency notes using a deep convolutional neural network, *IOP Conference Series: Materials Science and Engineering*, vol. 981(2), article no. 022018, 2020.
8. T. Li, P. Cao, Y. Yuan, L. Fan, Y. Yang and R. Feris, Targeted supervised contrastive learning for long-tailed recognition, *Proceedings of the IEEE/CVF Conference on Computer Vision and Pattern Recognition*, pp. 6918–6928, 2022.
9. Z. Lia, Y. Lin, Y. Cao, Y. Wei and Z. Zhang, Swin Transformer: Hierarchical vision transformer using shifted windows, *Proceedings of the IEEE/CVF International Conference on Computer Vision*, pp. 9992–10002, 2021.
10. Z. Liu, Y. Wang, Z. Tu, Y. Xiao and B. Tang, TriTransNet: RGB-D salient object detection with a triplet transformer embedding network, *Proceedings of the Twenty-Ninth ACM International Conference on Multimedia*, pp. 4481–4490, 2021.
11. J. Miao, C. Deng, H. Zhang and Q. Miao, Interactive channel attention for rotating component fault detection with strong noise and limited data, *Applied Soft Computing*, vol. 138(C), article no. 110171, 2023.
12. G. Miaoulis, I. Manev, M. Rauch and K. Kimball, Cross cultural analysis of purchasers' intention to wear a counterfeit luxury product in varying social situations, *Luxury Research Journal*, vol. 2(1-2), pp. 70–85, 2021.
13. Y. Pang, X. Zhao, T. Xiang, L. Zhang and H. Lu, Zoom in and out: A mixed-scale triplet network for camouflaged object detection, *Proceedings of the IEEE/CVF Conference on Computer Vision and Pattern Recognition*, pp. 2160–2170, 2022.
14. J. Peng, B. Zou and C. Zhu, A two-stage deep learning framework for counterfeit luxury handbag detection in logo images, *Signal, Image and Video Processing*, vol. 17(4), pp. 1439–1448, 2023.
15. A. Serban, G. Ilas and G. Porusniuc, SpotTheFake: An Initial Report on a New CNN-Enhanced Platform for Counterfeit Goods Detection, arXiv: 2002.06735v2 (`arxiv.org/abs/2002.06735v2`), 2020.
16. A. Sharma, L. Subramanian and E. Brewer, PaperSpeckle: Microscopic fingerprinting of paper, *Proceedings of the Eighteenth ACM Conference on Computer and Communications Security*, pp. 99–110, 2011.
17. T. Si, F. He, Z. Zhang and Y. Duan, Hybrid contrastive learning for unsupervised person re-identification, *IEEE Transactions on Multimedia*, vol. 25, pp. 4323–4334, 2023.

18. K. Teymournezhad, H. Azgomi and A. Asghari, Detection of counterfeit banknotes by security components based on image processing and GoogLeNet deep learning network, *Signal, Image and Video Processing*, vol. 16(6), pp. 1505–1513, 2022.
19. Q. Wang, B. Wu, P. Zhu, P. Li, W. Zuo and Q. Hu, ECA-Net: Efficient channel attention for deep convolutional neural networks, *Proceedings of the IEEE/CVF Conference on Computer Vision and Pattern Recognition*, pp. 11534–11542, 2020.
20. S. Woo, J. Park and J. Lee, CBAM: Convolutional block attention module, *Proceedings of the European Conference on Computer Vision*, pp. 3–19, 2018.
21. Y. Xia, Y. Xia, W. Li, R. Song, K. Cao and U. Stilla, ASFM-Net: Asymmetrical Siamese feature matching network for point completion, *Proceedings of the Twenty-Ninth ACM International Conference on Multimedia*, pp. 1938–1947, 2021.
22. J. Xie, M. Zhu and K. Hu, Improved seabird image classification based on a dual transfer learning framework and spatial pyramid pooling, *Ecological Informatics*, vol. 72, article no. 101832, 2022.
23. R. Xie, C. Hong and S. Zhu, Anti-counterfeiting digital watermarking algorithm for printed QR barcode, *Neurocomputing*, vol. 167, pp. 625–635, 2015.
24. R. Xie and P. Huang, An improved anti-counterfeiting printed QR watermarking algorithm based on a self-adaptive genetic algorithm, *IOP Conference Series: Materials Science and Engineering*, vol. 768(5), article no. 052002, 2020.
25. J. Xu, Z. Xiong and S. Bhattacharyya, PIDNet: A real-time semantic segmentation network inspired by PID controllers, *Proceedings of the IEEE/CVF Conference on Computer Vision and Pattern Recognition*, pp. 19529–19539, 2023.
26. P. Yee, K. Lim and C. Lee, DeepScene: Scene classification via a convolutional neural network with spatial pyramid pooling, *Expert Systems with Applications*, vol. 193, article no. 116382, 2022.
27. F. Yu, X. Xiu and Y. Li, A survey of deep transfer learning and beyond, *Mathematics*, vol. 10(19), article no. 3619, 2022.
28. F. Zhang, M. Li, G. Zhai and Y. Liu, Multi-branch and multiscale attention learning for fine-grained visual categorization, in *MultiMedia Modeling, Part I*, J. Lokoc, T. Skopal, K. Schoeffmann, V. Mezaris, X. Li, S. Vrochidis and I. Patras (Eds.), Springer, Cham, Switzerland, pp. 136–147, 2021.
29. J. Zhang and W. Slamu, Partial channel pooling attention beats convolutional attention, *Expert Systems with Applications*, vol. 237(C), article no. 121436, 2024.
30. X. Zhang, X. Hou, J. Gao, Z. Wang, C. Xu and D. Gao, Color evolution of dynamic persistent luminescence of $Zn_3Ga_2Ge_2O_{10}$: Cr^{3+}, Mn^{2+} phosphors for advanced anti-counterfeiting, *Journal of Materials Chemistry C*, vol. 11(47), pp. 16631–16637, 2023.
31. Y. Zhang, X. Zhang, J. Li, R. Qiu, H. Xu and Q. Tian, Semi-supervised contrastive learning with similarity co-calibration, *IEEE Transactions on Multimedia*, vol. 25, pp. 1749–1759, 2023.
32. M. Zhu, W. Min, J. Han, Q. Han and S. Cui, Improved channel attention methods via hierarchical pooling and reducing information loss, *Pattern Recognition*, vol. 148, article no. 110148, 2024.
33. F. Zhuang, Z. Qi, K. Duan, D. Xi, Y. Zhu and H. Zhu, A comprehensive survey of transfer learning, *Proceedings of the IEEE*, vol. 109(1), pp. 43–76, 2021.

Modeling and Reasoning About Digital Evidence Using Temporal Networks

Catherine Hoffmann and Krishnendu Ghosh

College of Charleston, Charleston, South Carolina, USA
ghoshk@cofc.edu

Abstract. The deluge of email and text communications has increased the need to develop efficient digital forensic analysis techniques for retrieving, organizing and reasoning about evidence. This chapter describes a temporal network methodology for organizing digital communications data to advance digital forensic analyses. An automated methodology that leverages temporal data organization is employed to extract relevant evidence. The methodology also enables digital forensic practitioners to visualize and reason about digital data using temporal network models of evidence. The effectiveness of the methodology is demonstrated using email and text datasets.

Keywords: Temporal Networks · Evidence Reconstruction · Evidence Reasoning · Email · Text Messages

1 Introduction

The prosecution of criminal activities requires evidence extraction and reasoning about the evidence. Efficiently extracting the relevant digital data [26] and reasoning about the data are vital to the accurate presentation of evidence. Due to the large amounts of digital data, digital evidence extraction and reasoning are challenging tasks [13, 16]. The diverse formats of digital data pose additional challenges [2, 14].

Details about criminal activities are often present in email and text communications. The time-stamped communications are helpful in understanding the sequences of events. This work emphasizes the organization of relevant evidence by leveraging the temporal properties of digital data. The goal is to construct timelines of evidence related to crimes based on the communications between the actors. Vital to creating such timelines are the time periods and frequencies of communications between a given actor and other actors and the chronology of the communications.

This chapter describes a methodology that derives temporal network representations from email and text communications. The time-stamped communications are leveraged to provide chronological sequences of events that support evidence collection and event reconstruction. The effectiveness of the methodology is demonstrated using email and text datasets.

Published by Springer Nature Switzerland AG 2026
E. Kurkowski and S. Shenoi (Eds.): DigitalForensics 2025, IFIP AICT 762, pp. 130–141, 2026.
https://doi.org/10.1007/978-3-032-09802-3_8

2 Background

This section describes temporal networks [4, 6] and natural language processing of digital forensic data [21].

2.1 Temporal Networks

Graph-based representations involving provenance graphs and evidence graphs have been leveraged in forensic analyses of digital data. A provenance graph comprises a set of labeled nodes denoting subjects and a set of edges denoting events that connect the objects [7]. Key applications of provenance graphs include intrusion detection and threat modeling based on attack history [25, 27]. Evidence graphs have been applied to network forensics [8]. In these applications, an evidence graph comprises a set of labeled nodes denoting source and target computers, and a set of edges denoting the interactions between the computers.

A temporal network is a graph-based formalism that incorporates the times corresponding to events of interest. Temporal networks comprising nodes connected by time-stamped edges are dynamic in that they change with time. These networks have been applied to time-stamped data such as click stream data and social networks [19].

A temporal network can be broken down into smaller temporal networks (elementary units) called motifs. A motif is a network of relationships involving just two nodes and their corresponding timestamps. Since time is a key component of criminal activities, the dynamic nature of temporal networks makes them an effective tool for digital forensic analysis. This work leverages temporal networks in a relatively new way in digital forensics to identify the principal criminal actors and indicators of criminal activity.

Another important, but less explored component of a temporal network, is a time-based pattern called a snapshot. Snapshots are static representations of patterns in a temporal network occurring within a specified time frame that are measured by their frequencies of occurrence [15].

Temporal networks are very effective for data exploration and analysis because they convey dynamic data and help identify dynamic, time-based patterns. Additionally, they are flexible and support fast querying. Alternative schemes such as traditional databases are better suited for static data representations. However, the database table format is rigid and requires a new query for each view.

2.2 Natural Language Processing

A large body of published literature deals with the applications of natural language processing in digital forensics, in particular, the extraction of relevant evidence [21]. Natural language processing methods have been used to mine digital data and create actionable intelligence for evidence collection and crime reconstruction [5]. The methods have also been applied to study text message communications [12], to mine the web for textual data residing on mobile devices [23], and to detect codewords in textual data to identify drug trafficking [20].

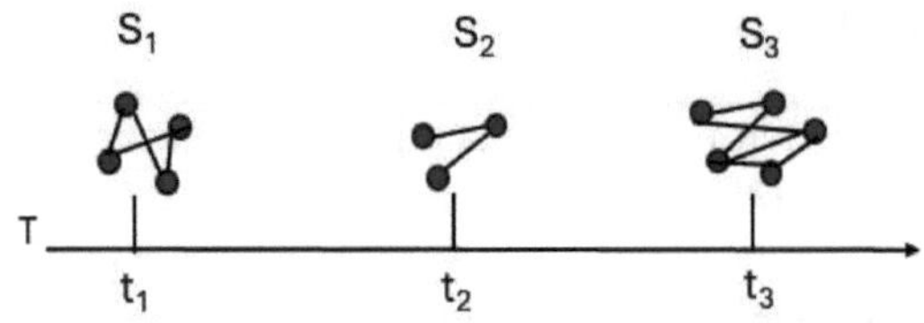

Fig. 1. Static temporal network T with event motifs S_1, S_2, S_3.

Natural language processing methods have been applied to study crimes that leverage social media such as recruiting actors for nefarious activities [18]. Codewords are commonly used in email and text communications by criminal actors to conceal illicit or malicious behavior. Takuro et al. [20] have developed a method for detecting codewords that do not appear in known-codeword lists by comparing the cosine similarities of words used with and without malicious intent.

3 Methodology

Constructing and reasoning with temporal networks are challenging due to their dynamic nature and growth. A static temporal network incorporating event motifs is constructed. An event motif is a network comprising edges that connect the nodes involved in a common event. In the context of this work, event motifs occur at specific timestamps.

Figure 1 shows a static temporal network T with event motifs S_1, S_2, S_3 occurring at times t_1, t_2, t_3, respectively. For example, at a specific date and time D, a set of email messages sent by an actor X and received by another actor Y is modeled as an event motif. In this case, the common event is the email received by actor Y at date and time D. The nodes of the event motif denote the sender and receivers of the email.

The assumption in evidence collection in the digital forensic context is that there is a chronological sequence of events following a specific timeline before a crime is committed. The temporal network representation of digital data is motivated by the following questions:

- What is the frequency of communications between each pair of actors in a given time frame? Analysis of communications provides insights into inappropriate behavior such as favoritism or discrimination in the workplace or in social situations [12]. In the digital forensics context, the questions could be phrased as forensic queries that focus on conversations about committing a specific crime during a certain time frame.
- Are codewords detectable using natural language processing methods? If so, it is necessary to extract the codewords [12], and to identify the actors involved in the communications and the time frames during which the communications occur. This question refers to the obfuscation of communications.

- Can specific language be identified and labeled as pertaining to criminal activities using natural language processing methods? If so, it is necessary to identify the actors who use this language and the associated time frames [24].
- Are there repeating communication patterns or event sequences involving the actors that can help identify criminal activities? If so, it is necessary to determine if the patterns and event sequences occur before or after a crime is committed [1].

The aforementioned queries have a common theme, namely extracting linguistic properties from the available data and organizing the data in a temporal network.

Constructing a static temporal network is a two-step process:

- The first step involves the application of natural language processing methods to extract event motifs. The timestamps in the dataset are used to construct the event motifs. Each event motif is labeled with a timestamp.
- The second step involves queries related to the events and event actors in the event motifs. Reasoning on the static temporal network can be performed at low or high levels of resolution. In the case of low resolution, a large time span is considered and the associated event motifs are collected. In the case of high resolution, the time span is limited and fewer event motifs are extracted. In both cases, a snapshot is created. The snapshot is a portion of the constructed temporal network occurring within the specific time span that contains all the event motifs in the time span.

4 Implementation

Two datasets were analyzed using static temporal networks. The goal was to evaluate the organization of the data to answer forensics-related queries focusing on the temporal representation of email and text messages in the two datasets.

The first dataset, Email Thread Summary Dataset [9], has a unique identifier for each email thread (`thread_id`), email thread subject (`subject`), email sent date and time (`timestamp`), email sender (`from`), email receiver(s) (`to`) and email content (`body`). The dataset contains interactions between objects (nodes) connected by timestamped edges [17].

A temporal network is constructed from the data by identifying the nodes – senders, receivers, thread id and subject, and the timestamped edges representing the interactions (sent emails) between pairs of nodes at the specified times. The data includes pairs of nodes and their corresponding timestamps ([`to`, `from`, `timestamp`]).

For each combination of two nodes (`thread_id` and `subject`, `to` and `from`, etc.), the pair of nodes is abstracted and attached to the associated `timestamp`. The `body` is excluded from each node pair because the large amount of data would render the tuples unreadable. However, the `body` of each email contains the main content and is accessible via its unique combination of `thread_id` and `timestamp`. For an email sent to multiple receivers, the receivers are stored in a list. In this case, the `to` list is split to a new pair for each receiver that maintains the same data as its corresponding node and timestamp. In addition, `timestamps` originally expressed as `date-time` objects that are not conducive to data processing are converted to `strings` for ease of data manipulation. The pairs of nodes represent portions of each email in the form of the event motif.

After the event motifs from the data are abstracted [15], the list of event motifs is integrated in the temporal network based on each timestamp. The construction of the temporal network with event motifs is implemented by initializing a temporal network using the `pathpy` Python package [19]. The temporal network is populated with event motifs expressed as nodes and edges. After the addition of each event motif, `pathpy` is used to construct the complete temporal network.

A snapshot of the temporal network is constructed using a method that takes three inputs – the temporal network, the relationship event motif to be searched and a timestamp (δ) specifying the timeframe used in the search. The method searches the temporal network for matching event motifs. The matching event motifs in the timeframe δ are added to the list of event motifs found in the snapshot.

The second dataset, Mobile Forensics Text Message Corpus [3, 12], used in the study contains 4,934 text messages, 289 of them drug-related. The data includes a binary representation of `class` (drug-related = 1 and non-drug-related = 0), a unique identifier for each contact (`subscriber`), the body of each text message (`message_body`), the date and time the message was sent or received in the format mm/dd/yy h:m AM/PM (`timestamp`), and incoming or outgoing message (`type`).

Note that the dataset contains the identity of one party in each communication, i.e., only the sender or receiver. The drug-related or non-drug-related message classification enables natural language processing to be applied to the message bodies with respect to drug-related queries.

5 Case Study Results

This section describes the results obtained using the temporal networks connecting event motifs constructed from the email and text message datasets. Data and scripts pertaining to the case study are available on zenodo (`zenodo.org/records/14635432`).

5.1 Email Dataset Analysis

The Email Thread Summary Dataset [9] containing Enron corporate email messages does not classify email as drug-related or non-drug-related as in the case of text messages in the Mobile Forensics Text Message Corpus [12]. However, the email dataset identifies the sender and receiver(s) of each email message, which enables email classification. Since the dataset is a corporate email corpus, it is unlikely to contain communications pertaining to drug-related criminal activities. Therefore, each email was classified as work-related or non-work-related, with a focus on non-work-related (suspicious) email.

The email dataset contains many mass email communications to employees. These communications were eliminated from consideration as they were unlikely to be non-work-related. Specifically, an email with ten or more receivers was deemed to be a mass email thread.

Several words related to non-work-related activities were selected and the threads containing one or more occurrences of these words were flagged for analysis. A total of 2,576 individuals sent email messages, with Kay Mann (826), Sara Shackleton (620) and Tana Jones (618) sending the most messages. Six hundred and ten individuals sent email identified as non-work-related. The three most common words related to non-work-related activities were party (2,644 occurrences), play (586) and beer (310). In all, 2,547 of the 21,684 email messages in the dataset were deemed to be non-work-related.

5.2 Text Message Dataset Analysis

Text messages in the Mobile Forensics Text Message Corpus [3, 12] were processed to create a temporal network whose event motifs were constructed based on the message timestamps. It is important to note that the dataset contains text messages identified by their senders or receivers, but not both.

The first step in the analysis was to search for known perpetrators (*ptr*) (i.e., subscribers) whose text messages contained keywords pertaining to criminal activities. Codewords were obtained from a list created by the Drug Enforcement Administration (DEA) [22], and seven words identified as potentially criminal were selected to be used as criminal activity keywords for the purpose of the study. The entire dataset was examined for malicious text messages containing a criminal activity keyword as well as a codeword and the subscribers involved were added to the known perpetrators list. A total of 31 known perpetrators were identified corresponding to the `subscriber_ids` 1, 2, 3, 4, 5, 6, 8, 9, 12, 13, 14, 15, 16, 17, 142, 143, 148, 149, 144, 145, 146, 154, 155, 156, 157, 31, 35, 38, 48, 49 and 63.

The frequency of communications (number of malicious messages sent) for each known perpetrator within each snapshot was computed. In the selected time frame, ptr_{48}, ptr_1 and ptr_3 were found to be involved more than any other known perpetrator with 188, 142 and 100 messages sent/received, respectively. However, these totals include all the messages sent by or received by known perpetrators and are, therefore, not necessarily malicious or drug-related. Since the known perpetrators did not exclusively send drug-related messages, inferring criminal activity based solely on their communications in a specific snapshot pattern would be inappropriate.

As a result, the search was narrowed to focus on snapshot patterns deemed to be definitely malicious when both messages in the snapshot patterns were tagged as `class` = 1 (drug-related). Of the 856 snapshot patterns found, 129 (15.07%) were identified as being definitely malicious. The frequencies of communications

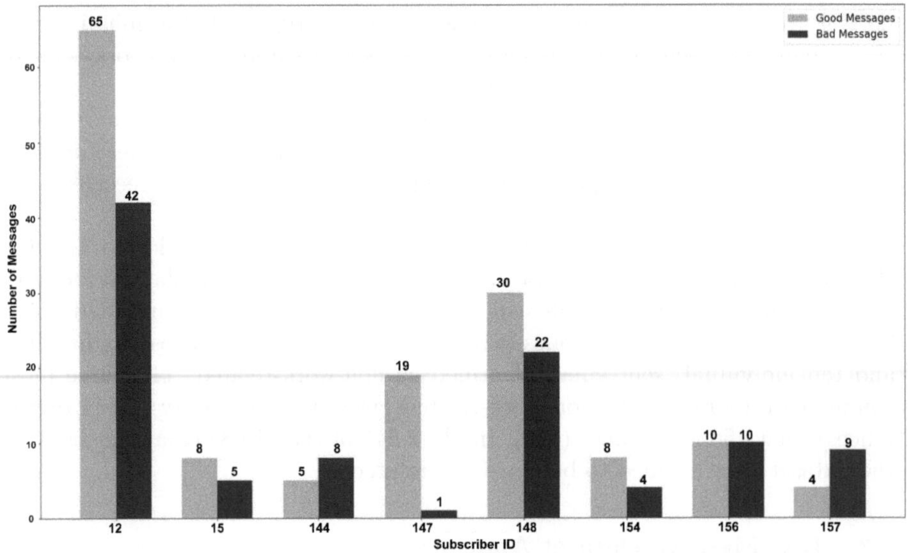

Fig. 2. Frequencies of good and bad text messages involving known perpetrators.

involving the known perpetrators involved in the definitely malicious snapshots were subsequently computed.

However, some known perpetrators sent or received significantly more messages than others, resulting in potentially misleading findings. Therefore, for each known perpetrator involved in at least ten messages, queries were executed to determine: (i) number of `incoming` and `class` = 0 messages, (ii) number of `incoming` and `class` = 1 messages, (iii) number of `outgoing` and `class` = 0 messages, and (iv) number of `outgoing` and `class` = 1 messages.

The queries revealed that ptr_{12} was involved in 107 messages (60.7% good and 39.3% bad), ptr_{15} was involved in 13 messages (61.5% good and 38.5% bad), ptr_{144} was involved in 13 messages (38.5% good and 61.5% bad), ptr_{147} was involved in 20 messages (95.0% good and 5.0% bad), ptr_{148} was involved in 52 messages (57.7% good and 42.3% bad), ptr_{154} was involved in 12 messages (66.7% good and 33.3% bad), ptr_{156} was involved in 20 messages (50.0% good and 50.0% bad) and ptr_{157} was involved in 14 messages (35.7% good and 62.5% bad). Figure 2 shows the frequencies of text messages classified as good and bad for the known perpetrators.

Next, known perpetrators whose sent or received messages were classified as malicious at least 50% of the time were identified. These known perpetrators – ptr_{144}, ptr_{148}, ptr_{156} and ptr_{157} – were deemed to be potential subjects of criminal investigations. The high volumes of messages sent and received in snapshots combined with the high percentage of malicious messages resulted in the flagging of the known perpetrators as having higher levels of involvement in criminal activities, and therefore, more likely to be involved in drug sales and distribu-

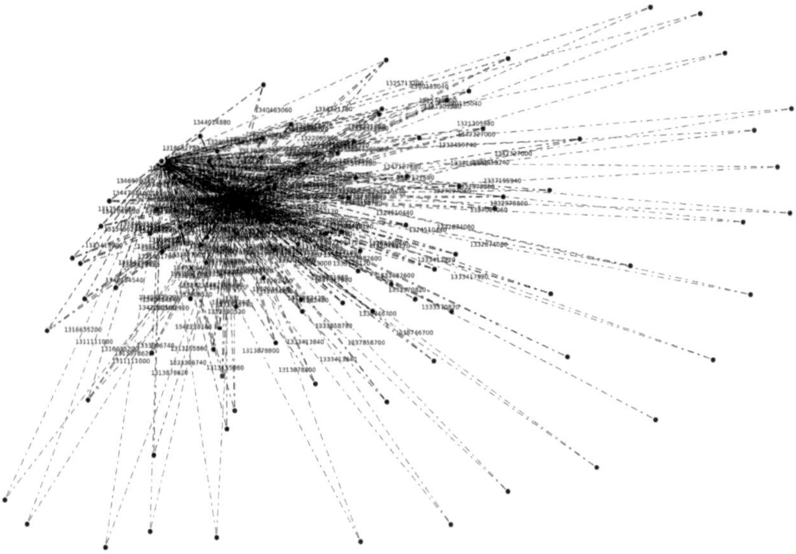

Fig. 3. Static temporal network of the Mobile Forensics Text Message Corpus.

tion. The known perpetrators whose messages were less frequently classified as malicious would be expected to be occasional or recreational drug users and not potential subjects of criminal investigations.

6 Static Temporal Network Queries

This section demonstrates examples of forensic-related querying of the text message corpus [3, 12]. The Python packages `pathpy` [19], `networkx` [11] and `Matplotlib` [10] were leveraged to create visualizations of the temporal networks. The `TemporalNetwork` method of `pathpy` was used to create the event motifs that comprise the two types of nodes representing subscribers (senders and receivers of text messages) and the message types (incoming or outgoing messages). The timestamps on the edges denote the connection times between node pairs in the event motifs.

Without specialized packages or libraries, a temporal network is displayed crudely as tuples containing data (e.g., (`sender`, `receiver` and `timestamp`)). Visualization techniques were employed in this work to fully utilize temporal networks. This ability is demonstrated by visualizations showing the breakdowns of temporal networks to event motifs.

Figure 3 shows the complete static temporal network of the text message dataset. All the node types (i.e., `subscriber`, `type` and `class`) are included along with the corresponding time-stamped edges. The `subscriber_id` and `type` (incoming or outgoing) are nodes in the event motifs. The edges connect the se-

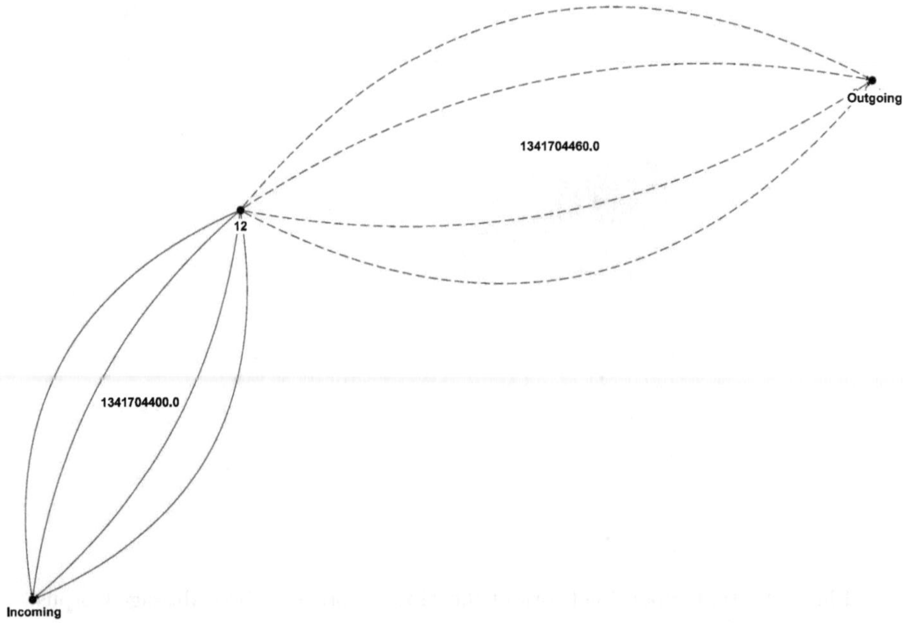

Fig. 4. Event motif $ptr_A \rightarrow ptr_{12} \rightarrow ptr_C$ within 24 hours.

quence of nodes $s_1, t_1, s_2, t_2, \ldots, s_n, t_n$ where $s_1, s_2, \ldots, s_n$ and $t_1, t_2, \ldots, t_n$ correspond to `subscriber_ids` and `types`, respectively. The edges connecting event motifs populate the temporal network and are labeled with the corresponding timestamps.

Figure 4 shows all the snapshots representing communications by a known perpetrator ptr_{12} that match the event motif pattern $ptr_A \rightarrow ptr_{12} \rightarrow ptr_C$ within 24 hours of involvement in an identified criminal activity. The pattern represents an incoming text message from an arbitrary known perpetrator ptr_A to ptr_{12} followed by an outgoing message from ptr_{12} to an arbitrary known perpetrator ptr_C. The event motif comprises three nodes, `incoming`, ptr_{12} and `outgoing`, connected by 130 edges labeled with timestamps. The number of edges with timestamped labels corresponds to the number of text messages sent to or sent by ptr_{12} in each pattern within the specified 24-hour period.

Figure 5 shows all the event motifs corresponding to the pattern $ptr_A \rightarrow ptr_X \rightarrow ptr_C$ within 24 hours of involvement in an identified criminal activity. The pattern represents an incoming message from an arbitrary known perpetrator ptr_A to any identified known perpetrator ptr_X, followed by an outgoing message from the identified known perpetrator ptr_X to an arbitrary known perpetrator ptr_C. The event motif considers all the `subscriber_ids` with the pattern. The temporal network contains 28 nodes – `incoming` and `outgoing` nodes and nodes corresponding to known perpetrators with `subscriber_ids` 1, 2, 3,

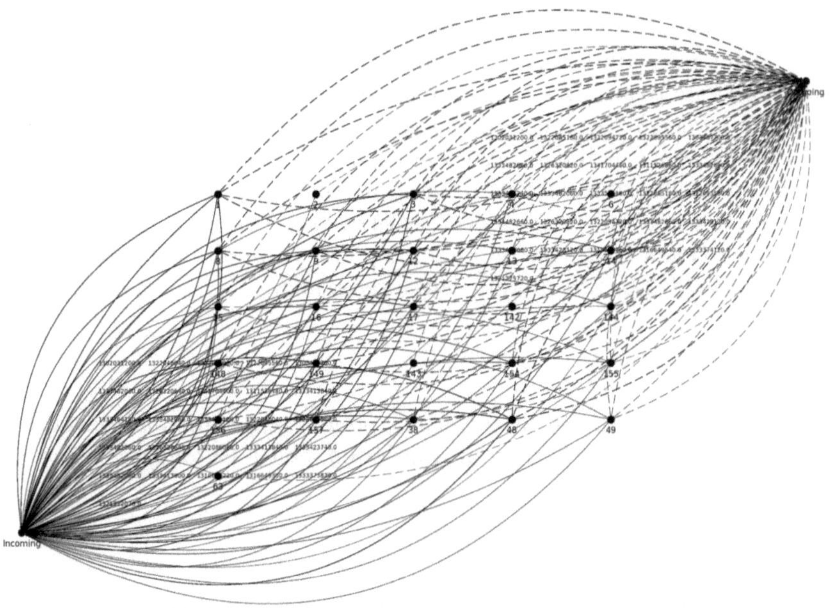

Fig. 5. Event motif $ptr_A \rightarrow ptr_X \rightarrow ptr_C$ within 24 hours.

4, 6, 8, 9, 12, 13, 14, 15, 16, 17, 142, 143, 148, 149, 144, 154, 155, 156, 157, 38, 48 49 and 63 – that are connected by 1,712 timestamped edges.

The following research questions are addressed by the temporal network representations of digital data from the text message dataset:

- **R1:** What is the time period where an individual contacted a set of individuals or a specific individual, and what are the contact frequencies? The output of the query is shown in Figure 4 and specifies the time period in which an individual is contacted. The numbers associated with the timestamped edges correspond to the contact frequencies.
- **R2:** What is the order of the communications between a set of individuals? Specifically, who first contacted whom, etc.? The timestamped edges in the output for the query pattern $ptr_A \rightarrow ptr_X \rightarrow ptr_C$ in Figure 5 illustrate the order of the communications between the set of individuals. Additionally, the timestamped edges identify the chronology of the contacts.
- **R3:** Who are the individual(s) who initially contacted the suspect and who are the individual(s) that the suspect subsequently contacted? The nodes labeled with `subscriber_ids` in the successive event motifs – constructed recursively on the nodes representing perpetrators and connected via timestamped edges – correspond to the individuals who were contacted by individuals suspected of criminal activity.

7 Conclusions

This chapter describes an automated methodology for organizing digital communications data to advance forensic analysis. The methodology leverages temporal network models of evidence to enable digital forensic practitioners to visualize and reason about digital data such as email and text messages. The effectiveness of the methodology is demonstrated using email and text datasets.

Future work will employ deep-learning-based natural language processing methods to identify textual information precisely. Additionally, the methodology will be extended to incorporate causal reasoning.

Acknowledgement

This research was funded by the School of Sciences, Mathematics and Engineering at the College of Charleston, Charleston, South Carolina.

References

1. B. Arregui-Garcia, A. Longa, Q. Lotito, S. Meloni and G. Cencetti, Patterns in temporal networks with higher-order egocentric structures, *Entropy*, vol. 26(3), article no. 256, 2024.
2. D. Barradas, T. Brito, D. Duarte, N. Santos and L. Rodrigues, Forensic analysis of communication records of messaging applications from physical memory, *Computers and Security*, vol. 86, pp. 484–497, 2019.
3. Cyber Security Lab, Mobile Forensics Text Message Corpus, Purdue University, Calumet, Indiana (`web.archive.org/web/20130921043042/http://cybersecurity.cit.purduecal.edu/content/tmcorpus.html`), 2012.
4. P. Holme and J. Saramaki, Temporal networks, *Physics Reports*, vol. 519(3), pp. 97–125, 2012.
5. D. Hughes, P. Rayson, J. Walkerdine, K. Lee, P. Greenwood, A. Rashid, C. May-Chahal and M. Brennan, Supporting law enforcement in digital communities through natural language analysis, in *Computational Forensics*, S. Srihari and K. Franke (Eds.), Springer, Berlin Heidelberg, Germany, pp. 122–134, 2008.
6. A. Li, S. Cornelius, Y. Liu, L. Wang and A. Barabasi, The fundamental advantages of temporal networks, *Science*, vol. 358(6366), pp. 1042–1046, 2017.
7. Z. Li, Q. Chen, R. Yang, Y. Chen and W. Ruan, Threat detection and investigation with system-level provenance graphs: A survey, *Computers and Security*, vol. 106, article no. 102282, 2021.
8. C. Liu, A. Singhal and D. Wijesekera, Creating integrated evidence graphs for network forensics, in *Advances in Digital Forensics IX*, G. Peterson and S. Shenoi (Eds.), Springer, Berlin Heidelberg, Germany, pp. 227–241, 2013.
9. M. Mamdouh, Email Thread Summary Dataset (`www.kaggle.com/datasets/marawanxmamdouh/email-thread-summary-dataset`), 2024.
10. Matplotlib Development Team, Matplotlib: Visualization with Python (`matplotlib.org`), 2024.
11. NetworkX Developers, NetworkX: Network Analysis in Python (`networkx.org`), 2024.

12. D. O'Day and R. Calix, Text message corpus: Applying natural language processing to mobile device forensics, *Proceedings of the IEEE International Conference on Multimedia and Expo Workshops*, 2013.
13. M. Olivier, Digital forensics and the big data deluge – Some concerns based on Ramsey theory, in *Advances in Digital Forensics XVI*, G. Peterson and S. Shenoi (Eds.), Springer, Cham, Switzerland, pp. 3–26, 2020.
14. A. Orebaugh and J. Allnutt, Data mining instant messaging communications to perform author identification for cybercrime investigations, *Digital Forensics and Cyber Crime*, S. Goel (Ed.), Springer, Berlin Heidelberg, Germany, pp. 99–110, 2009.
15. A. Paranjape, A. Benson and J. Leskovec, Motifs in temporal networks, *Proceedings of the Tenth ACM International Conference on Web Search and Data Mining*, pp. 601–610, 2017.
16. M. Pollitt and A. Whitledge, Exploring big haystacks: Data mining and knowledge management, in *Advances in Digital Forensics II*, M. Olivier and S. Shenoi (Eds.), Springer, Boston, Massachusetts, pp. 67–76, 2006.
17. M. Saqr, Temporal network analysis: Introduction, methods and analysis with R, in *Learning Analytics Methods and Tutorials: A Practical Guide Using R*, M. Saqr and S. Lopez-Pernas (Eds.), Springer, Cham, Switzerland, pp. 541–567, 2024.
18. J. Scanlon and M. Gerber, Automatic detection of cyber-recruitment by violent extremists, *Security Informatics*, vol. 3(5), 2014.
19. I. Scholtes, When is a network a network? Multi-order graphical model selection in pathways and temporal networks, *Proceedings of the Twenty-Third ACM SIGKDD International Conference on Knowledge Discovery and Data Mining*, pp. 1037–1046, 2017.
20. H. Takuro, S. Yuichi, Y. Tahara and A. Ohsuga, Codeword detection in microblogs focusing on differences in word use between two corpora, *Proceedings of the International Conference on Computing, Electronics and Communications Engineering*, pp. 103–108, 2020.
21. D. Ukwen and M. Karabatak, Review of NLP-based systems in digital forensics and cybersecurity, *Proceedings of the Ninth International Symposium on Digital Forensics and Security*, 2021.
22. U.S. Drug Enforcement Administration, Drug Slang Code Words, DEA Intelligence Report DEA-HOU-DIR-020-17, Springfield, Virginia (`www.dea.gov/documents/2017/2017-05/2017-05-01/drug-slang-code-words`), 2017.
23. K. Vertanen and P. Kristensson, Mining, analyzing and modeling text written on mobile devices, *Natural Language Engineering*, vol. 27(1), pp. 1–33, 2021.
24. D. Wright, Corpus approaches to forensic linguistics: Applying corpus data and techniques in forensic contexts, in *The Routledge Handbook of Forensic Linguistics*, M. Coulthard, A. May and R. Sousa-Silva (Eds.), London, United Kingdom, pp. 611–627, 2020.
25. Y. Xie, D. Feng, Z. Tan and J. Zhou, Unifying intrusion detection and forensic analysis via provenance awareness, *Future Generation Computer Systems*, vol. 61(C), pp. 26–36, 2016.
26. M. Yang and K. Chow, An information extraction framework for digital forensic investigations, in *Advances in Digital Forensics XI*, G. Peterson and S. Shenoi (Eds.), Springer, Cham, Switzerland, pp. 61–76, 2015.
27. M. Zipperle, F. Gottwalt, E. Chang and T. Dillon, Provenance-based intrusion detection systems: A survey, *ACM Computing Surveys*, vol. 55(7), article no. 135, 2022.

Digital Forensics Frameworks

A Comprehensive Workflow for Cloud Forensics

Pranitha Sanda[1], Digambar Pawar[2], Radha Vedala[3], and Keshav Shrivas[1]

[1] C.R. Rao Advanced Institute of Mathematics, Statistics and Computer Science, Hyderabad, India
pranitha.sanda@gmail.com
[2] University of Hyderabad, Hyderabad, India
[3] Institute for Development and Research in Banking Technology, Hyderabad, India

Abstract. The vast majority of cloud computing environments do not provide built-in support for cloud forensics. Current incident response solutions for cloud environments primarily focus on detection and mitigation, and lack structured approaches for supporting forensic investigations. This chapter attempts to bridge the gap by proposing a comprehensive workflow for investigating cloud incidents. Best practices implemented by leading cloud service providers are incorporated in the workflow. The integration of a cloud anti-forensics module in the workflow is a novel feature that distinguishes it from other approaches.

Keywords: Cloud Forensics · Cloud Anti-Forensics · Workflow

1 Introduction

Digital forensics deals with the identification, collection, analysis, preservation and presentation of digital evidence in court proceedings [7]. Cloud forensics is the "cloud computing application of digital forensics [that combines] traditional computer forensics, small-scale digital device forensics and network forensics" [27]. It extends digital forensics to cloud environments, which are shared collections of rapidly-reconfigurable networked resources that include networks, servers, storage, apps and services. Cloud forensics involves collecting cloud forensic artifacts, preparing the artifacts for forensic analysis, conducting forensic analysis and preserving the artifacts and ensuring their integrity.

The process of conducting investigations, the types of evidence and several other elements associated with cloud cases differ from conventional digital media cases. Due to cloud privacy restrictions, digital forensic practitioners do not have direct access to the physical resources and are not directly involved in evidence collection. Indeed, cloud service providers are the only source of cloud evidence. Additional challenges to cloud forensic investigations are imposed by virtualization, multi-tenancy, endless storage and remote access. A National Institute of Standards and Technology (NIST) report [9] details the challenges facing cloud forensics. Key challenges pertain to anti-forensics, architecture, data collection, data processing, standard operating procedures, training and legal issues.

The growth of cloud computing has greatly increased the number of cloud investigations conducted by cloud service providers and law enforcement [31].

Published by Springer Nature Switzerland AG 2026
E. Kurkowski and S. Shenoi (Eds.): DigitalForensics 2025, IFIP AICT 762, pp. 145–156, 2026.
https://doi.org/10.1007/978-3-032-09802-3_9

Malik et al. [18] estimate that the compound annual growth rate (CAGR) for cloud forensics is approximately 16.53% and that the global cloud forensics market will reach $36.9 billion by 2031.

This work focuses on a workflow for cloud forensics that includes the often-overlooked aspect of cloud anti-forensics. Best practices instituted by leading cloud service providers such as Amazon Web Services, Microsoft Azure and Google Cloud Platform are integrated to address cloud forensics as well as cloud anti-forensics. An analysis of forensic procedures adopted by major cloud service providers [28] has identified logs, disk storage and memory as the primary containers of forensic artifacts; as a result, this work considers each of these types of artifacts. Additionally, this work considers how cloud environments – with their centralized monitoring and controlled infrastructures – offer more effective means for detecting and mitigating anti-forensic activity compared with unregulated computing environments. The ultimate objective is to specify a comprehensive, robust and resilient workflow that enhances cloud forensic capabilities while countering malicious efforts to manipulate or destroy digital evidence.

2 Related Research

This section discusses key research related to cloud forensics challenges and cloud forensics frameworks.

2.1 Cloud Forensic Challenges

Several researchers have discussed the challenges facing cloud forensics and the efforts made to overcome them. Manral et al. [19] have classified the challenges as provider-driven, incident-driven and cloud-forensics-driven based on consumers and resources. Pichan et al. [24] have conducted a comparative review of the technical difficulties facing each stage in cloud forensics – identification, collection, analysis, preservation and presentation. Also, they discuss solutions put forth by researchers, cloud service providers and government organizations.

Zawoad and Hasan [35] have examined cloud forensics challenges through the lens of cloud service paradigms such as infrastructure as a service (IaaS), platform as a service (PaaS) and software as a service (SaaS). Martini and Choo [20] have detailed the technological obstacles and suggested solutions for public and private cloud infrastructures. Ruan et al. [27] have studied the difficulties along three dimensions – technological, administrative and legal. Kwon and Choi [14] have emphasized the problem of "credibility of cloud evidence" – it is untrustworthy due to the multi-tenancy in cloud environments and the many actors involved in cloud forensic processes. Clearly, the collection, storage and integrity of cloud evidence are key issues in cloud forensics.

2.2 Cloud Forensics Frameworks

Several researchers have proposed cloud forensics frameworks that provide structured approaches for investigating cases involving cloud environments. Akilal and

Kechadi [1] have proposed the integration of forensics in the system design and development stages to comply with system and software engineering standards. The principal focus is forensics by design with an emphasis on cloud computing. Key factors such as security, privacy and resilience are integrated with forensics by design in compliance with International Standards Organization (ISO) standards.

Simou et al. [32, 33] have specified a cloud-forensics-enabled framework that allows software engineers to design cloud services that support forensic investigations. Seven forensic constraints are identified and the associated feature diagrams that support the design of forensics-enabled cloud devices are provided [32]. In subsequent work, Simou et al. [33] validate cloud forensics readiness using a real-world case study, demonstrating how organizations can assess readiness and improve compliance with forensic investigation standards.

Prakash et al. [25] have presented a framework for cloud investigations based on a survey of 104 experts in cloud computing/digital forensics. The framework was subsequently validated by surveying 20 experts who emphasized the need for persistent log storage, data segregation techniques and legal frameworks that support international collaboration.

Alex and Kishore [2] have proposed a forensics monitoring plane (FMP) setup outside cloud premises to reduce the dependence on cloud providers. Forensic tools are incorporated to monitor inbound and outbound cloud connections. The monitored data is imaged, encrypted and stored in separate forensic servers in a secure environment. The forensic tools also capture images of network traffic and cloud virtual machines (VMs). However, the approach introduces additional challenges such as maintaining user privacy as stipulated by service level agreements, ensuring trust, intercepting benign requests and responses, and handling the additional computational overhead.

Most cloud forensics frameworks assume cloud service providers to be trusted entities. In contrast, Ye et al. [34] have proposed a solution for untrusted cloud environments. They leverage a multilayer compressed counting bloom filter (ML-CCBF) to locate attacked cloud nodes, verify the reliability of evidence and ensure the integrity of provenance data captured by monitoring cloud logs.

Khanafseh et al. [13] have conducted a comprehensive review of digital forensics frameworks with an emphasis on cloud forensics. They compare cloud forensics frameworks based on evidence identification, collection, analysis, preservation and reporting, and identify their limitations.

AlSaed et al. [4] have proposed a framework that ensures evidence integrity. Evidence metadata is captured before uploading evidence to the cloud and is compared after downloading the evidence from the cloud to check its integrity. Apache Spark is employed to analyze large volumes of cloud log data for timeline construction to gain information such as hits per hour and hits per IP address.

Moric et al. [21] discuss the forensic capabilities of Microsoft Azure using native Azure tools such as unified audit logs (UALs) and Azure Data Explorer with the Kusto Query Language (KQL). They demonstrated how KQL can be used to identify failed login attempts, suspicious privilege escalations, etc. They also evaluated the framework by performing a forensic investigation of a ransomware attack. Additionally, they discussed the incorporation of artificial intelligence (AI) techniques to enhance forensic capabilities.

Rani and Geethakumari [26] have proposed a framework that detects anti-forensic attacks in cloud environments by identifying suspicious packets. Anti-forensic attacks hinder cloud forensic investigations by erasing or obfuscating evidence, which make the attacks difficult to trace. Rani and Geethakumari introduced a three-stage system that identifies suspicious packets using signature analysis and anomaly detection, proceeds to mark them for traceback and monitors the virtual machines that generate the packets.

Recent work on cloud forensics frameworks focuses on conceptual frameworks and prototype frameworks. The conceptual work tends to incorporate forensic capabilities during the software engineering design phase based on standards and expert opinion. The prototype-based work focuses on cloud logs. However, only two works cited above [26, 34] discuss the anti-forensic aspects. Rani et al. [26] discuss anti-forensics in cloud environments and identify suspicious packets using signature analysis, but they ignore the other aspects of cloud forensics. Ye et al. [34] consider cloud environments to be untrusted and assume that evidence may be tampered, but they do not use the term anti-forensics. The proposed cloud forensics workflow attempts to bridge the gap by providing a holistic approach that considers cloud forensics and cloud anti-forensics.

3 Comprehensive Cloud Forensics Workflow

In cloud forensics, it is important to emphasize anti-forensics and forensics equally. Therefore, the proposed workflow incorporates two primary modules for cloud anti-forensics and cloud forensics. The cloud anti-forensics module proactively checks for anti-forensic activity engaged by adversaries by continuously monitoring cloud artifacts for suspicious activity before incidents occur. Regulated and centrally-controlled cloud environments provide the flexibility to monitor virtual instance activity. The cloud forensics module supports the investigation of incidents after they have occurred. It leverages traditional forensic approaches that identify, collect, analyze and preserve evidentiary cloud artifacts.

Figure 1 shows the comprehensive cloud forensics workflow. The workflow supports the collection, analysis and preservation of cloud artifacts using existing forensic tools. However, the capabilities of current tools need to be extended to handle cloud artifacts.

3.1 Cloud Anti-Forensics Module

Adversaries typically engage in anti-forensic activity before an incident is reported, seeking to eliminate traces of evidence from being left behind. Therefore, it is imperative to monitor a cloud environment continuously to check if any anti-forensic activity is occurring.

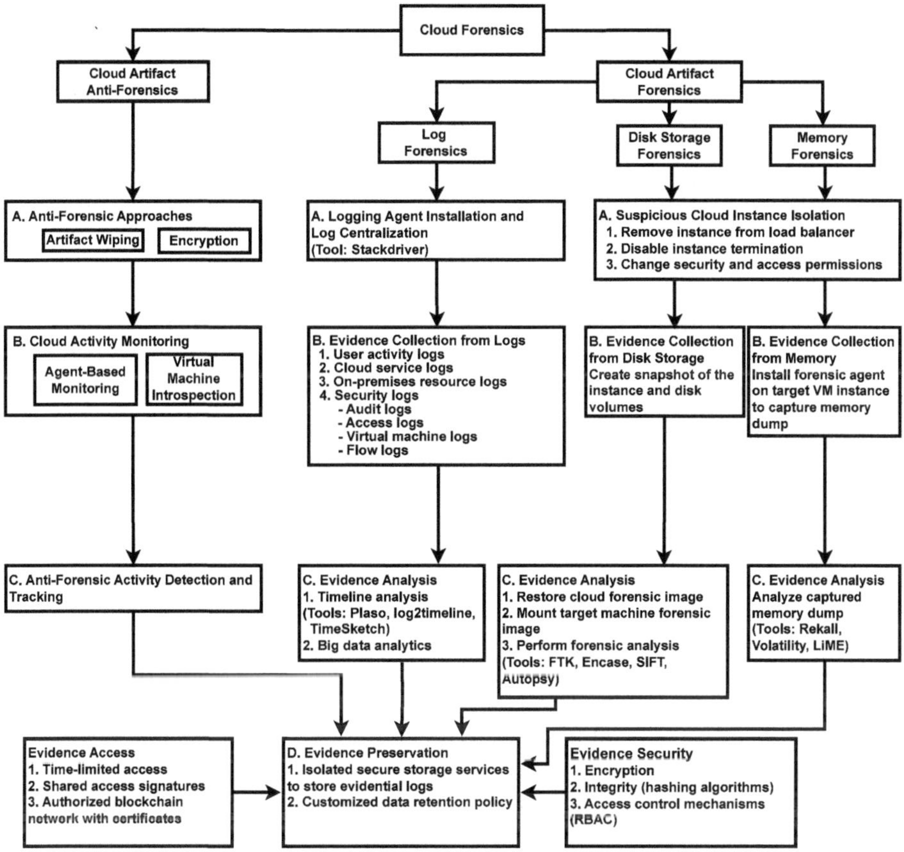

Fig. 1. Comprehensive cloud forensics workflow.

Anti-Forensic Approaches. Anti-forensic approaches include artifact wiping, data hiding and trail obfuscation [5, 6, 8, 11, 17, 31]. Artifact wiping is employed to remove traces of evidence by overwriting file content multiple times; the permanent damage to data makes recovery impossible. Data hiding is often employed to conceal data to hinder investigations; two common methods are encryption and steganography. Trail obfuscation is a deliberate effort to alter or destroy evidence. The most common methods involve compression bombs, distributed denial-of-service attacks, proxy servers and IP and MAC address spoofing.

Monitoring Cloud Activity. Cloud environments must be monitored for anti-forensic activity. This is accomplished by monitoring at the virtual machine level or by performing virtual machine introspection (VMI). Agent-based virtual machine monitoring installs system monitoring tools on targeted cloud virtual machines. In contrast, virtual machine introspection monitors virtual machines at the hypervisor layer. Virtual machine introspection has garnered significant attention due to its isolation from virtual machines and its comprehensive, but semantically less, visibility into virtual machine operations.

Anti-Forensics Detection Tools. Traditional detection tools detect anti-forensic activity based on the signatures left by anti-forensics tools following their execution [3, 10, 12, 15, 22]. Anti-forensic approaches such as artifact wiping and encryption can be detected via statistical/information theoretic techniques. Both approaches involve frequent write system calls that are analyzed to identify wiping [30] and encryption [16, 23]. For example, P. P. Sanda et al. [30] have analyzed the patterns in sequences of system calls invoked by wiping tools. Ad-ditional techniques and tools are required for anti-forensics detection to ensure the integrity of evidence in cloud environments.

3.2 Cloud Forensics Module

Cloud artifacts are typically found in three containers – logs, disk storage and memory. During cloud forensics, it is vital to ensure effective artifact collection, analysis, security and preservation. However, in the case of disk storage and memory forensics, before the collection process, it is necessary to isolate the targeted instance from the cloud environment to mitigate the effects of an incident. In particular, virtual instance termination must be disabled to prevent the virtual instance from terminating abruptly. Furthermore, the security permissions of the virtual instance should be changed immediately to prevent evidence tampering by the adversary.

Logs. Logs provide timestamped data for every activity, rendering them crucial to event reconstruction, incident response and timeline creation.

Log analysis initiates with log data collection from various cloud environment resources. Based on the type of resource and type of content logged, logs are classified as user activity logs, cloud service logs, on-premises resource logs and security logs. Security logs are classified as audit logs, access logs, virtual machine logs and flow (network) logs. To collect log data from on-premises resources, it is necessary to install a logging agent on each resource.

Table 1 provides details about the different types of logs. Since log data comes from different sources, the data formats may differ. Therefore, it is necessary to convert the data to a standard format.

The next step is log analysis. Since the volume of logs generated in a cloud environment is massive, big data analytics is typically used for analysis. Leading cloud service providers use big data analytics for cloud logs; examples are Amazon Kinesis, Azure HDInsight and Google BigQuery.

Due to the volume of cloud logs, the potential exists that logs could be overwritten due to limited storage capacity. It is vital to ensure that log retention policies are in place to ensure complete incident reconstruction. The log retention

Table 1. Logs and log data.

Logs		**Purpose**
User Activity Logs		Troubleshooting, accountability, analytics, incident response, security monitoring, compliance
Cloud Service Logs		Performance monitoring, cost management, access management, security monitoring, compliance
On-Premises Resource Logs		Performance monitoring, compliance, auditing, backup and disaster recovery, security monitoring
Security Logs	Audit Logs	Troubleshooting, monitoring, compliance
	Access Logs	Performance monitoring, troubleshooting, security, compliance
	Virtual Machine Logs	Managing, troubleshooting, securing virtual infrastructures
	Flow Logs	Troubleshooting, securing network activity, monitoring

policy varies based on cloud service provider – for example, Amazon's is ten years, Azure's is 730 days and Google's is 360 days [29]. Government regulations mandate the preservation of logs. Cloud service providers that fail to adhere to the regulations are exposed to legal action.

Disk Storage. Disk storage forensics in cloud environments is challenging due to distributed storage, virtualization and multi-tenancy. To mitigate evidence loss, it is crucial to rapidly identify the targeted instances, isolate them from load balancers and disable their termination. Stopping a cloud instance from terminating is crucial to preserve volatile data and maintain evidence integrity. In particular, auto-termination must be disabled and the instance must be stopped or suspended manually.

Before any analysis, a snapshot of the target instance and all the associated volumes must be created. This preserves the state of disk storage and supports evidence recovery. Hash values of the snapshot must be computed and preserved to ensure evidence integrity. As in traditional digital forensics, a dedicated forensic workstation equipped with the appropriate forensic tools is required. An image file with all the forensic tools used for analysis must be created. Following a cloud incident, the image is restored in a secure environment and the target instance is mounted on the forensic image, following which forensic analysis can proceed.

Memory. Cloud memory forensics involves the analysis of volatile random-access memory (RAM) from cloud-based instances to gain insights about user activity and system behavior. The practice is of great significance because it provides details about the executing processes, data in an unencrypted state, passwords, etc. Combining memory forensics with log forensics and disk storage forensics helps create a comprehensive understanding of a cloud incident.

The initial steps in memory forensics are the same as those in disk storage forensics – isolate the instance, disable termination and change access policies. However, it is required to install a forensic agent on the targeted virtual instance in order to capture the memory dump of the instance. Example agents used for memory dump acquisition are Amazon's Systems Manager (SSM) Agent and Google's GRR Rapid Response [29]. The memory dumps are subsequently analyzed using digital forensic tools such as Volatility, Rekall and LiME.

4 Security and Preservation

A secure storage environment preserves the evidentiary cloud artifacts and ensures their integrity. For the duration of the forensic investigation, a secure storage environment with access control mechanisms must be deployed so that only authorized users can access the evidence. Additional mechanisms such as time-limited access and shared access signatures may be used to strengthen security. Time-limited access may be implemented via access permissions with expiration policies and temporary credentials such as tokens or keys. Shared Access Signature (SAS) provided by Azure enables authorized individuals to access evidentiary artifacts with restricted permissions (read, write, delete, etc.) on specific resources (e.g., blobs and files) within defined time frames.

Cloud investigations involve multiple individuals, and the possibility exists that they may collude to tamper with the evidence. To address this issue, evidence metadata and investigation findings should be secured in a private blockchain. Blockchain technology intrinsically guarantees the integrity of evidence and investigation findings captured as blockchain transactions. The blockchain participants are vetted and authorized to access the evidence and investigation findings.

Previous research [29] has developed an architecture that integrates blockchain technology and cloud forensics to secure evidentiary metadata and investigation findings. The evidence metadata includes hash values, MAC timestamps, logs and key investigation documents. The architecture has demonstrated acceptable performance, reduced overhead and increased reliability. Cloud service providers are encouraged to leverage blockchain technology in their cloud forensics frameworks to support transparency, integrity and auditability.

5 Discussion

This research effort has adopted and refined the best practices employed by leading cloud service providers and attempted to integrate them in a unified and

Table 2. Comparative analysis of cloud forensics frameworks.

Framework Contribution	**Cloud Forensics Framework Support**			
	Forensics			**Anti-Forensics**
	Log Forensics	**Disk Forensics**	**Memory Forensics**	
Forensics by design [1]	✓	✓	✓	×
Forensics by design [32, 33]	✓	✓	×	×
Guidelines based on a cloud forensics survey [25]	✓	✓	×	×
Forensics monitoring plane outside cloud [2]	✓	×	×	×
Tamper-proof framework using MLCCBF [34]	✓ ✓	× ×	× ×	✓ ✓
Apache Spark for timeline construction using cloud logs [4]	✓	×	×	×
Forensic capabilities of Azure using native Azure tools and AI [21]	✓	✓	×	×
Detecting anti-forensic attacks in cloud [26]	×	×	×	✓
Proposed workflow: Forensics and anti-forensics	✓	✓	✓	✓

comprehensive cloud forensics workflow. The workflow incorporates a cloud anti-forensics module, a critical, but largely overlooked, component of cloud forensic investigations. In the research literature, only Rani et al. [26] have considered this aspect, but they did not emphasize other aspects of cloud forensics.

Indeed, a review of the literature reveals that a significant gap exists with regard to addressing cloud anti-forensics. Most researchers have primarily viewed cloud forensics frameworks at the software engineering design level. Meanwhile, implementation-oriented research has tended to concentrate on cloud log analysis, overlooking other critical cloud artifacts. In contrast, the proposed workflow considers log forensics as well as disk storage forensics and memory forensics.

Table 2 presents a comparative analysis of cloud forensics frameworks in the literature, including the proposed workflow. The comparison underscores the enhanced forensic capabilities introduced by the proposed workflow, especially its inclusion of multiple forensic data sources (logs, disk storage and memory) and its coverage of cloud anti-forensics.

6 Conclusions

The vast majority of cloud computing environments do not provide built-in support for cloud forensics. Current incident response solutions focus on detection and mitigation but lack structured approaches for cloud forensics. The conceptual workflow described in this chapter incorporates the best practices employed by leading cloud service providers. The workflow also considers cloud anti-forensics, a largely overlooked component of cloud forensic investigations. Cloud forensics implementations also tend to concentrate on cloud log analysis, ignoring other cloud artifacts. The workflow is comprehensive because it considers log forensics as well as disk storage forensics and memory forensics.

Most cloud forensics frameworks, including the workflow described in this chapter are conceptual in nature. Future research will attempt to implement the cloud forensics and cloud anti-forensics modules, transitioning the current workflow to a useable framework for real-world cloud environments.

References

1. A. Akilal and M. Kechadi, An improved forensic-by-design framework for cloud computing with systems engineering standard compliance, *Forensic Science International: Digital Investigation*, vol. 40, article no. 301315, 2022.
2. M. Alex and R. Kishore, Forensics framework for cloud computing, *Computers and Electrical Engineering*, vol. 60, pp. 193–205, 2017.
3. R. AlHarbi, A. AlZahrani and W. Bhat, Forensic analysis of anti-forensic file-wiping tools on Windows, *Journal of Forensic Sciences*, vol. 67(2), pp. 562–587, 2022.
4. Z. AlSaed, M. Jazzar, A. Eleyan, T. Bejaoui and S. Popoola, An integrated framework implementation for cloud forensics investigation using a logging tool, *International Conference on Smart Applications, Communications and Networking*, 2022.
5. K. Conlan, I. Baggili and F. Breitinger, Anti-forensics: Furthering digital forensic science through a new extended, granular taxonomy, *Digital Investigation*, vol. 18(S), pp. S66–S75, 2016.
6. S. Garfinkel, Anti-forensics: Techniques, detection and countermeasures, *Proceedings of the Second International Conference on i-Warfare and Security*, pp. 77–84, 2007.
7. S. Garfinkel, Digital forensics research: The next 10 years, *Digital Investigation*, vol. 7(S), pp. S64–S73, 2010.
8. R. Harris, Arriving at an anti-forensics consensus: Examining how to define and control the anti-forensics problem, *Digital Investigation*, vol. 3(S), pp. 44–49, 2006.
9. M. Herman, M. Iorga, A. Salim, R. Jackson, M. Hurst, R. Leo, R. Lee, N. Landreville, A. Mishra, Y. Wang and R. Sardinas, NIST Cloud Computing Forensic Science Challenges, NIST Interagency/Internal Report (NISTIR) 8006, National Institute of Standards and Technology, Gaithersburg, Maryland, 2020.
10. G. Horsman, Digital tool marks (DTMs): A forensic analysis of file wiping software, *Australian Journal of Forensic Sciences*, vol. 53(1), pp. 99–111, 2019.
11. A. Jain and G. Chhabra, Anti-forensic techniques: An analytical review, *Proceedings of the Seventh International Conference on Contemporary Computing*, pp. 412–418, 2014.

12. D. Joo, J. Lee and D. Jeong, A reference database of Windows artifacts for file-wiping tool execution analysis, *Journal of Forensic Sciences*, vol. 68(3), pp. 856–870, 2023.
13. M. Khanafseh, M. Qatawneh and W. Almobaideen, A survey of various frameworks and solutions in all branches of digital forensics with a focus on cloud forensics, *International Journal of Advanced Computer Science and Applications*, vol. 10(8), pp. 610–629, 2019.
14. S. Kwon and J. Choi, An agent-based adaptive monitoring system, in *Agent Computing and Multi-Agent Systems*, Z. Shi and R. Sadananda (Eds.), Springer, Berlin Heidelberg, Germany, pp. 672–677, 2006.
15. E. Lee, S. Lee, H. Kwon, S. Lee and G. Kim, Identification of data wiping tools based on deletion patterns in ReFS $Logfile, *Forensic Science International: Digital Investigation*, vol. 46(S), article no. 301607, 2023.
16. K. Lee, J. Lee, S. Lee and K. Yim, Effective ransomware detection using entropy estimation of files for cloud services, *Sensors*, vol. 23(6), article no. 3023, 2023.
17. H. Majed, H. Noura and A. Chehab, Overview of digital forensics and anti-forensic techniques, *Proceedings of the Eighth International Symposium on Digital Forensics and Security*, 2020.
18. A. Malik, D. Bhatti, T. Park, H. Ishtiaq, J. Ryou and K. Kim, Cloud digital forensics: Beyond tools, techniques and challenges, *Sensors*, vol. 24(2), article no. 433, 2024.
19. B. Manral, G. Somani, K. Choo, M. Conti and M. Gaur, A systematic survey of cloud forensics challenges, solutions and future directions, *ACM Computing Surveys*, vol. 52(6), article no. 124, 2019.
20. B. Martini and K. Choo, Cloud forensic technical challenges and solutions: A snapshot, *IEEE Cloud Computing*, vol. 1(4), pp. 20–25, 2014.
21. Z. Moric, V. Dakic, A. Kapulica and D. Regvart, Forensic investigation capabilities of Microsoft Azure: A comprehensive analysis and its significance in advancing cloud cyber forensics, *Electronics*, vol. 13(22), article no. 4546, 2024.
22. K. Park, J. Park, E. Kim, C. Cheon and J. James, Anti-forensic trace detection in digital forensic triage investigations, *Journal of Digital Forensics, Security and Law*, vol. 12(1), article no. 8, 2017.
23. K. Patel and S. Parameswaran, SHIELD: A software hardware design methodology for security and reliability of MPSoCs, *Proceedings of the Forty-Fifth ACM/IEEE Design Automation Conference*, pp. 858–861, 2008.
24. A. Pichan, M. Lazarescu and S. Soh, Cloud forensics: Technical challenges, solutions and comparative analysis, *Digital Investigation*, vol. 13, pp. 38–57, 2015.
25. V. Prakash, A. Williams, L. Garg, P. Barik and R. Dhanraj, Cloud-based framework for performing digital forensic investigations, *International Journal of Wireless Information Networks*, vol. 29, pp. 419–441, 2022.
26. D. Rani and G. Geethakumari, A framework for the identification of suspicious packets to detect anti-forensic attacks in a cloud environment, *Peer-to-Peer Networking and Applications*, vol. 14, pp. 2385–2398, 2021.
27. K. Ruan, J. Carthy, T. Kechadi and M. Crosbie, Cloud forensics, in *Advances in Digital Forensics VII*, G. Peterson and S. Shenoi (Eds.), Springer, Berlin Heidelberg, Germany, pp. 35–46, 2011.
28. P. Sanda, D. Pawar and V. Radha, An insight into cloud forensic readiness by leading cloud service providers: A survey, *Computing*, vol. 104, pp. 2005–2030, 2022.

29. P. Sanda, D. Pawar and V. Radha, Blockchain-based tamper-proof and transparent investigation model for cloud VMs, *The Journal of Supercomputing*, vol. 78, pp. 17891–17919, 2022.
30. P. Sanda, D. Pawar and R. Vedala, WiDeS: Wiping detection using system calls – An anti-forensic resistant approach, *Proceedings of the Twenty-Second IEEE International Conference on Trust, Security and Privacy in Computing and Communications*, pp. 1695–1703, 2023.
31. B. Sartin, Anti-Forensics – Distorting the evidence, *Computer Fraud and Security*, vol. 2006(5), pp. 4–6, 2006.
32. S. Simou, C. Kalloniatis, S. Gritzalis and V. Katos, A framework for designing cloud forensic-enabled services (CFeS), *Requirements Engineering*, vol. 24, pp. 403–430, 2019.
33. S. Simou, C. Kalloniatis, S. Gritzalis, V. Katos and M. Psalidas, Revised forensic framework validation and cloud forensic readiness, *International Journal of Electronic Governance*, vol. 14(1-2), pp. 236–263, 2022.
34. F. Ye, Y. Zheng, X. Fu, B. Luo, X. Du and M. Guizani, TamForen: A tamper-proof cloud forensic framework, *Transactions on Emerging Telecommunications Technologies*, vol. 33(4), article no. e4178, 2022.
35. S. Zawoad and R. Hasan, Cloud Forensics: A Meta-Study of Challenges, Approaches and Open Problems, arXiv: 1302.6312 (arxiv.org/abs/1302.6312), 2013.

A Unified Cyber Threat Intelligence and Digital Forensics and Incident Response Framework for Proactive Threat Detection and Mitigation

Anurag Chandra[1] and Sheeba Armoogum[2]

[1] Defence and Aviation, New Delhi, India
[2] University of Mauritius, Reduit, Mauritius
s.armoogum@uom.ac.mu

Abstract. The rapid evolution of cyber threats, including advanced persistent threats, zero-day vulnerabilities and ransomware attacks, requires a paradigm shift in cyber security strategies. Traditional cyber threat intelligence frameworks and digital forensics and incident response frameworks have been effective, but they often operate independently, leading to inefficiencies and delayed responses to complex threats.
This chapter describes a unified artificial-intelligence-enhanced framework that bridges the gaps of the individual frameworks by offering tailored solutions for diverse organizational needs. The unified framework integrates proactive threat intelligence and reactive digital forensics and incident response, bridging independent operations and enhancing real-time adaptability. Ethical governance is embedded throughout the framework, ensuring compliance with standards and regulations, transparency and accountability in artificial-intelligence-driven processes. It enhances scalability, adaptability and ethical alignment by accommodating organizations at different stages of cyber security maturity. Also, it empowers organizations to transition from reactive to proactive security measures, reduces redundancies and addresses the dynamic nature of modern cyber threats.

Keywords: Cyber Threat Intelligence · Digital Forensics · Incident Response · Artificial Intelligence · Ethical Governance · Unified Framework

1 Introduction

Cyber security is evolving under immense pressure from advanced persistent threats, zero-day vulnerabilities and ransomware attacks. These threats target vulnerabilities in traditional security infrastructures, often exposing inefficiencies in the defensive frameworks [9]. A 2023 ENISA report [13] analyzing the cyber security landscape highlights the sophistication of cyber threats and weaknesses inherent in conventional security infrastructures. Despite technological advancements, many organizations face difficulties integrating two essential cyber security components – cyber threat intelligence (CTI) and digital forensics and incident response (DFIR). The lack of cohesion between the two frameworks

Published by Springer Nature Switzerland AG 2026
E. Kurkowski and S. Shenoi (Eds.): DigitalForensics 2025, IFIP AICT 762, pp. 157–181, 2026.
https://doi.org/10.1007/978-3-032-09802-3_10

often results in independent operations, leading to inefficiencies and delayed responses to cyber incidents [50]. A NIST Special Publication [45] discusses the development of cyber-resilient systems and identifies challenges in current security frameworks, reinforcing the need for an integrated approach. Additionally, gaps in traditional security methodologies [5] justify the need to integrate CTI and DFIR processes.

Cyber threat intelligence enables organizations to systematically collect, process and disseminate threat intelligence in order to proactively identify and mitigate threats [51]. The Intelligence Cycle [38], a foundational CTI framework, facilitates structured data collection, threat analysis and intelligence dissemination to improve cyber security decision-making [45]. However, traditional CTI frameworks often operate reactively instead of proactively, reducing their ability to adapt to the evolving cyber threat landscape.

Conversely, DFIR emphasizes a structured approach for identifying, mitigating and recovering from security incidents by leveraging forensic methodologies and incident response best practices. The NIST Incident Response Framework [45] outlines a systematic approach to managing security incidents. However, it emphasizes post-incident analysis and recovery instead of proactive threat mitigation.

The Diamond Model of Intrusion Analysis [5] maps cyber adversary tactics and techniques. It focuses on the relationships between attackers, their capabilities, the infrastructures they exploit and their victims. The MITRE ATT&CK Framework [35] provides a structured knowledge base of adversarial behaviors, tactics, techniques and procedures, helping strengthen detection, defense and mitigation strategies against cyber threats. Despite their benefits, the independent application of these models without a comprehensive integration strategy can lead to vulnerabilities that are exploitable by sophisticated cyber attacks that target gaps in defense mechanisms. An integrated approach that combines CTI and DFIR, enhanced by artificial-intelligence-driven automation and real-time intelligence sharing, can strengthen organizational resilience and significantly improve cyber security postures [49].

Artificial intelligence (AI) is revolutionizing cyber security by enhancing CTI and DFIR, addressing existing gaps and improving operational efficiency. Techniques such as deep learning and graph neural networks (GNNs) have identified cyber threat patterns, providing better predictive capabilities [12]. Additionally, predictive analytics enables organizations to assess emerging risks proactively, while AI-driven automation improves threat detection and response, mitigating potential attacks more effectively. However, adopting AI in cyber security presents several challenges, including scalability issues, training dataset biases, ethical concerns and regulatory compliance [33]. According to Gonzalez-Granadillo et al. [17], maintaining transparency, accountability and fairness in AI-driven solutions is a priority because opaque decision-making can reduce trust in automated security systems.

The increasing complexity of cyber threats and the need for integrated defense strategies also present challenges. Disconnected CTI and DFIR workflows lead to inefficiencies, resulting in delays in threat detection, analysis and response that render organizations vulnerable to evolving threats and attacks [20]. The immense volume of threat data and the need for real-time analysis also complicate cyber security operations, often delaying the generation of practical insights. Furthermore, existing frameworks frequently lack the adaptability to combat new threats such as zero-day vulnerabilities. Ethical and regulatory concerns, including data privacy and algorithmic transparency, affect the credibility and adoption of AI-driven solutions.

To address these gaps, this chapter proposes the Unified AI-Enhanced CTI-DFIR Framework. The unified framework integrates an enhanced CTI framework designed to leverage AI for real-time, predictive threat intelligence along with an enhanced DFIR framework that focuses on AI-driven automation for detection, containment and recovery. The Unified AI-Enhanced CTI-DFIR Framework bridges isolated operations, encourages proactive threat management and ensures ethical compliance. The conceptual nature of the framework emphasizes qualitative metrics to evaluate its effectiveness, including scalability, adaptability and transparency.

The significance of the Unified AI-Enhanced CTI-DFIR Framework lies in its ability to transition organizations from reactive to proactive cyber security measures. The framework enhances organizational resilience by streamlining workflows, reducing redundancies and addressing complex cyber threats. Moreover, the incorporation of ethical governance ensures that AI-enabled processes are transparent, equitable and compliant with standards and regulations to engender stakeholder trust.

2 Related Work

Integrating CTI and DFIR is essential to address sophisticated cyber threats. CTI involves the systematic collection, analysis and dissemination of information about potential threats to enable organizations to anticipate and mitigate risks proactively [17]. DFIR concentrates on structured responses to security incidents, encompassing detection, containment, eradication and recovery [46]. The two frameworks often operate independently despite their complementary objectives, leading to inefficiencies in addressing advanced threats and increasing incident response times.

2.1 CTI and DFIR Limitations

Current tools such as IBM QRadar XDR [23], Microsoft Sentinel [34] and Palo Alto Cortex XSOAR [40] represent advancements in CTI-DFIR integration. IBM QRadar XDR utilizes AI-driven analytics to prioritize threats and automate response workflows. However, its complexity and the expertise required for configuration and maintenance make it inaccessible to smaller organizations [22]. Microsoft Sentinel engages cloud-native machine learning for scalable threat detection, but it is tied to the Microsoft ecosystem, which limits its adaptability to heterogeneous environments. Palo Alto Cortex XSOAR enhances security orchestration, automation and response (SOAR) capabilities with predefined playbooks for threat intelligence and incident response. However, it faces challenges with unknown and evolving threats because it relies on static workflows that hinder real-time adaptability [26].

Scalability challenges further exacerbate the limitations. Tools such as Splunk Enterprise Security [53] demand considerable computational resources, rendering them impractical for resource-constrained organizations [52]. Vendor lock-in is another limitation because platforms designed for proprietary ecosystems obstruct interoperability [39]. Furthermore, most systems depend on basic anomaly detection and lack sophisticated AI models capable of recognizing complex attack patterns and predicting future threats [41].

2.2 Real-World Case Studies

The SolarWinds supply chain attack of 2020 [31] highlighted the inadequacy of CTI frameworks in correlating anomalous activities across networks. Despite using advanced monitoring tools, many organizations failed to detect the intrusion for months, underscoring the reactive nature of DFIR workflows [28]. The MOVEit file transfer software breach of 2023 exploited a zero-day vulnerability that exposed the limitations of static threat detection mechanisms. Another significant example is the Colonial Pipeline ransomware attack of 2021 that disrupted fuel supplies across the Eastern United States [10]. Although CTI systems provided prior intelligence on the ransomware campaign, the lack of integration with incident response processes delayed containment efforts, highlighting the need for the real-time application of threat intelligence in DFIR workflows.

2.3 Foundational Models

The Intelligence Cycle and Diamond Model of Intrusion Analysis are foundational frameworks for CTI and DFIR, respectively. The Intelligence Cycle involves planning, collection, processing, analysis, dissemination and feedback. Its structured approach ensures systematic threat intelligence generation but struggles with real-time adaptability in dynamic threat landscapes. Integrating AI in the Intelligence Cycle enhances flexibility, enabling iterative feedback loops and proactive threat management [38].

The Diamond Model focuses on the relationships between adversaries, capabilities, infrastructures and victims, providing a detailed view of intrusion events. While it offers technical depth, the lack of contextual integration limits its utility in operational workflows. Embedding AI in the Diamond Model can uncover complex patterns, especially related to multistage attacks and advanced persistent threats [5].

2.4 Comparative Analysis

Other frameworks such as the Cyber Kill Chain [21], MITRE ATT&CK [35] and Structured Threat Information Expression (STIX) [42] have significantly contributed to CTI and DFIR. The Cyber Kill Chain divides cyber attacks into stages, emphasizing detection and disruption. However, its linear nature hinders responses to dynamic and multistage threats [4]. MITRE ATT&CK categorizes adversarial tactics, techniques and procedures, providing a comprehensive knowledge base for threat analysis. While it is effective for categorization, MITRE ATT&CK lacks mechanisms for real-time adaptability and seamless integration with incident response workflows. STIX provides a standardized language for sharing threat intelligence across platforms but it focuses primarily on data sharing instead of operational capabilities [42].

In contrast, the Intelligence Cycle and Diamond Model excel at providing strategic as well as tactical insights. The structured methodology of the Intelligence Cycle is well-suited for systematic intelligence generation whereas the focus of the Diamond Model on adversary relationships supports detailed threat characterization. Integrating these models in a unified framework would enable organizations to leverage their complementary strengths, helping bridge the gap between proactive intelligence and reactive incident response.

2.5 Enhancing CTI and DFIR Using AI

Artificial intelligence has emerged as a transformative enabler of CTI-DFIR integration [12]. Machine learning models such as graph convolutional networks (GCNs) can analyze complex relationships within indicators of compromise, uncovering hidden patterns in sophisticated attacks [3, 30]. Machine learning algorithms enhance predictive analytics, enabling organizations to anticipate future threat vectors and allocate resources. For example, IBM QRadar XDR integrates CTI insights in DFIR workflows, automating evidence collection, containment and remediation [24]. AI-powered platforms also facilitate real-time adaptability by dynamically updating threat models based on evolving attack patterns, addressing the static nature of traditional frameworks. Additionally, advanced AI models facilitate the correlation of data from diverse sources, closing gaps in the dissemination and operationalization of threat intelligence.

Ethical governance frameworks are crucial in addressing algorithmic bias and the lack of transparency in AI systems [7]. Adopting principles of fairness and transparency ensures that AI-enabled systems align with standards and regulations, promoting trust and accountability during deployment [14].

2.6 Unified Framework Justification

The limitations of current systems and insights drawn from real-world case studies highlight the need for a unified framework that integrates CTI and DFIR processes. The proposed Unified AI-Enhanced CTI-DFIR Framework is designed to address the inefficiencies and fragmentation of current systems. The framework integrates enhanced CTI and DFIR frameworks to bridge isolated operations, automate workflows and embed ethical governance as a foundational layer.

3 Enhanced CTI Framework

This section provides an overview of the proposed Enhanced CTI Framework, describes the framework process and discusses its limitations and enhancements.

3.1 Framework Overview

The Enhanced CTI Framework addresses the evolving landscape of cyber threats by integrating principles from established intelligence models such as the Intelligence Cycle and Diamond Model of Intrusion Detection. The framework offers a comprehensive, cyclical approach to threat identification, analysis and mitigation, aligning with the dynamic nature of cyber threats. It ensures that cyber security teams can continuously enhance their threat detection and response capabilities by incorporating stages that encompass planning, data acquisition, processing, analysis, dissemination and iterative feedback. The cyclical process promotes proactive threat hunting, enabling the identification of emerging threats before they escalate. Integrating AI and advanced analytics facilitates the refinement of the framework, ensuring its effectiveness against complex, ever-changing adversarial tactics.

Several CTI frameworks support threat detection, analysis and mitigation strategies, but they differ in their strengths and limitations [42]. Understanding the distinct capabilities of the frameworks provides the context for refining and optimizing CTI processes, including their integration with AI-driven automation and ethical governance models [1]:

- **Cyber Kill Chain [21]:** This framework tracks attacker actions through seven sequential phases – reconnaissance, weaponization, delivery, exploitation, installation, command and control, and actions on objectives. The Cyber Kill Chain offers a structured visualization of the attack progression, making it easier for defenders to detect and disrupt attacks at various stages. However, it is primarily reactive and based on historical attack patterns that limit its ability to address emerging and evolving threats. The static approach also may leave gaps in proactive threat detection and prevention, rendering integration with AI-driven analytics and predictive threat modeling essential to enhancing its effectiveness.
- **MITRE ATT&CK Framework [35]:** This framework provides a comprehensive knowledge base of adversarial tactics, techniques and procedures that are essential to detecting and preventing cyber attacks. The framework maps how adversaries operate in networks, enabling organizations to enhance their threat detection and mitigation strategies. While MITRE ATT&CK is useful for understanding attack techniques and behaviors, its implementation can be complex, requiring technical expertise and seamless integration in security operations environments. However, Alevizos and Dekker [1] note that AI-driven automation has facilitated the adoption of MITRE ATT&CK in SOAR platforms, improving incident response efficiency.

- **Intelligence Cycle Framework [38]:** This framework follows a structured process comprising direction, collection, processing, analysis, dissemination and feedback. Its iterative flow ensures continuous intelligence updates, enhancing the ability to respond effectively to emerging threats. Its primary strength is the emphasis on iterative improvement and intelligence dissemination, which enables cyber security teams to refine and strengthen their defenses over time. However, a significant limitation is that a traditional intelligence cycle framework lacks technical implementation details, requiring substantial customization and integration with AI-driven analytics to be effective in modern cyber security operations.
- **Diamond Model of Intrusion Analysis [5]:** This framework focuses on understanding the relationships between adversaries, capabilities, infrastructures and victims, offering a structured methodology for contextual threat analysis. It highlights the need to analyze the interactions among these elements to enhance the comprehension of cyber incidents. While the framework provides valuable insights, it lacks native automation and advanced analytics capabilities that limit its scalability in real-world cyber security environments. Recent studies suggest that integrating AI-driven threat correlation and real-time analytics can improve adaptability and predictive capabilities. Additionally, hybrid approaches that combine the Diamond Model with frameworks such as MITRE ATT&CK could enhance its operational effectiveness by mapping adversary tactics to specific incidents in a structured manner.

3.2 Framework Process

The Enhanced CTI Framework shown in Figure 1 offers a structured methodology for enhancing cyber security postures via CTI. The framework begins with raw data collection and culminates in informed security actions. It incorporates a data collection layer, centralized data store, analysis layer, knowledge generation layer, dissemination layer and response layer. A feedback loop facilitates continuous improvement through AI-driven contributions and ethical governance, reinforcing the adaptability to evolving threats.

The foundational data collection layer [1] focuses on gathering threat-related data from diverse sources. The layer integrates indicators of compromise such as malicious IP addresses, file hashes and domain names, enriched with AI-powered web crawlers to enhance relevance and accuracy. It also logs network activity data that is processed by AI anomaly detection models to provide real-time insights. Additionally, an open-source intelligence (OSINT) component leverages publicly available information (e.g., from forums and industry blogs) and AI tools to prioritize data pertaining to emerging threats and threat actor tactics [1].

The centralized data store consolidates all the collected threat data in a unified repository, ensuring consistency and accuracy throughout the framework. AI facilitates efficient storage and retrieval by standardizing data formats through data normalization, validating completeness and accuracy [16] using AI-assisted

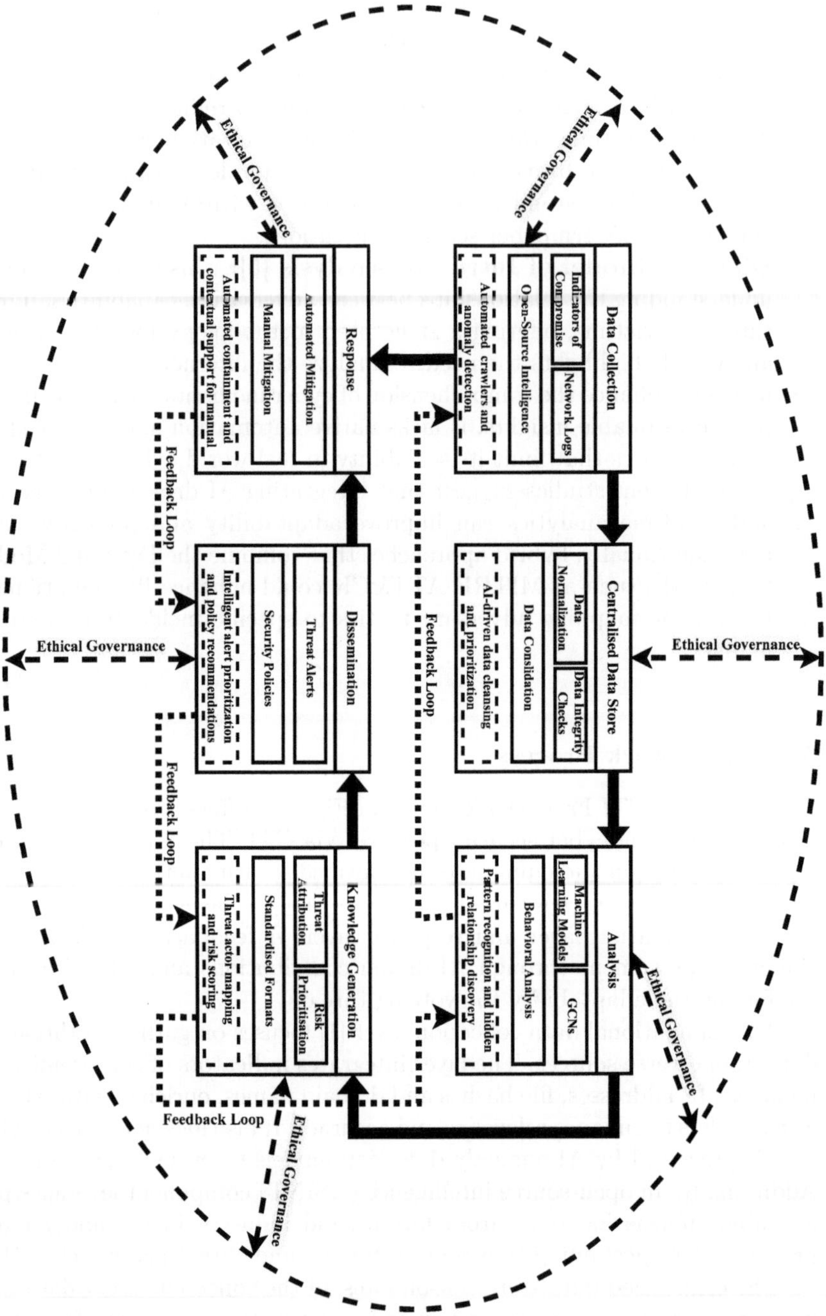

Fig. 1. Enhanced CTI Framework.

integrity checks and consolidating relevant inputs from diverse sources. This process enhances the accessibility and reliability of the data for downstream analysis, ensuring that threat intelligence is actionable and current in evolving cyber security environments.

The analysis layer extracts meaningful insights from raw data using AI techniques. Machine learning models detect patterns, anomalies and potential threats to provide proactive threat intelligence. Graph convolutional networks (GCNs) [55] analyze relationships and dependencies in datasets to uncover hidden connections and improve anomaly detection in cyber security environments.

The knowledge generation layer transforms analysis results into actionable intelligence, ensuring usability and compatibility across various systems. This includes threat attribution where AI maps threats to actors and campaigns, and risk prioritization where threats are ranked by severity and likelihood. Intelligence is structured using standardized formats [42] such as STIX and Trusted Automated Exchange of Indicator Information (TAXII), facilitating seamless integration and sharing with other security tools.

The dissemination layer ensures that refined intelligence reaches stakeholders in a timely and prioritized manner. AI enhances this process by automating the delivery of threat alerts and updating security policies based on AI analysis of current trends. Additionally, AI-driven threat intelligence platforms facilitate the real-time sharing and correlation of security data [36], improving situational awareness and proactive defense strategies. The layer helps maintain a proactive defense by keeping stakeholders informed and prepared to mitigate emerging cyber threats.

The response layer focuses on executing actions to mitigate threats. AI-driven automated mitigation triggers predefined responses such as isolating infected systems and blocking malicious traffic, which enhance reaction speed and reduce human intervention [1]. Additionally, AI-driven threat intelligence platforms provide contextual recommendations to support human-led responses in complex threat scenarios, improving decision-making and efficiency in incident resolution. The combination of automation and expert oversight ensures comprehensive and adaptive threat mitigation in dynamic cyber security environments.

The feedback loop is a vital mechanism for continuously refining and enhancing all the framework layers [1]. Insights from the response layer inform the dissemination process, improving the prioritization of future alerts and strengthening proactive cyber security strategies. Feedback from the dissemination layer enhances the accuracy of threat attribution and risk prioritization in the knowledge generation layer, further refining analytical models in the analysis layer. Additionally, adjustments to data collection layer strategies help focus on the most impactful data sources, promoting a dynamic and adaptive intelligence cycle that effectively responds to evolving cyber threats.

AI is integrated in every stage of the framework. Automated crawlers and anomaly detection tools ensure comprehensive and real-time data acquisition in the data collection layer, enhancing the accuracy of threat intelligence [11]. In the centralized data store, AI-driven processes optimize data cleansing, validation and prioritization, providing high-integrity threat data for further analysis. The analysis layer benefits from AI-powered pattern recognition and relationship discovery, improving anomaly detection and reducing false positives in cyber threat investigations. The knowledge generation layer employs AI for threat actor mapping and risk scoring, facilitating proactive threat mitigation. AI also supports the dissemination layer by prioritizing alerts, automating policy recommendations and enhancing security posture through adaptive decision-making. In the response layer, AI enables automated containment, predictive threat response and contextual support for manual interventions, contributing to an integrated and resilient cyber security ecosystem.

The framework is embued with ethical governance principles that ensure compliance, transparency, fairness and trust. Compliance with regulations is upheld and explainable AI ensures that AI-driven decisions are auditable and understandable [19]. Regular audits mitigate potential biases in AI models, promoting fairness and stakeholder trust through validated and accountable processes. This comprehensive integration of AI contributions and ethical governance renders the Enhanced CTI Framework a robust, adaptive system for proactive cyber security. The integration also ensures effective anticipation, analyses and responses while preserving transparency and trust.

3.3 Limitations and Enhancements

Frameworks such as the Cyber Kill Chain, MITRE ATT&CK and Diamond Model provide valuable insights into cyber threat detection and analysis, but they have some limitations. For example, the Cyber Kill Chain is highly structured but reactive, concentrating primarily on historical attack patterns and unable to anticipate future threats [4]. MITRE ATT&CK presents a comprehensive knowledge base of adversarial behaviors, but needs significant technical expertise for effective implementation. The Intelligence Cycle emphasizes iterative improvement, but it often lacks the necessary technical specificity for practical applications. The Diamond Model offers influential contextual insights, but it struggles with automation and scalability when addressing complex threats.

In contrast, the proposed Enhanced CTI Framework incorporates advanced AI capabilities and automation, addressing gaps in existing models by predictively identifying threats, automating incident responses and continuously being refined by the iterative feedback loop. The inclusion of ethical governance ensures that decision-making processes are transparent and aligned with organizational values, rendering the framework a more holistic solution than existing frameworks. While integrating advanced analytics and AI increases the implementation complexity, it offers the potential for effective, adaptive and scalable threat intelligence that is crucial to responding to the cyber threat landscape.

4 Enhanced DFIR Framework

This section describes the proposed Enhanced DFIR Framework and compares it against current DFIR frameworks.

4.1 Framework Overview

The Enhanced DFIR Framework shown in Figure 2 offers a structured and adaptive methodology for managing security incidents effectively, minimizing damage and strengthening cyber security resilience. The framework incorporates AI and ethical governance principles, contributing to continuous refinement and real-time adaptability to emerging cyber threats as well as compliance with standards and regulations.

The preparation stage helps establish organizational readiness via proactive measures, AI-driven analytics and ethical governance. AI-based predictive models evaluate high-risk scenarios to optimize resource allocation and develop dynamic incident response plans. Simulated AI-powered attack scenarios enhance team preparedness by providing real-world training environments tailored to evolving cyber threats. AI-driven decision support systems assist in streamlining resource acquisition in order to deploy the most effective security technologies [54]. Additionally, regulatory compliance and ethical governance frameworks are integrated in the planning process to facilitate the adherence to international standards and regulations. Secure AI-powered communications platforms facilitate seamless coordination among key stakeholders, enhancing situational awareness and response efficiency [18, 32].

The containment, eradication and recovery stage attempts to limit the spread of incidents, eliminate root causes and restore normal operations. AI-powered predictive analytics evaluates attack patterns and recommends optimal containment strategies to support rapid responses to security incidents. Automated malware removal systems neutralize threats with minimal manual intervention and AI-driven data recovery mechanisms ensure the integrity and confidentiality of restored information [44]. AI-based vulnerability assessment tools prioritize patching and system hardening efforts, concentrating on critical areas to enhance security resilience. During the recovery phase, AI is employed to verify the functionality and security of restored systems, minimizing downtime and expediting the return to full functionality. Ethical governance is integrated throughout the process to ensure compliance with regulatory requirements, maintain transparency and uphold stakeholder trust in cyber security operations.

The post-incident activity stage promotes continuous learning and enhances cyber security resilience. AI-driven automation is vital to producing incident reports that document timelines, actions taken, evidence collected and lessons learned, ensuring adherence to standards and regulations. Advanced analytics assists in identifying root causes and vulnerabilities, helping refine response strategies and bolster cyber security training programs. Additionally, insights from previous incidents are anonymized and shared with trusted stakeholders to improve collective intelligence and strengthen cyber security [20]. Ethical governance is crucial during the post-incident activity stage to ensure that incident information is shared responsibly while maintaining data privacy, regulatory compliance and stakeholder trust.

A comprehensive feedback loop mechanism ensures that lessons learned from all the stages contribute to an evolving and resilient framework. Insights from

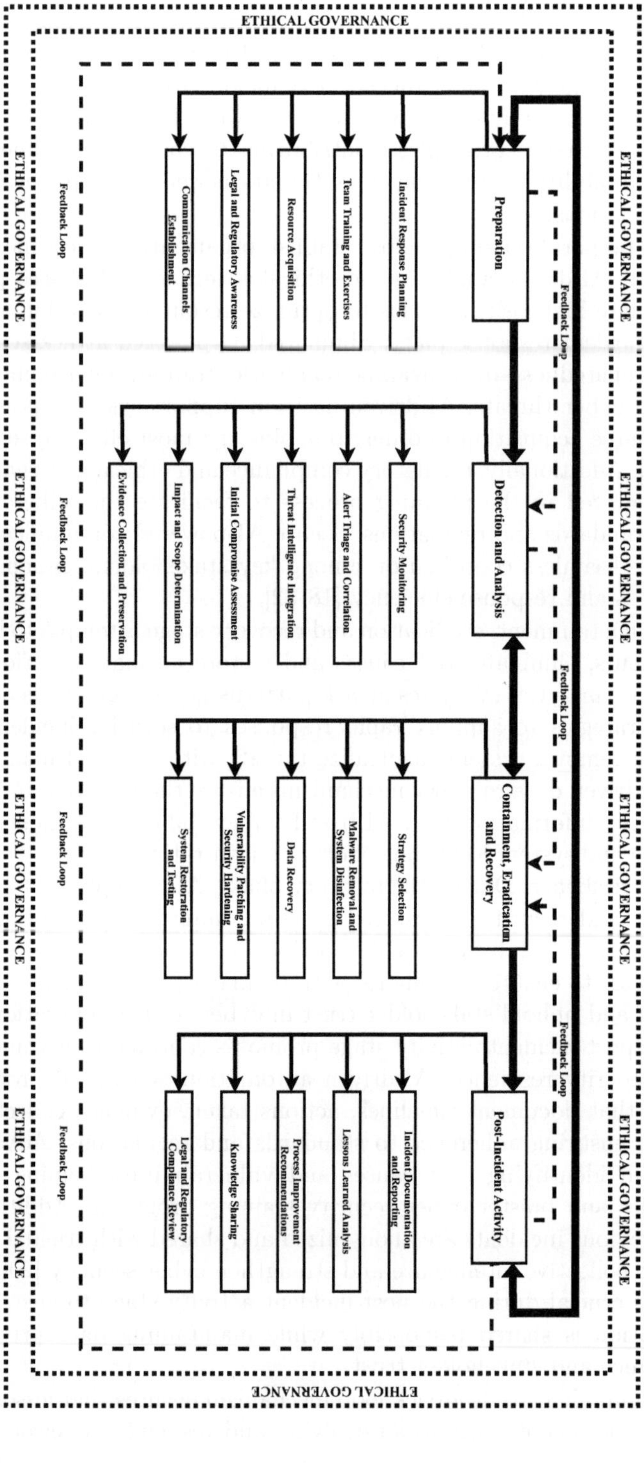

Fig. 2. Enhanced DFIR Framework.

post-incident reviews inform the preparation stage, enhancing resource allocation and refining response plans [45]. Data from the containment and recovery phases enhances detection and analysis methodologies, ensuring that evolving threats are addressed. The iterative design of the feedback mechanism allows for continuous improvement supported by AI-driven analytics that dynamically updates workflows, threat detection algorithms and automated decision-making processes in real time to strengthen organizational security postures.

AI plays a key role across all the Enhanced DFIR Framework stages – streamlining workflows, enhancing threat detection and enabling data-driven decision-making. AI algorithms automate repetitive tasks, provide predictive insights and intelligently prioritize actions to reduce response times and improve accuracy in cyber security operations. Ethical governance principles are integrated throughout the framework to enhance transparency, regulatory compliance and fairness in AI-driven security measures [6]. Explainable AI advances accountability by making AI-based decisions auditable and interpretable, fostering trust among stakeholders. Periodic audits and rigorous assessments mitigate biases to ensure that AI models remain ethical, unbiased and aligned with security standards and regulatory requirements. The integration strengthens organizational resilience against evolving cyber threats while maintaining ethical and responsible AI-driven cyber security postures.

In summary, the proposed Enhanced DFIR Framework provides a resilient and adaptive structure for incident response. Enhancing AI-driven efficiencies improves threat detection, streamlines workflows and advances overall decision-making. Ethical governance principles are embedded throughout the framework to ensure transparency, compliance and trust in cyber security operations. Incorporating a dynamic feedback loop supports continuous learning and process optimization to enable organizations to proactively address evolving threats and maintain robust security postures in an increasingly complex cyber landscape.

4.2 Comparative Analysis

DFIR frameworks offer structured methodologies for managing cyber security incidents, mitigating damage and advancing organizational security. The proposed Enhanced DFIR Framework builds on existing models by incorporating an iterative approach that leverages AI capabilities and embeds ethical governance. This section assesses the proposed framework against established models such as the NIST Cybersecurity Framework [37], ISO/IEC 27035 [25], SANS Ultimate Guide [47], CREST [8], FIRST CSIRT [15] and MITRE ATT&CK [35], evaluating their advantages, limitations and relevance in the evolving cyber security landscape [48].

The preparation stage of the proposed framework emphasizes proactive measures to achieve comprehensive readiness via structured incident response planning, team training, resource allocation, legal compliance and secure communications channels. AI-driven analytics is pivotal to identifying high-risk scenarios, optimizing resource distribution and simulating advanced threat environments in order to enhance preparedness. The integration of adaptive learning models helps refine response strategies and enable teams to manage complex incidents. Unlike conventional frameworks that offer overarching risk management strategies, the proposed framework embeds AI-driven automation for real-time decision-making and dynamic response refinement [45]. Furthermore, structured guidelines ensure that legal and compliance considerations are integrated seamlessly to enhance the efficiency and effectiveness of incident preparedness strategies.

The detection and analysis stage of the proposed framework leverages AI to enhance anomaly detection, correlate threat intelligence and streamline forensic analysis to improve incident identification speed and accuracy. AI-driven systems continuously monitor network activities, detect behavioral anomalies and provide real-time threat intelligence, enabling security teams to respond proactively to emerging risks. Traditional approaches, such as those outlined in structured incident response guidelines, offer foundational methodologies but often lack the adaptive, AI-powered capabilities to address sophisticated cyber threats. Frameworks such as adversarial tactics mapping provide valuable insights into attacker behavior, but they primarily focus on classification instead of real-time response. The proposed framework addresses these limitations by integrating AI-powered analytics to provide enhanced situational awareness, automate forensic workflows and generate actionable intelligence for effective cyber security operations.

The containment, eradication and recovery stage of the proposed framework emphasizes real-time threat containment, malware elimination, vulnerability management and system recovery. AI-powered analytics assesses attack vectors, predicts adversary movements and facilitates automated threat isolation to reduce response time and enhance security resilience. AI-driven remediation tools proactively identify compromised assets, neutralize threats with minimal manual intervention and verify the integrity of the restored systems. Additionally, AI-enhanced vulnerability detection supports prioritized patching and system hardening to reinforce cyber defenses against future attacks [27]. Traditional containment frameworks mainly focus on manual processes, providing procedural guidance but often lacking predictive automation that could expedite recovery. The proposed framework integrates AI to improve efficiency and precision and ensure compliance with regulatory requirements. Moreover, it embeds ethical governance to maintain transparency and trust in AI-driven cyber security operations.

The post-incident activity phase of the proposed framework prioritizes continuous improvement through AI for incident documentation, adversarial pattern recognition and process refinement. AI-driven automation streamlines incident reporting by capturing key timelines, actions taken and evidence collected to create structured documentation that complies with standards and regulations. Advanced analytics assists in identifying attack patterns and root causes, providing actionable recommendations to enhance future incident response strategies. Traditional frameworks emphasize post-incident reviews but often lack AI-driven mechanisms that dynamically adapt detection and mitigation workflows to respond to evolving cyber threats. By embedding AI in the post-incident activity phase, the proposed framework can facilitate continuous learning, enhance cyber security readiness and ensure proactive adaptation to new attack vectors [45].

The ethical governance layer of the proposed framework is a crucial component that is often overlooked in traditional models. It ensures adherence to standards and regulations, enhances transparency through explainable AI and mitigates biases in AI-driven decision-making. The embedding of ethical principles in AI-enabled cyber security operations helps foster trust among stakeholders and promotes responsible AI deployment [17]. Unlike conventional models that primarily focus on technical and procedural aspects, ethical considerations are integrated to safeguard against the unintended consequences of automated security responses. While current models such as CREST and FIRST CSIRT emphasize ethical security practices and inter-team collaboration, they lack explicit mechanisms to address the broader implications of AI governance in forensic investigations and incident response strategies. In contrast, the proposed framework embeds ethical oversight in all AI-driven processes to ensure accountability, fairness and compliance with evolving cyber security standards and regulations.

In conclusion, the proposed Enhanced DFIR Framework enhances cyber security practices by integrating AI across all the stages to improve threat detection, streamline containment processes and refine post-incident analysis. While established frameworks such as ISO/IEC 27035 and the SANS Ultimate Guide provide structured procedural guidance, they lack the adaptability needed to effectively address evolving cyber threats. The AI-enhanced approach of the proposed framework engages a dynamic, data-driven response strategy that strengthens cyber security resilience. Moreover, integrating ethical governance principles in the framework promotes transparency, accountability and compliance with standards and regulations, making it a robust and forward-looking model for digital forensics and incident response that addresses contemporary security challenges.

5 Unified AI-Enhanced CTI-DFIR Framework

The Unified AI-Enhanced CTI-DFIR Framework shown in Figure 3 merges the strengths of the Enhanced CTI Framework and the Enhanced DFIR Framework to create a comprehensive framework for tackling contemporary cyber security challenges. The integration facilitates seamless collaboration between proactive threat intelligence and reactive incident response.

The preparation and risk mitigation stage of the unified framework establishes the foundation for cyber security readiness by integrating insights from CTI and structured DFIR practices. AI-powered predictive models play a crucial role in identifying potential security risks and support the development of adaptive incident response strategies tailored to evolving cyber threats. Advanced simulation techniques enhance training exercises to equip security teams with the skills to manage sophisticated attack scenarios. AI-driven tools streamline resource allocation by recommending appropriate security technologies based on real-time threat intelligence. Ethical governance principles embedded in the stage ensure compliance with standards and regulations, maintain transparency

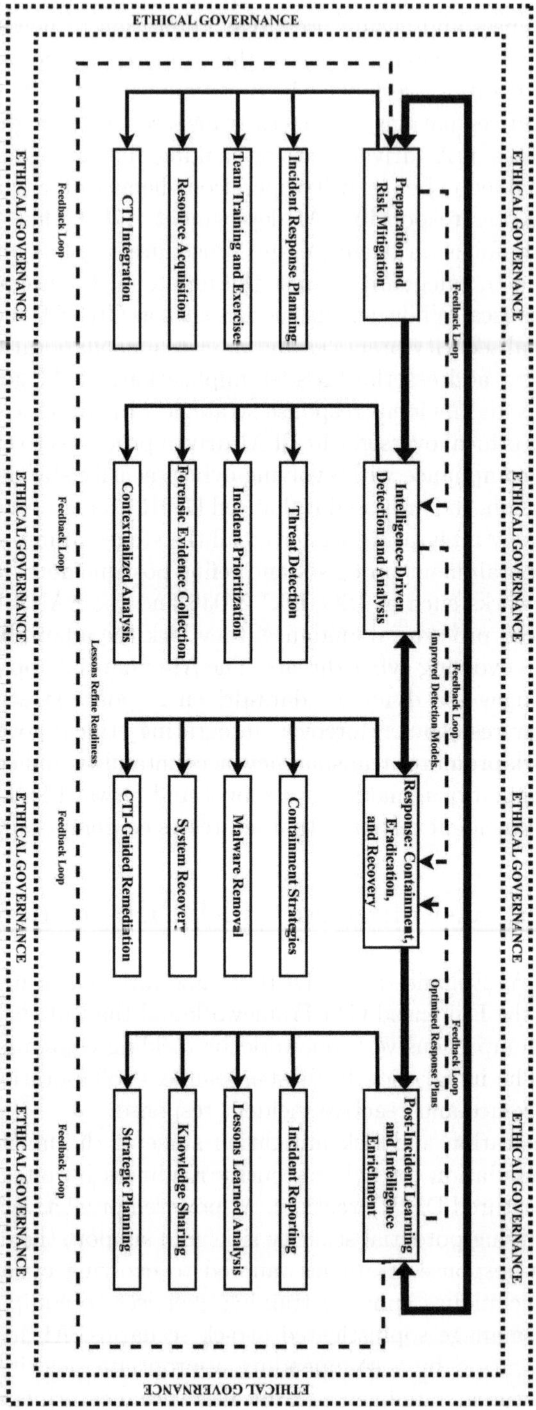

Fig. 3. Unified CTI-DFIR Framework.

in security protocols and uphold fairness in training methodologies. A dynamic feedback loop continuously refines risk assessment models by incorporating insights from past incidents, optimizing readiness strategies and improving overall organizational resilience in the face of cyber threats.

The detection and contextualized analysis stage of the unified framework integrates the CTI and DFIR workflows to enhance threat identification and analysis. AI-driven threat detection systems engage machine learning and advanced analytics to monitor network activities, detect behavioral anomalies and correlate them with indicators of compromise and adversarial tactics, techniques and procedures [2]. The contextualized approach prioritizes threats based on severity, impact and adversarial intent, supporting informed triage and response actions. Automated forensic data collection ensures the integrity and admissibility of digital evidence while AI-driven behavioral analysis identifies patterns across attack surfaces to detect multistage threats. The continuous feedback loop refines detection models to enhance anomaly identification and proactive threat mitigation strategies. Ethical governance principles embued in the framework reinforce transparency, accountability and adherence to forensic best practices, ensuring that AI-driven security decisions align with standards and regulations.

The containment, eradication and recovery stage of the unified framework integrates CTI insights to enhance containment strategies, eliminate threats and ensure system restoration. AI-driven mechanisms facilitate rapid containment by isolating compromised systems, preventing lateral movements and minimizing operational disruptions. Automated malware tools detect and eliminate malicious artifacts while AI-powered threat intelligence helps identify and neutralize advanced attacks. Enhanced remediation processes leverage CTI to apply security patches, adjust configurations and strengthen system defenses against recurrent threats. The continuous feedback loop refines mitigation strategies and updates threat intelligence models, improving organizational response capabilities. Ethical governance is crucial to maintaining data privacy, ensuring compliance with standards and regulations, and fostering trust in AI-driven cyber security practices.

The post-incident learning and intelligence enrichment stage of the unified framework ensures that insights from past incidents are systematically analyzed to strengthen future cyber security measures. AI-driven automation facilitates the creation of incident reports that capture key findings, response actions and outcomes to support data-driven decision-making. These reports are crucial to refining security strategies, directing investment priorities and optimizing organizational cyber security policies. AI also enhances root cause analysis and pattern recognition, providing valuable intelligence to CTI systems to enhance proactive threat detection and mitigation efforts. Collaboration with trusted partners enables effective knowledge sharing that promotes collective defense against cyber threats. Ethical governance mechanisms ensure data privacy and compliance. The continuous feedback loop refines cyber security workflows to support adaptive and resilient cyber security postures against evolving threats.

AI contributions are deeply integrated in the unified framework to automate repetitive security tasks, enhance predictive threat modeling and deliver practical insights that enhance decision-making. AI-driven analytics increases detection accuracy and response times, enabling organizations to manage their cyber risks effectively. Ethical governance is integrated in AI processes to ensure transparency, fairness and compliance with standards and regulations. Techniques for bias mitigation and explainability are incorporated to build trust in AI-driven cyber security solutions. The continuous feedback loop optimizes AI models and CTI/DFIR workflows to improve adaptability based on real-world incident data, strengthening the overall resilience of cyber security defenses.

The Unified CTI-DFIR Framework provides a comprehensive approach to cyber security by seamlessly integrating proactive intelligence gathering with reactive incident response. The framework enhances threat detection, incident containment and forensic investigation capabilities by leveraging AI-driven automation, advanced analytics and structured governance. Ethical governance ensures that AI-driven cyber security applications are transparent, accountable and compliant with standards and regulations. The iterative feedback mechanisms embedded in the framework engender continuous improvement and enable organizations to stay ahead of emerging cyber threats. Adopting the unified framework would enable organizations to enhance their cyber security resilience, mitigate sophisticated cyber risks and build trust in an increasingly complex threat landscape.

5.1 Comparative Analysis

Several advanced platforms – such as IBM QRadar XDR [23], Microsoft Sentinel [34] and Palo Alto Cortex XSOAR [40] – have made significant strides in integrating CTI and DFIR. These platforms enhance threat detection, automate incident responses and streamline security operations. However, their limitations include dependence on proprietary ecosystems, deployment complexity and real-time adaptability challenges. The proposed Unified AI-Enhanced CTI-DFIR Framework addresses these limitations by leveraging AI, ethical governance and a continuous feedback loop to enhance operational efficiency. By incorporating AI-driven predictive analytics, cross-platform interoperability and governance mechanisms, the proposed framework offers improved scalability, adaptability and compliance to enable organizations to effectively combat sophisticated cyber threats.

AI Integration and Predictive Capabilities. A significant strength of the unified framework is its AI-driven architecture. AI models can continually learn from real-time data and adapt to evolving cyber threats, providing a predictive capability that helps anticipate emerging threats, recognize complex attack patterns and dynamically adjust security measures. Unlike traditional detection mechanisms, AI enhances proactive defense strategies by automating threat intelligence processing, improving anomaly detection and supporting adaptive incident response. By utilizing continuous model refinement and real-time feedback, the unified framework surpasses current tools such as IBM QRadar XDR, Microsoft Sentinel and Palo Alto Cortex XSOAR that primarily focus on rule-based detection instead of predictive threat mitigation.

Although AI is integrated to varying degrees in current cyber security platforms, most implementations focus on detection instead of prediction. For example, IBM QRadar XDR uses AI-powered analytics to evaluate and prioritize threats, but it is limited by predefined rules and detection workflows that limit its adaptability. Similarly, Palo Alto Cortex XSOAR relies on playbooks to automate response mechanisms, but it often struggles to adjust dynamically to new and evolving threats. Several security tools leverage traditional anomaly detection techniques but lack advanced AI-driven models capable of identifying sophisticated multistage attack sequences and anticipating future threats. In contrast, the proposed unified framework incorporates a dynamic AI-powered feedback loop, enabling systems to continually learn and refine their threat detection and mitigation processes in real time. This integration gives organizations an adaptive advantage, enhancing their ability to anticipate and neutralize emerging cyber threats before they escalate.

Ethical Governance and Transparency. The integration of ethical governance in the proposed unified framework provides a significant advantage over existing cyber security solutions. Ethical governance ensures that AI-driven threat detection and incident response processes adhere to the principles of fairness, transparency, accountability and privacy protection. As AI continues to evolve as a fundamental component of cyber security operations, it is essential to address ethical issues such as bias mitigation, explainability and regulatory compliance. The proposed framework embeds ethical oversight at every stage of the CTI-DFIR lifecycle, ensuring the responsible deployment of AI driven security mechanisms. The incorporation of comprehensive governance policies and compliance measures enables organizations to build trust in AI-powered cyber security solutions while remaining aligned with legal and ethical standards [29].

Cyber security platforms such as IBM QRadar XDR, Microsoft Sentinel and Palo Alto Cortex XSOAR are effective at threat detection and incident response, but they lack clearly defined ethical governance frameworks. The platforms emphasize threat prioritization and detection but do not integrate mechanisms to ensure that AI-driven processes align with ethical considerations such as transparency, fairness and privacy protection. Without explicit governance models, AI-driven cyber security decisions could inadvertently introduce biases, compromise regulatory compliance or undermine trust in automated security measures. The proposed unified framework addresses these gaps by embedding ethical decision-making in every stage of threat intelligence and incident response. It engages a balanced approach that integrates robust cyber security with ethical accountability by prioritizing transparency in AI models, ensuring alignment with standards and regulations and implementing responsible AI principles.

Scalability and Flexibility. Scalability is a crucial advantage provided by the proposed unified framework. Traditional security tools often require significant computational resources, making them less accessible to organizations with limited budgets. The proposed framework integrates AI-driven automation and cloud-native technologies to optimize resource utilization and ensure efficient scaling across diverse infrastructures. The modular architecture facilitates adaptive deployment that dynamically adjusts cyber security operations based on real-time threat intelligence. All the while, AI models continually enhance detection and response capabilities, enhancing the framework's ability to handle increased data loads and evolving attack landscapes. By promoting interoperability and eliminating rigid dependencies on proprietary ecosystems, the framework manifests a flexible, future-ready cyber security paradigm [43].

In contrast, traditional security solutions such as IBM QRadar XDR, Microsoft Sentinel and Palo Alto Cortex XSOAR have scalability limitations due to their reliance on complex configurations and resource-intensive operations. While cloud-native architectures improve scalability, platform dependencies limit their adaptability in heterogeneous information technology environments. Furthermore, predefined playbooks and static workflows in automated platforms may struggle to manage large-scale data processing and real-time threat response effectively. The proposed unified framework addresses these challenges by integrating AI-driven automation, dynamic resource allocation and adaptive security mechanisms. By optimizing resource utilization and enabling seamless scalability, it provides a more agile and efficient cyber security solution for organizations of varying sizes and operational needs [43].

Adaptability to Emerging and Evolving Threats. The proposed unified framework addresses the complexities related to emerging threats and previously unknown attack vectors. By utilizing AI-driven analytics, the framework can identify novel attack techniques, anticipate future cyber threats and dynamically adjust security protocols in real time. Such adaptability is crucial in the rapidly changing threat landscape where conventional security tools relying on static workflows or predefined rule-based detection systems often fail to address new or sophisticated attacks. The framework integrates advanced behavioral analysis, machine learning models and predictive threat intelligence to strengthen proactive defense mechanisms, ensuring that organizations can swiftly adapt and respond to evolving cyber security challenges.

Current security solutions such as IBM QRadar XDR and Palo Alto Cortex XSOAR primarily rely on predefined rule sets and structured playbooks for automated incident response. While the systems are effective at handling known threat scenarios, they often struggle to adapt to sophisticated, multistage attacks that evolve beyond their static detection parameters. The proposed framework addresses this limitation by leveraging real-time feedback and AI-driven threat intelligence to enhance detection and response. The integration of adaptive learning models and dynamic rule evolution continually refines the ability to identify and mitigate emerging novel attack vectors, significantly improving the resilience of cyber security operations.

Vendor Lock-In and Interoperability. The proposed unified framework addresses the challenge of vendor lock-in, a drawback in many current cyber security solutions. Platforms such as IBM QRadar XDR, Microsoft Sentinel and Palo Alto Cortex XSOAR generally operate in proprietary ecosystems, which hinders their ability to integrate smoothly with third-party security tools. This dependency restricts flexibility, preventing organizations from adopting a diverse security infrastructure that incorporates solutions from multiple vendors. For example, Microsoft Sentinel is optimized for Microsoft cloud environments. Similarly, Palo Alto Cortex XSOAR is designed for the Palo Alto Networks ecosystem, which impacts its adaptability in environments that require broader interoperability. In contrast, the proposed framework emphasizes open standards, cross-platform compatibility and seamless integration with diverse security solutions. By engaging an application-programming-interface-driven architecture and modular components, the framework provides operational flexibility, enabling organizations to build adaptable cyber security infrastructures free from vendor lock-in constraints.

The proposed Unified AI-Enhanced CTI-DFIR Framework is exceptionally flexible, supporting seamless integration across diverse environments and compatibility with third-party security solutions. The framework eliminates the dependence on single-vendor ecosystems and improves interoperability with cyber security tools by utilizing open standards and a modular architecture. Such adaptability is essential for organizations that seek a unified security strategy while preserving operational efficiency and minimizing integration complexity.

6 Conclusions

The proposed Unified AI-Enhanced CTI-DFIR Framework systematically integrates cyber threat intelligence, digital forensics, incident response and artificial intelligence with ethical governance principles. The framework addresses key challenges such as response coordination, operational fragmentation and the need for adaptable and scalable solutions in complex threat environments. It supports the transition from reactive to proactive cyber security by enabling predictive analytics, automated mitigation workflows and continuous feedback loops. These capabilities are particularly valuable in responding to evolving cyber threats, including advanced persistent threats and zero-day exploits.

While existing tools offer significant incident detection and handling capabilities, the unified framework seeks to augment the tools by providing deeper contextualization, faster decision-making and greater operational synergies between intelligence gathering and forensic response. Ethical governance is a foundational part of the framework that reinforces the alignment with data privacy, transparency and compliance with standards and regulations. The alignment helps build trust in AI-driven decisions and encourages responsible innovation in cyber security operations.

Designed to be modular and scalable, the framework can support organizations at varying levels of maturity and resource availability. Rather than positioning itself as a replacement for established systems, the framework offers a structured model that may be adapted to address emerging cyber security needs.

Future research will further develop the framework by integrating federated learning, explainable AI and cross-institutional sharing of threat intelligence. These enhancements will improve robustness, resilience and transparency across diverse digital ecosystems.

References

1. L. Alevizos and M. Dekker, Towards an AI-enhanced cyber threat intelligence processing pipeline, *Electronics*, vol. 13(11), article no. 2021, 2024.
2. J. Al-Saraireh and A. Masarweh, A novel approach for detecting advanced persistent threats, *Egyptian Informatics Journal*, vol. 23(4), pp. 45–55, 2022.
3. O. Boyaci, A. Umunnakwe, A. Sahu, M. Narimani, M. Ismail, K. Davis and E. Serpedin, Graph neural networks based detection of stealth false data injection attacks in smart grids, *IEEE Systems Journal*, vol. 16(2), pp. 2946–2957, 2022.
4. B. Bryant and H. Saiedian, A novel kill-chain framework for remote security log analysis with SIEM software, *Computers and Security*, vol. 67, pp. 198–210, 2017.
5. S. Chen, T. Pai and C. Sun, Applying the Diamond Model of intrusion analysis with generative pre-trained transformer 3, *Proceedings of the International Conference on Consumer Electronics – Taiwan*, pp. 289–290, 2023.
6. T. Clancy, D. Robbins, O. Eris, L. Booker and K. Enos, A Sensible Regulatory Framework for AI Security, MITRE Corporation, McLean, Virginia (www.mitre.org/sites/default/files/2023-06/PR-23-1943-A-Sensible-Regulatory-Framework-For-AI-Security_0.pdf), 2023.
7. N. Correa, C. Galvao, J. Santos, C. Del Pino, E. Pinto, C. Barbosa, D. Massmann, R. Mambrini, L. Galvao, E. Terem and N. de Oliveira, Worldwide AI ethics: A review of 200 guidelines and recommendations for AI governance, *Patterns*, vol. 4(10), article no. 100857, 2023.
8. CREST, Cyber Security Incident Response Procurement Guide, Version 1, Coventry, United Kingdom (www.crest-approved.org/wp-content/uploads/2022/04/CSIR-Procurement-Guide-1.pdf), 2013.
9. Cybersecurity and Infrastructure Security Agency, Enabling Distributed Security in Cyberspace – Building a Healthy and Resilient Cyber Ecosystem with Automated Collective Action, Arlington, Virginia (www.dhs.gov/xlibrary/assets/nppd-cyber-ecosystem-white-paper-03-23-2011.pdf), 2011.
10. Cybersecurity and Infrastructure Security Agency, The attack on Colonial Pipeline: What we've learned and what we've done over the past two years, *Blog*, Arlington, Virginia (www.cisa.gov/news-events/news/attack-colonial-pipeline-what-weve-learned-what-weve-done-over-past-two-years), May 7, 2023.
11. R. Das and R. Sandhane, Artificial intelligence in cyber security, *Journal of Physics: Conference Series*, vol. 1964, article no. 042072, 2021.

12. D. Dunsin, M. Ghanem, K. Ouazzane and V. Vassilev, A comprehensive analysis of the role of artificial intelligence and machine learning in modern digital forensics and incident response, *Forensic Science International: Digital Investigation*, vol. 48, article no. 301675, 2024.
13. European Union Agency for Cybersecurity, ENISA Threat Landscape 2023, Athens, Greece (www.enisa.europa.eu/sites/default/files/publications/ENISAThreatLandscape2023.pdf), 2023.
14. J. Fjeld, N. Achten, H. Hilligoss, A. Nagy and M. Srikumar, Principled Artificial Intelligence: Mapping Consensus in Ethical and Rights-Based Approaches to Principles for AI, Berkman Klein Center Research Publication No. 2020-1, Harvard University, Cambridge, Massachusetts, 2020.
15. Forum of Incident Response and Security Teams, FIRST CSIRT Services Framework, Version 2.1, Cary, North Carolina (www.first.org/education/csirt_services_framework), 2019.
16. S. Gong and C. Lee, Cyber threat intelligence framework for incident response in an energy cloud platform, *Electronics*, vol. 10(3), article no. 239, 2021.
17. G. Gonzalez-Granadillo, S. Gonzalez-Zarzosa and R. Diaz, Security information and event management (SIEM): Analysis, trends and usage in critical infrastructures, *Sensors*, vol. 21(14), article no. 4759, 2021.
18. Hamirul, Darmawanto, N. Elsyra and Syahwami, The role of artificial intelligence in government services: A systematic literature review, *Open Access Indonesia Journal of Social Sciences*, vol. 6(3), pp. 998–1003, 2023.
19. R. Hamon, H. Junklewitz and I. Sanchez, Robustness and Explainability of Artificial Intelligence – From Technical to Policy Solutions, EUR 30040, Publications Office of the European Union, Luxembourg, Luxembourg, 2020.
20. Y. He, L. Maglaras, A. Aliyu and C. Luo, Healthcare security incident response strategy – A proactive incident response (IR) procedure, *Security and Communication Networks*, vol. 2022(1), article no. 2775249, 2022.
21. E. Hutchins, M. Cloppert and R. Amin, Intelligence-Driven Computer Network Defense Informed by Analysis of Adversary Campaigns and Intrusion Kill Chains, White Paper, Lockheed Martin Corporation, Bethesda, Maryland (www.lockheedmartin.com/content/dam/lockheedmartin/rms/documents/cyber/Gaining_the_Advantage_Cyber_Kill_Chain.pdf), 2011.
22. International Business Machines, Palo Alto networks acquires IBM QRadar SaaS assets, Press Release (www.ibm.com/new/announcements/palo-alto-networks-ibm-qradar-saas), September 4, 2024.
23. International Business Machines, IBM QRadar XDR Connect, Armonk, New York (www.ibm.com/products/qradar-xdr-connect), 2025.
24. International Business Machines, Network Detection and Response (NDR) Solutions, Armonk, New York (www.ibm.com/products/qradar-siem/ndr), 2025.
25. International Organization for Standardization, ISO/IEC 27032:2023, Cybersecurity – Guidelines for Incident Management, Geneva, Switzerland, 2023.
26. J. Jacobs, S. Romanosky, O. Suciu, B. Edwards and A. Sarabi, Enhancing vulnerability prioritization: Data-driven exploit predictions with community-driven insights, *Proceedings of the IEEE European Symposium on Security and Privacy Workshops*, pp. 194–206, 2023.
27. R. Jones, M. Omar, D. Mohammed, C. Nobles and M. Dawson, Harnessing the speed and accuracy of machine learning to advance cybersecurity, *Proceedings of the Congress in Computer Science, Computer Engineering and Applied Computing*, pp. 418–421, 2023.

28. G. Karantzas and C. Patsakis, An empirical assessment of endpoint detection and response systems against advanced persistent threat attack vectors, *Journal of Cybersecurity and Privacy*, vol. 1(3), pp. 387–421, 2021.
29. B. Li, P. Qi, B. Liu, S. Di, J. Liu, J. Pei, J. Yi and B. Zhou, Trustworthy AI: From principles to practices, *ACM Computing Surveys*, vol. 55(9), article no. 177, 2022.
30. S. Li, Q. Zhou, R. Zhou and Q. Lv, Intelligent malware detection based on graph convolutional network, *The Journal of Supercomputing*, vol. 78(3), pp. 4182–4198, 2022
31. M. Marelli, The SolarWinds hack: Lessons for international humanitarian organizations, *International Review of the Red Cross*, vol. 104(919), pp. 1267–1285, 2022.
32. N. Mat, N. Jamil, Y. Yusoff and M. Kiah, A systematic literature review on advanced persistent threat behaviors and its detection strategy, *Journal of Cybersecurity*, vol. 10(1), article no. tyad023, 2024
33. J. Meister, R. Akram and K. Markantonakis, Deep learning application in security and privacy – Theory and practice: A position paper, in *Information Security Theory and Practice*, O. Blazy and C. Yeun (Eds.), Springer, Cham, Switzerland, pp. 129–144, 2019.
34. Microsoft, Microsoft Sentinel Documentation, Redmond, Washington (`learn.microsoft.com/en-us/azure/sentinel`), 2025.
35. MITRE Corporation, MITRE ATT&CK v17.1, McLean, Virginia (`attack.mitre.org/versions/v17`), 2025.
36. B. Naik, A. Mehta, H. Yagnik and M. Shah, The impacts of artificial intelligence techniques in augmentation of cybersecurity: A comprehensive review, *Complex and Intelligent Systems*, vol. 8(2), pp. 1763–1780, 2021.
37. National Institute of Standards and Technology, Framework for Improving Critical Infrastructure Cybersecurity, Version 1.1, Gaithersburg, Maryland (`nvlpubs.nist.gov/nistpubs/cswp/nist.cswp.04162018.pdf`), 2018.
38. C. Nolan, Understanding the Intelligence Cycle, Edited by Mark Phythian, New York: Routlege, 2013, *Journal of Strategic Security*, vol. 8(4), pp. 114–116, 2015.
39. J. Opara-Martins, R. Sahandi and F. Tian, Critical analysis of vendor lock-in and its impact on cloud computing migration: A business perspective, *Journal of Cloud Computing: Advances, Systems and Applications*, vol. 5, article no. 4, 2016.
40. Palo Alto Networks, What is Extended Detection and Response (XDR)? Santa Clara, California (`www.paloaltonetworks.com/cyberpedia/what-is-extended-detection-response-XDR`), 2024.
41. S. Rajapaksha, H. Kalutarage, M. Al-Kadri, A. Petrovski, G. Madzudzo and M. Cheah, AI-based intrusion detection systems for in-vehicle networks: A survey, *ACM Computing Surveys*, vol. 55(11), article no. 237, 2022.
42. A. Ramsdale, S. Shiaeles and N. Kolokotronis, A comparative analysis of cyber-threat intelligence sources, formats and languages, *Electronics*, vol. 9(5), article no. 824, 2020.
43. M. Repetto, D. Striccoli, G. Piro, A. Carrega, G. Boggia and R. Bolla, An autonomous cybersecurity framework for next-generation digital service chains, *Journal of Network and Systems Management*, vol. 29(4), article no. 37, 2021.
44. M. Rhode, P. Burnap and A. Wedgbury, Real-time malware process detection and automated process killing, *Security and Communication Networks*, vol. 2021(1), article no. 8933681, 2021.
45. R. Ross, V. Pillitteri, R. Graubart, D. Bodeau and R. McQuaid, Developing Cyber-Resilient Systems: A Systems Security Engineering Approach, NIST Special Pub-

lication 800-160, Volume 2, Revision 1, National Institute of Standards and Technology, Gaithersburg, Maryland, 2021.
46. E. Salfati and M. Pease, Digital Forensics and Incident Response (DFIR) Framework for Operational Technology (OT), NIST Interagency/Internal Report (NISTIR) 8428, National Institute of Standards and Technology, Gaithersburg, Maryland, 2021.
47. SANS Institute, The Ultimate Guide to Getting Started in Digital Forensics and Incident Response (DFIR), White Paper, Rockville, Maryland (`www.sans.org/white-papers/ultimate-guide-getting-started-digital-forensics-incident-response`), 2024.
48. N. Saqib, V. Germanos, W. Zeng and L. Maglaras, Mapping of the security requirements of GDPR and NISD, *EAI Endorsed Transactions on Security and Safety*, vol. 7(24), article no. e2, 2020.
49. I. Sarker, M. Furhad and R. Nowrozy, AI-driven cybersecurity: An overview, security intelligence modeling and research directions, *SN Computer Science*, vol. 2, article no. 173, 2021.
50. N. Serketzis, V. Katos, C. Ilioudis, D. Baltatzis and G. Pangalos, Actionable threat intelligence for digital forensics readiness, *Information and Computer Security*, vol. 27(2), pp. 273–291, 2019.
51. B. Shin and P. Lowry, A review and theoretical explanation of the "cyberthreat-intelligence (CTI) capability" that needs to be fostered in information security practitioners and how this can be accomplished, *Computers and Security*, vol. 92, article no. 101761, 2020.
52. F. Skopik, M. Landauer and M. Wurzenberger, Blind spots of security monitoring in enterprise infrastructures: A survey, *IEEE Security and Privacy*, vol. 20(6), pp. 18–26, 2022.
53. Splunk, Splunk Enterprise Security, San Francisco, California (`www.splunk.com/en_us/pdfs/product-briefs/splunk-enterprise-security.pdf`), 2024.
54. A. Zacharis and C. Patsakis, AiCEF: An AI-assisted cyber exercise content generation framework using named entity recognition, *International Journal of Information Security*, vol. 22(5), pp. 1333–1354, 2023.
55. M. Zhang, H. Tong, J. Xu and R. Maciejewski, Graph convolutional networks: A comprehensive review, *Computational Social Networks*, vol. 6, article no. 11, 2019.

Author Index

Published by Springer Nature Switzerland AG 2026
E. Kurkowski and S. Shenoi (Eds.): DigitalForensics 2025, IFIP AICT 762, p. 183, 2026.
https://doi.org/10.1007/978-3-032-09802-3

MIX
Papier aus verantwortungsvollen Quellen
Paper from responsible sources
FSC® C105338

If you have any concerns about our products,
you can contact us on
ProductSafety@springernature.com

In case Publisher is established outside the EU,
the EU authorized representative is:
Springer Nature Customer Service Center GmbH
Europaplatz 3, 69115 Heidelberg, Germany

Printed by Libri Plureos GmbH
in Hamburg, Germany